PRAISE FOR
RETAIL DISRUPTORS

'Hard discounters are a proven concept with plenty of opportunities to expand both in geographies around the world as well as in different product categories and more business sectors. It is critical to everyone in business to fully understand these developments. This book provides the best possible insights regarding the phenomenon of hard discounting, as [both] a learning about business models and as a valuable base for day-to-day and strategic decisions. A book worth every minute to read.' **Harry Brouwer, Executive Vice President, Unilever Food Solutions – Global**

'A must-read for any brand marketer. Hard discounters have come like a "thief in the night", responsible for reducing manufacturer brand sales by half trillion dollars annually. Many national brands stuck their heads in the sand and are now under the hammer to defend their brands against the hard discounter "brands". Yes, while we were asleep at the wheel, Aldi, Lidl and others built "brand" connections with consumers. Is it too late to save your brand? You'd better hope not.' **John Gerrie, Chairman, FMCG Association ANZ**

'*Retail Disruptors* is a seminal work that defines the strategy, tactics and impact of the global hard discounter phenomenon. It's essential reading for everyone that competes with or sells to this dynamic sector of retailing.' **John Failla, Founder, Store Brands Decisions, US**

'Finally a book that analyses the discounters from an international, global perspective! Most publications focus on national markets. Not this book. This makes the book definitely a "must read" for everyone professionally involved in the retail business today. But also shoppers, interest groups, investors and policy makers can learn from the unique insights and considerations revealed in the book. **Philippe Gruyters, Managing Director European Marketing Distribution (EMD), Europe's largest grocery alliance**

'Professors Steenkamp and Sloot have written a "must-read" for anyone interested in retail. The book allows one to truly understand the disruptive powers of discount formulas. It should therefore be on every retail professional's night stand.' **Dave Pieters, former General Manager, Coles Australia**

'In the last 25 years, hard discounters have achieved remarkable success in the Western world. So far, conventional retailers and brand manufacturers have failed to find the right answers as to how to deal with this retail disruption. The very insightful book by Steenkamp and Sloot uncovers the primary secrets of the hard discount business model. It will be very helpful for retailers and marketers around the world to understand why they are so successful. Just one warning: understanding hard discounters doesn't mean that you can beat them!' **Kees Buur, former Buying Director Health and Beauty, A.S. Watson Benelux**

Retail Disruptors

The spectacular rise and impact
of the hard discounters

Jan-Benedict Steenkamp
with Laurens Sloot

First published in Great Britain and the United States in 2019 by Kogan Page Limited

2nd Floor, 45 Gee Street	c/o Martin P Hill Consulting	4737/23 Ansari Road
London EC1V 3RS	122 W 27th St, 10th Floor	Daryaganj
United Kingdom	New York NY 10001	New Delhi 110002
www.koganpage.com	USA	India

© Jan-Benedict Steenkamp and Laurens Sloot, 2019

ISBN   978 0 7494 8347 0
E-ISBN   978 0 7494 8348 7

British Library Cataloguing-in-Publication Data

A CIP record for this book is available from the British Library.

Library of Congress Cataloging-in-Publication Data

Names: Steenkamp, Jan-Benedict E. M., author. | Sloot, Laurens, author.
Title: Retail disruptors : the spectacular rise and impact of the hard
    discounters / Jan-Benedict Steenkamp and Laurens Sloot.
Description: 1 Edition. | New York, NY : Kogan Page Ltd, [2018] | Includes
    bibliographical references and index.
Identifiers: LCCN 2018026418 (print) | LCCN 2018037577 (ebook) | ISBN
    9780749483487 (ebook) | ISBN 9780749483470 (pbk.) | ISBN 9780749483487
    (eISBN)
Subjects: LCSH: Discount houses (Retail trade) | Hypermarkets. | Grocery
    trade. | Retail trade.
Classification: LCC HF5469 (ebook) | LCC HF5469 .S74 2018 (print) | DDC
    381/.149–dc23

Typeset by Integra Software Services, Pondicherry
Print production managed by Jellyfish
Printed and bound by CPI Group (UK) Ltd, Croydon, CR0 4YY

To Valarie Steenkamp, my soulmate in everything, and to the three 'disruptors' in my life, Iris, Tristan, and Alex Steenkamp. They are proof that disruption is to be cherished rather than feared.

Jan-Benedict Steenkamp

To my mother who gave me the gift of self-confidence and to Gerdien whose love and dedication makes our family strong and happy.

Laurens Sloot

CONTENTS

07   How conventional retailers can compete with hard discounters 118

08   Strategies to reduce procurement costs 146

PART THREE Brand manufacturer strategies versus hard discounters 165

09   Competition – creating winning brand propositions versus private labels 167

LIST OF FIGURES

LIST OF TABLES

LIST OF ABBREVIATIONS

B2B	Business to business
B2C	Business to consumer
CEO	Chief executive officer
CFO	Chief financial officer
CMO	Chief marketing officer
CPG	Consumer packaged goods
EBIT	Earnings before interest and taxes
EBITDA	Earnings before interest, taxes, depreciation, and amortization
EDLP	Every day low prices
HiLo	High-low (regular price is relatively high but products are frequently in promotion)
M&A	Mergers and acquisitions
R&D	Research and development
SG&A	Selling, general and administrative expenses
SKU	Stock keeping unit

ABOUT THE AUTHORS

Jan-Benedict Steenkamp (Dr honoris causa; PhD, MSc, BSc [all summa cum laude]) is C. Knox Massey Distinguished Professor of Marketing at the University of North Carolina's Kenan-Flagler Business School where he was Chairman of Marketing from 2006 to 2018. He is an Honorary Professor at the European Institute for Advanced Studies in Management, Fellow of the European Marketing Academy, and Fellow at the Institute for Sustainable Growth at Fudan University (Shanghai). He is chairman of the International Advisory Board of the Institute of Nation(al) Branding at ECNU (Shanghai) and member of the governmental Committee of Global Experts of the Chinese Association of Quality. He is a member of the selection committee of the Spinoza Prize, nicknamed the Dutch Nobel Prize. He also is executive director of AiMark, an institute that bridges the academic world and leading CPG and market research companies. His areas of expertise include branding, retailing and private labels, global marketing, and marketing strategy.

A prolific writer, he is the author of *Product Quality* (Van Gorcum, 1989), *Private Label Strategy: How to beat the store brand challenge* (Harvard Business School Press, 2007), *Brand Breakout: How emerging market brands will go global* (Palgrave Macmillan, 2013), and *Global Brand Strategy: Worldwise marketing in the age of branding* (Palgrave MacMillan, March 2017). *Brand Breakout* was selected as Best Business Book 2013: Globalization by Booz & Co. His books have been translated into various languages, including Chinese. He has published two articles in the *Harvard Business Review*. More academic papers have appeared in *Academy of Management Journal, Journal of Marketing, Journal of Marketing Research, Journal of Retailing,* and *Strategic Management Journal*, among others. He has written 10 cases, available through The Case Centre. His work has received over 40,000 citations.

One of the world's leading thinkers on global strategy, branding, and private labels, he has taught, consulted, and given executive seminars on all continents. His work has been featured in *The Wall Street Journal, Financial Times, The Economist, The New York Times, Bloomberg Businessweek*, newspapers in China, Europe, India, and South Korea, and he has been interviewed on television and radio in the US, China, Europe, South Africa, and India.

A native of the Netherlands, he has taught at universities in Belgium, the Netherlands, Austria, China, India, Spain, South Africa, the UK, and the US. He has been recognized as 'Teaching All Star' by UNC's MBA programme.

The Royal Netherlands Academy of Sciences has awarded him the Muller Lifetime Prize for 'exceptional achievements in the area of the behavioural and social sciences'. It was the first time the prize had been awarded to an academic in any area of business administration. He has received an honorary doctorate from Aarhus University (Denmark) and lifetime achievement honours from the American Marketing Association and the European Marketing Academy.

Laurens Sloot (PhD, MSc) is the Anton Dreesmann Professor of Retail Marketing at the University of Groningen (the Netherlands). He started his academic career in 1992 as an assistant professor at Erasmus University Rotterdam and was selected teacher of the year in 1994. He finished his dissertation on assortment management in 2006. In 2007, he became associate professor of retail marketing at the University of Groningen and was appointed as (part-time) Anton Dreesmann Professor of Retail Marketing in 2011.

While working at Erasmus University in 1997 he started EFMI Business School. Since then this institute has developed into a leading educational and research institute for senior and top executives from food retailers and food manufacturers. In 2000, he launched the Master of Food Management programme, which is one of the most successful senior executive programmes in the Dutch food industry. Each year, he gives about 100 keynote speeches, workshops and in-company trainings for top and senior executives in the field of grocery retailing and CPG manufacturing. In 2017, he was named Food Manager of the year by the Dutch food industry.

His areas of expertise include retailing strategies, new business models, retailer-supplier relationships, category management, and retail mix. He has written about 10 articles in leading marketing journals, including the *Journal of Marketing Research* and the *Journal of Retailing*. He is frequently interviewed by the Dutch media about issues in food retailing and brand manufacturing.

He is an avid player of poker, which he regards as a game of skill where the long-term results are based on a player's mathematical and psychological abilities, but where the short-term outcomes are mainly a matter of luck. He has attended the World Series of Poker multiple times and finished 220th in the main event in 2010.

Also by the authors:

Jan-Benedict Steenkamp, *Product Quality* (Assen, The Netherlands: Van Gorcum, 1989).

Laurens Sloot, *Understanding Consumer Reactions to Assortment Unavailability* (Rotterdam, The Netherlands: ERIM, 2006).

Nirmalya Kumar and Jan-Benedict Steenkamp, *Private Label Strategy: How to meet the store brand challenge* (Cambridge, MA: Harvard Business School Press, 2007).

Nirmalya Kumar and Jan-Benedict Steenkamp, *Brand Breakout: How emerging market brands will go global* (New York: Palgrave MacMillan, 2013).

Jan-Benedict Steenkamp, *Global Brand Strategy: World-wise marketing in the age of branding* (New York: Palgrave MacMillan, 2017).

PREFACE

The first wave of private labels disrupting the consumer packaged goods industry occurred in the period between 1980 and 2010. This stage was led by 'conventional' (full-service) retailers like Kroger, Tesco, Albert Heijn, Coles, and Carrefour. Their model was to compete with so-called copycat private labels that sell for around 30 per cent less than quality-equivalent national brands. With the exception of Germany, hard discounters played a minor role. Brand manufacturers lost hundreds of billions of dollars in revenues to these retailers, but since all conventional retailers more or less followed the same business model, competition among them was fierce but predictable and manageable.

We are now in the eye of a new storm rolling in over the consumer packaged goods industry – that of hard discounters who completely redefine value for money. Unlike conventional retailers whose assortment largely consists of national brands, private labels account for somewhere between 70 and 90 per cent of hard discounters' assortment. This means that hard discounters have (literally) little space for national brands at all. Through a sophisticated sourcing and assortment strategy, hard discounters are able to deliver high-quality products at prices that are 50 per cent below quality-equivalent national brands and around 30 per cent below those of the copycat private labels of conventional retailers. They have achieved operational efficiencies that even Walmart cannot dream of. But this time around, retailers will be hit as hard as national brand manufacturers because hard discounters have redefined the price-value curve in the industry.

Many retail and brand managers are befuddled by the success of hard discounters. How can consumers flock in ever greater numbers to these small, austere stores, with their small assortment and few – if any – of the brands that people were thought to love so much? Surely this has to be a fluke? Unfortunately for them, systematic underestimation of this new threat has led to dramatic decreases in the market share of conventional retailers and brand manufacturers alike in market after market – first in Germany, next in France, the Netherlands, and Belgium, and most recently in Poland, the UK, Italy, and Australia. Hard discounters have now set their sight on the ultimate prize: the US, the biggest grocery market in the world.

What makes hard discounters so successful? And what can other retailers do in response? What should brand manufacturers do? Answering these questions is tough under any circumstances, but, in this case, it is hindered by the fact that the two leading global champions, Aldi and Lidl, are privately held and rather secretive. Not that this has limited their success; Lidl's mother company, Schwarz Gruppe, is the third-largest grocery retailer in the world with a presence in 29 countries in 2018, while Aldi is at number five, with stores in 20 countries. Both are bigger than such giants as AEON, Ahold Delhaize, Tesco, Auchan, Albertsons, or Rewe. The purpose of this book is to lift the veil of secrecy covering hard discounters. We will detail the hard discounter business model and the strategies followed by key players and in key countries. This sets the stage for the development of counterstrategies. As the great Chinese military strategist Sun Tzu wrote around 500 BC, 'If you know the enemy and know yourself, you need not fear the result of a hundred battles'. We will document that incumbent retailers and brand manufacturers are anything but helpless. Indeed, some will actually profit from working with hard discounters.

ACKNOWLEDGEMENTS

This book is the result of a long journey through the ever more volatile waters of hard discounters, 'conventional' retailers, and brand manufacturers. In our journey, we were fortunate to be able to draw on the insights and feedback of colleagues, companies, and marketing practitioners. We are deeply grateful to our colleagues in the marketing discipline. Special thanks go to Katrijn Gielens (UNC Kenan-Flagler) for her many detailed insights. Her knowledge of retailing in all its formats continues to amaze us every day. We are also grateful to Barbara Deleersnyder (Tilburg University) and Oliver Koll (University of Innsbruck) for their detailed feedback on strategies to work successfully with hard discounters, and to Marcel van Aalst (EFMI Business School) and Ruben Lautenbag (Simon-Kucher & Partners) for sharing their research and ideas on the impact of hard discounters. We gratefully acknowledge the intellectual contributions of Kusum Ailawadi (Dartmouth College), Marnik Dekimpe, Inge Geyskens, and Els Gijsbrechts (Tilburg University), Kristopher and Agnieszka Keller (UNC Kenan-Flagler), Nirmalya Kumar (Singapore Management University), Koen Pauwels (Northeastern University), John Roberts (University of New South Wales), Anne ter Braak and Lien Lamey (KU Leuven), Harald van Heerde (Massey University), Peter Verhoef (University of Groningen), and Auke Hunneman (BI Norwegian Business School).

This book would not have been possible without close collaboration with a large number of companies. We are grateful for the data support of the market research agencies GfK, Kantar Worldpanel, and Europanel, and of EFMI Business School. Over the years, we have worked with many firms to test our ideas in the real world. Ahold Delhaize, Bunge, Jumbo, Plus, Procter & Gamble, Reckitt Benckiser, Superunie, and Unilever have been especially supportive.

We are grateful to a number of individual managers who have provided us with specific feedback and information over the years including Alfred Dijs (AiMark), John Gerrie (ProBrands Australia), Philippe Gruyters (EMD), Richard Herbert (Europanel), Koen de Jong (IPLC), Hans Kisjes (Essity), José Antonio Lombardía (DIA), Helen Passingham-Hughes (Europanel), Jeff Schomburger (P&G), Greg Seminara (Export Solutions), Herman Sievers (Lidl), Andreas Vente (Aldi), and Koen Hazewinkel (Store Europe).

A special word of thanks goes to Paul Polman, Unilever's CEO and a true visionary in the industry. He identified the threat posed by hard discounters before almost anybody else in the industry. When he was P&G's President Europe, he took then-CEO A G Lafley to the competitor he feared the most. He did not take Lafley to the headquarters of Nestlé, Unilever, or Reckitt Benckiser. No, they visited a lowly Aldi store. He told us this story a long time ago, and it provided the impetus, first for an article in the *Harvard Business Review*, and now for this book.

We have had the privilege to test and refine our ideas in lectures to participants at conferences on all continents and in various MBA and executive programmes. We learned as much from them as they learned from us. We further thank David Ernsthausen (UNC Kenan-Flagler's Librarian) and Irene van Berlo (EFMI Business School) for excellent research support. If there existed a report or database somewhere in the known universe about a topic we were looking for, they were able to find it. We thank Erin Mitchell for her invaluable help during the entire project.

Finally, we want to acknowledge all the brand and retailer executives who work hard every day to enrich the lives of all of us as consumers, by offering high-quality brands or private labels. If they find this book useful, it will be worth all of our efforts.

How hard discounters are disrupting the traditional retail model

Hard discounters emerged in post-war Europe, especially in war-devastated Germany, where, in the 1960s, small austere stores began to appear, carrying a lean selection of private-label items displayed in their shipping cartons. Founded by the Albrecht brothers, these stores bore the banner Aldi (from Albrecht Discount). Why would you want to even go to such an outlet, commonly referred to as a hard-discount store? Because the prices were rock-bottom. You could fill up your shopping cart for a fraction of the price you had to pay in conventional ('full-service') supermarkets.

Aldi enjoyed success among low-income shoppers, and, by the early 1970s, Aldi's market share in grocery retailing in Germany was around 5 per cent.[1] Inspired by Aldi's success, other retailers in Germany copied the hard-discount format – most successfully Lidl, the flagship of the Schwarz Group. The hard-discount format was also adopted outside of Germany, including in Denmark (Netto), France (Leader Price), Italy (EuroSpin), Norway (REMA 1000), Poland (Biedronka), Spain (DIA), Turkey (BIM), and the United States (Trader Joe's, Save-A-Lot) to name a few.

Ascendancy of hard discounters

No longer do hard discounters operate at the fringes of the modern Western retailscape. With sales of US $90–100 billion each in 2017, Schwarz and Aldi are two of the largest grocery retailers in the world (Table 1.1). Moreover,

Table 1.1 Global Top 20 grocery retailers in 2017

Company	Country of origin	Global grocery revenues ($ bn)	CAGR 2012– 2017 (%)	Dominant operational format	# Countries of operation	Revenues from foreign operations (%)
Walmart	US	314.4	1.6	Hypermarket/Superstore	28	27
Kroger	US	100.1	2.2	Supermarket	1	–
Schwarz	Germany	97.6	6.4	Discount store	29	63
Carrefour	France	96.2	2.3	Hypermarket /Superstore	33	59
Aldi	Germany	91.8	7.2	Discount store	20	69
Seven & I	Japan	90.7	–	Convenience store	19	38
Costco	US	76.5	4.9	Warehouse Club	12	28
Ahold Delhaize	Netherlands	70.6	–	Supermarket	11	79
Tesco	UK	60.5	–2.8	Hypermarket Superstore	8	24
Rewe	Germany	56.8	2.4	Supermarket	11	28
Edeka	Germany	56.7	3.1	Supermarket	1	–
AEON	Japan	54.2	–	Hypermarket Supermarket	11	6
Auchan	France	50.1	3.3	Hypermarket	14	72
Albertsons	US	49.3	–	Supermarket	1	–

					Worldwide	
Alibaba	China	48.0	49.2	Online channel		6
Casino	France	39.7	0	Supermarket	17	14
Woolworths	Australia	38.2	1.2	Supermarket	3	10
E. Leclerc	France	36.7	2.6	Hypermarket	7	17
Walgreens Boots Alliance	US	34.7	–	Drug store	9	22
ITM	France	34.2	2.4	Supermarket	4	10

NOTE Revenues refer to grocery (edible grocery, health and beauty products, and household and pet care) only. CAGR = compound annual growth rate, based on the currency of the country of origin. CAGR for Kroger is corrected for the acquisition of Harris Teeter. CAGR for Seven & I, Ahold Delhaize, AEON, Albertsons, AEON, and Walgreens Boots Alliance are not reported because of multiple large takeovers or mergers. For #countries of operation, we included only countries where revenues exceeded $10 million.

SOURCE Authors' calculations based on 2017 data from Planet Retail the organic growth rate of Aldi and Lidl over the period 2012–2017 was higher than about any other top retailer, except Alibaba, which benefits from the great willingness of Chinese consumers to purchase groceries online and the less developed brick-and-mortar infrastructure in China.

Table 1.1 further shows that Aldi and Lidl's reach is not restricted to their home market. Faced with saturation in Germany, both hard discounters have embarked on an aggressive strategy of international expansion. They earn more than 60 per cent of their revenues from foreign operations. Aldi is present in 18 countries in Europe, as well as in Australia and the United States. Lidl is present in 28 European countries and entered the United States in 2017.

While Aldi and Lidl are renowned as the giants among the discounters, there are a number of fast-growing challengers, some of which have expanded outside their home market as well (Table 1.2). Take Biedronka, Jerónimo Martins' hard-discount chain in Poland. Over the period 2012–2017, it achieved a compound annual growth rate (CAGR) of 11.2 per cent. Along the way, the Polish retailscape was fundamentally changed. In 2017, nearly one out of every three zlotys spent on grocery products was allocated to a hard discounter.

Back to basics: what is a hard discounter?

Hard-discount retailers offer basic goods and daily necessities at the lowest possible prices, while maintaining high-quality standards. A hard-discount store differs from discount supermarkets or hypermarkets like Asda, Kaufland, or Walmart. Hard-discount stores are typically about 8,000–15,000 square feet, less than one-tenth the size of a Walmart Supercenter, with comparably lower staffing levels. To reduce costs, hard discounters often display items on shipping pallets and in the boxes in which they arrive. The store is minimally decorated and offers a limited assortment of consumer packaged goods and perishables – typically less than 2,000 stock-keeping units (SKUs). In contrast, the average US supermarket carried 40,000 to 50,000 SKUs in 2017, while a Walmart Supercenter sells over 100,000 grocery and non-grocery items.[2] Offering a limited assortment of products enables hard discounters to provide a high volume of basic goods and helps to streamline efficient operations.

Private labels feature prominently in the assortment of hard discounters. Over 50 per cent of BIM and DIA's SKUs are private label, while the share of private label in Trader Joe's exceeds 80 per cent and, in Aldi, 90 per cent.

The relative emphasis on private labels is the key differentiator between hard discounters and brand discounters such as Dollar General, Dollar Tree, Netto Marken-Discount, or Poundland. Hard discounters have deep expertise on how their products are produced, who can produce them, and what trade-offs they need to make. The large revenues combined with their small number of SKUs mean that the volume per SKU is very large. Aldi and Lidl, for example, are the No. 1 and No. 2 sellers of self-branded grocery products worldwide in 2018. As a result, they are able to take a 'grind it to powder' approach to costs, driving out every fractional cent of cost without compromising on quality. This allows hard discounters to outcompete other retailers on price. Indeed, most international comparisons of prices across retail stores have designated the hard discounter the winner.

Hard discounters as brands

Brands give us meaning in our role as consumers. Any product that is not a brand will inherently have limited market appeal. Why do brands matter? Because 1) brands make decision making easier, and 2) brands are a quality assurance. However, brands do not necessarily have to be *manufacturer* brands. Increasingly, the discount banner name is becoming a brand in its own right.

1 Hard discounters make decision making easier

Brands ease consumer decision making. The human brain stores product knowledge in associate networks largely organized around the brand. If you recognize a brand and have some knowledge about it, then you can easily access and use related product knowledge in your decision making. You need not engage in additional thought or data processing to make a purchase decision. Which brand is healthier? Which is more appealing to my children? Which one provides better performance (eg removing stains) or tastes better? Absent brands, you need to study each offering and analyse product details before you can choose between them. Most people do not want to expend this time and effort on their everyday purchases.

Shopping at a supermarket with 40,000 SKUs and countless varieties of laundry detergent or peanut butter brands does not make for easy decision making. How much easier it is to shop at Trader Joe's, with only the Trader Joe's brand name and few options per category (except for its wine!). Hard

Table 1.2 Global Top 10 discount store operators in 2017

Company (country of origin)	Discount banner(s)	Total discount banner revenues ($ bn)	Discount type	CAGR 2012–2017 (%)	# Countries of operation	Total number of outlets	Average store size (sq ft)
Aldi (Germany)	Aldi, Trader Joe's, Hofer	101.3	Hard	7.2	20	11,210	9,156
Schwarz (Germany)	Lidl	80.6	Hard	7.1	29	10,697	10,346
Dollar General (US)	Dollar General	23.9	Brand	8.4	1	14,325	7,420
Dollar Tree (US)	Dollar Tree, Family Dollar	21.7	Brand	7.2	2	14,450	7,841
Edeka (Germany)	Netto Marken-Discount	15.0	Brand	2.4	1	4,182	8,036
Rewe (Germany)	Penny	14.0	Hard	1.7	6	2,165	7,724
Jerónimo Martins (Portugal)	Biedronka	12.7	Hard	11.2	1	2,741	6,727

DIA (Spain)	DIA, Minipreço	10.1	Hard	3.5	5	6,993	4,453
BIM (Turkey)	BIM	6.9	Hard	20.4	3	6,685	3,208
Reitangruppen (Norway)	REMA 1000	5.7	Hard	−1.3	5	609	10,407

NOTE CAGR for Dollar Tree is corrected for the acquisition of Family Dollar in 2015. CAGR calculated for ongoing operations. Revenues include grocery and non-grocery.
SOURCE Authors' calculations based on 2017 data from Planet Retail

discounters provide unparalleled simplicity to time-harassed consumers. Often, we want simplicity, not overwhelming choice.

Branding consultancy Siegel+Gale tracks consumer perceptions of brand simplicity around the world. They define brand simplicity as brands that are easy to understand, transparent and honest, make customers feel valued, are innovative and fresh, and are useful. They found that in the period 2009–2017, a stock portfolio comprised of publicly traded 'simplest' brands in their Global Top 10 had outperformed the S&P 500 and the (German) DAX by a factor of three, and that 61 per cent of consumers were more likely to recommend the brand to others. So, which brands constituted the global Top 2 in 2017? Aldi and Lidl. This is what Siegel+Gale wrote about #1, Aldi:

> With its simple, consistent store layouts, Aldi offers affordable, high-quality goods combined with a stress-free customer experience. Because the discount supermarket chain mostly carries exclusive products, customers don't have to choose between the typical and sometimes overwhelming array of brands and prices.[3]

2 Hard discounters as quality assurance

Second, consumers value brands for the quality assurance they provide. As the former chief marketing officer (CMO) of Unilever, Simon Clift said:

> A brand is the contract between a company and consumers. And the consumer is the judge and jury. If (s)he believes a company is in breach of that contract either by underperforming or reducing quality service rendering, the consumer will simply choose to enter a contract with another brand.[4]

Executives who invest in brands know these investments would yield poor returns if the brands failed to fulfil their promises; therefore, companies have a strong incentive to deliver on quality. Consumers intuitively understand this connection and use brand name as an indicator of product quality.

In the past, this meant that consumers relied on the manufacturer brand. But nowadays, consumers around the world increasingly rely on the hard discounter banner as quality signal – the Germans call it 'Aldi Qualität'. And they are right to do so. An analysis of test results reported by the German consumer testing agency Stiftung Warentest revealed that 81 per cent of Aldi products across 26 packaged goods categories were rated 'excellent' or 'good', versus 64 per cent of the premium brands and 85 per cent of the market leaders.[5] Lidl was voted the best retailer in produce in the Netherlands for six out of eight years in the period 2010–2017.[6] This is especially noteworthy, as hard discounters in the past had little, if any, produce, which is logistically very complex. These and other widely publicized quality kudos increase the confidence of consumers in relying on the hard discounter brand name as a quality guarantee.

Retail disruptors as a sign of our times

In the past, hard discounters were primarily frequented by the poor. Not anymore. Three important developments have made hard discounters increasingly attractive for middle-class and even high-income consumers.

Stagnating incomes

While the top incomes have increased substantially over the decade 2007–2017, middle incomes have largely stagnated. In Britain, real wages fell every year between 2009 and 2014, the longest decline since the mid-1800s and in 2018 were still some 3 per cent below 2007.[7] In Italy, nominal wages in 2016 were still below their 2006 levels.[8]

To make ends meet, many middle-income families began shopping at hard-discount stores in order to keep living standards high. Take the UK, where in 2017, middle-class shoppers account for 60 per cent of shoppers at Aldi and Lidl. Only one out of every four shoppers comes from the group of working-class semi- and unskilled manual workers, which used to be the typical demographic of shoppers at Aldi and Lidl.

The impact of recessions

Recessions favour hard discounters. The German weekly magazine *Stern* quoted the mother of the Albrecht brothers in 2002: 'The harder the times, the better off Aldi is.' *Time* magazine commented in 2008: 'Spooked by the gravest economic crisis in decades [ie the 2008 recession], Americans are curtailing their spending. They're making fewer trips to supermarkets and migrating from grocers like Albertsons and Whole Foods to deep discounters like Aldi and Save-A-Lot.' *Forbes* argued in 2009 that, during harsh economic times, discounters come to be in a better position than many of the conventional retailers because they offer value merchandise at a time when customers are watching their pennies.[9]

But harsh times do not last forever. What happens afterwards? Many have speculated that hard-discounter buying is something that occurs in recessions and will reverse afterwards. In the worsening economic climate in Europe in 2008, Tesco's chief financial officer dismissed any idea that the success of discounters would endure by saying that they were merely having a 'moment in the sun'.[10] Unfortunately for Tesco, he was wrong.

A systematic examination of data from 15 Western European countries spanning two decades reveals that hard discounter share increases both in bad times *and* in good times. However, hard discounter share does increase faster during a recession, but that extra jolt in a recession is not lost when good economic times return.[11] For example, in the early 2000s, the German economy was not doing well. The hard discounters profited handsomely, seeing their market share increase from 19.6 per cent in 2000 to 26.3 per cent in 2003. While growth slowed afterwards to 26.4 per cent in 2004 and 27.5 per cent in 2006, there was no fallback.[12] Why do we not see a return to conventional retailers? Because as new hard-discount shoppers learn that the quality, assortment, and shopping experience is actually better than they had expected, a significant proportion of them remain loyal to the hard discounter, even after the necessity to economize on expenditures is over. The onward march of hard discounters continues across business cycles.

Smart shopping phenomenon

Where you shop has always been one of the great social signifiers in Britain. According to shopping folklore, for the middle classes it is Marks & Spencer, for the upper-middle class Waitrose, and Morrisons is the stronghold of lower-middle-class Britain.[13] Yet, in 2017, one out of every two Britons shopped at Aldi or Lidl. Why? Stagnating incomes are one explanation, but there is more. Increasingly, it is considered 'smart' shopping to purchase hard-discounter products of (supposedly) comparable quality for a much lower price, rather than being 'ripped off' by high-priced manufacturer brands or the store brands offered by the likes of Tesco, Kroger, or Coles. The smart shopping phenomenon is not restricted to Britain, or even to groceries. It is a global trend in consumer behaviour. Shopping for lower-priced brands can be found in investing (eg Vanguard), airlines (Spirit, Ryanair), furniture (Ikea), consumer electronics (Vizio, Media Market), apparel (Primark, H&M), automotive (Dacia, Daihatsu), and healthcare (Aravind, Teva).[14]

Smart shopping provides positive motivation to shop at hard discounters. You shop at Lidl or Trader Joe's, not because you *have to*, but because you *want to*. It is now cool to shop in a savvy way. Germans call this positive motivation 'Ich bin doch nicht blöd' (I'm not stupid) and 'Geiz ist geil' (stinginess is cool). Hard discounter shoppers are now found among all socioeconomic strata and in all product categories. In one country after the other, there is no longer a stigma attached to shopping at a hard discounter. Take 51-year-old British teacher Janet Wadsworth, who abandoned UK grocery giant Tesco for discounter Aldi after the German chain opened a store near her home in the English village of St Bees. 'It used to be that people might have been embarrassed to be seen at Aldi,' she said in an interview with the *Wall Street Journal*, 'but I think that's gone'.[15] Clive Black, a retail analyst at UK-based Shore Capital, called this 'one of the biggest changes in consumer attitudes we've seen in a generation,' adding, 'you now see plenty of Audis, BMWs, and Mercedes parked outside Aldi and Lidl – it's now seen as a badge of honour'.[16]

Implications for retailers and brands

The preceding developments in hard discounters and the response by consumers have put tremendous growth and profitability pressure on conventional retailers and manufacturer brands. Any social stigma attached to being seen shopping at a hard discounter is receding as consumers in countries from Germany to Australia have shifted an ever-increasing portion of their grocery purchases to hard discounters.

The biggest disruption in grocery retailing in half a century

Wherever hard discounters appear, the grocery retailscape is profoundly changed. In 2014, Dalton Philips, then CEO of Morrisons, the UK's fourth-largest retailer, called the rise of hard discounters 'the biggest challenge facing the industry since the 1950s and the advent of the supermarket'.[17] It also cost him his job. According to the British press, he was fired in January 2015 after failing to arrest the decline in sales, largely attributed to the success of Aldi and Lidl.[18] Andy Clarke, the CEO of Walmart's subsidiary Asda, the UK's second-largest grocery chain, called the new competitive environment created by Aldi and Lidl 'the worst storm in retail history'.[19]

In Germany, hard discounters accounted for three out of every ten euros spent on grocery purchases – or €60 billion – in 2017.[20] The rise of hard discounters costs conventional retailers directly via lost sales and indirectly via downward pressure on prices. Prices at hard discounters tend to be 33 to 50 per cent below those at other retailers (direct effect). These retailers have responded to the hard-discount attack by reducing the prices of national brands, as well as their own store brands (indirect effect). We conservatively estimate that the combined effect puts the annual revenue lost by conventional retailers due to the rise of hard discounters at €100 billion in 2017.

Aldi entered Australia in 2001, and, by 2017, had cost conventional retailers like Woolworths and Coles AU $16 billion in lost annual revenues.[21] Auchan's fightback against the likes of Aldi and Lidl squeezed its operating margins in France from a fairly robust 4 per cent in 2009 to 0.3 per cent in 2016, while Casino had to revise down its profits several times.

UK retailers long thought themselves impervious to the hard discounter threat, seemingly secure behind their sophisticated private-label architecture, consisting of three price/quality tiers – value, standard, and premium – along with speciality and niche private labels. Yet, in the period 2012–2017, the combined market share of Aldi and Lidl more than doubled to 12 per cent. The effect on the Big Four UK retailers was devastating. While market leader Tesco's revenues in the UK had nearly doubled in the preceding decade, they declined by 6 per cent in these last years. To shore up its home market, it drastically curtailed its international ambitions, withdrawing from countries like the United States, South Korea, Japan, and China. Morrisons was even more affected – its revenues declined by 13 per cent.[22] The revenues of Sainsbury's and Asda also declined. Stock prices of the three listed main players Tesco, Sainsbury's, and Morrisons decreased by 35 to 50 per cent between January 2014 and January 2016.

There is no end in sight. What should perhaps worry conventional retailers most is that the discounters have proven themselves adept at moving upmarket, even as they retain most of their efficiencies. Lidl now stocks a limited range of branded goods alongside its cheaper own-label items. Aldi used to be known for canned and packaged foods, but has introduced fresh and delicatessen products.

Manufacturer brands feeling the pressure

Manufacturer brands have been hurt by the rise of private labels, which by 2017 had captured 21.2 per cent of consumer packaged goods sales in the United States, and 36.5 per cent in Western Europe, according to Europanel. While this is bad enough, manufacturer brands are doubly hurt by the shift from conventional retailers, where manufacturer brands account for 50 to 75 per cent of total sales, to hard discounters, where private labels account for 50 to 90 per cent of total sales. When A G Lafley, then CEO of Procter & Gamble, visited the company's European headquarters in 2001, Paul Polman, then P&G's president for Europe (and now the CEO of Unilever), took him to visit P&G's most dangerous competitor: not the headquarters of Henkel, Nestlé, or Unilever, but an Aldi store. Polman explained to us: 'Aldi hardly sells any national brands. That makes it very difficult to compete as they own the channel at the same time.' The rise of hard discounters poses a triple-whammy threat to brand manufacturers:

1 Any private-label item bought at a hard discounter is a sale lost to brand manufacturers.

2 The success of hard discounters compels other retailers to put more emphasis on their own store brands to try to be more price competitive.

3 Brand manufacturers feel the pressure to reduce prices, or at least to restrain price increases, in order to retain market share. For example, Procter & Gamble was forced to cut the prices of Always sanitary napkins by 17 per cent and Pampers diapers by 11 per cent to remain competitive in Germany against Aldi's private labels.

We conservatively estimate that by 2017, the success of hard discounters has been responsible for reducing manufacturer brand sales by half a trillion dollars *annually*.[23] That amount exceeds the combined sales of Procter & Gamble, Unilever, Nestlé, L'Oréal, Coca-Cola, and PepsiCo in that same year by a wide margin.

The next frontier: The United States

In the United States, hard discounters have been less of a factor in grocery retailing than in other developed countries. The hard discounter banners Aldi, Trader Joe's, and Save-A-Lot accounted for a modest 2.6 per cent of grocery sales in the United States in 2017 (the brand discounters Dollar General and Dollar Tree accounted for another 2.5 per cent). We believe this is going to change. Why? Three reasons stand out: consumer receptivity, market opportunity, and hard discounters' plans.

1 *Consumer receptivity to hard discounters*

In the past, US consumers, like UK shoppers before them, exhibited relatively little interest in shopping with hard discounters. This is ever less the case. This is what Vanessa Zimmerman wrote in a comment on an article in *Supermarket News* in 2015, announcing that Lidl was coming to the United States: 'Come to San Diego, please! I shopped your store for two months while I was in Ireland and became addicted.'[24]

We have seen that stagnating household incomes have been an engine of hard discounter growth in various European countries. The situation in the United States is only slightly better on average. Between 2000 and 2016, the average real income increased on average 0.9 per cent per year – hardly impressive by any standard. Moreover, income growth was not evenly spread across regions and income strata. The median household income, adjusted for the cost of living, was lower in 2016 than in 2000 in more than 80 per cent of urban areas.[25]

2 Market opportunity

The US grocery market is huge, and, as such, attractive for just about any retailer. Yet, the United States lacks nationwide deep-discount grocery chains. The chain that comes closest is Walmart; however, consumer satisfaction with Walmart is low. In a survey conducted in 2017 by the American Customer Satisfaction Index, Walmart was ranked last out of all major US grocery chains on customer satisfaction. Compare this with Trader Joe's, which was ranked #2, and Aldi, ranked #3.[26]

3 Hard discounters' plans

Aldi has reached an inflection point in its market success. The growth rate has increased from a 'low' of 5.8 per cent in 2012 to 13.9 per cent in 2017 (Figure 1.1). Aldi's value proposition is strong. Prices can be as much as 40 per cent below conventional supermarkets and 25 per cent less than big-box discounters like Walmart.[27]

In response to Lidl's entry into the United States, Aldi announced in June 2017 a dramatic acceleration of its previously cautious expansion plans. It plans to open 900 new stores by 2022, bringing its total to 2,500 – the same as Kroger had in 2017. While Aldi is expanding aggressively, its subsidiary (but independently operated) Trader Joe's covers the more upscale segment of the market. Its expansion is going more slowly, but that is by design, not by any lack of demand. Trader Joe's operated around 500 stores in 2017, which generated around US $10 billion in sales.

And then there is Lidl, which opened its first stores in the United States in June 2017. Although only time will tell how successful Lidl will be in

Figure 1.1   Aldi in the United States

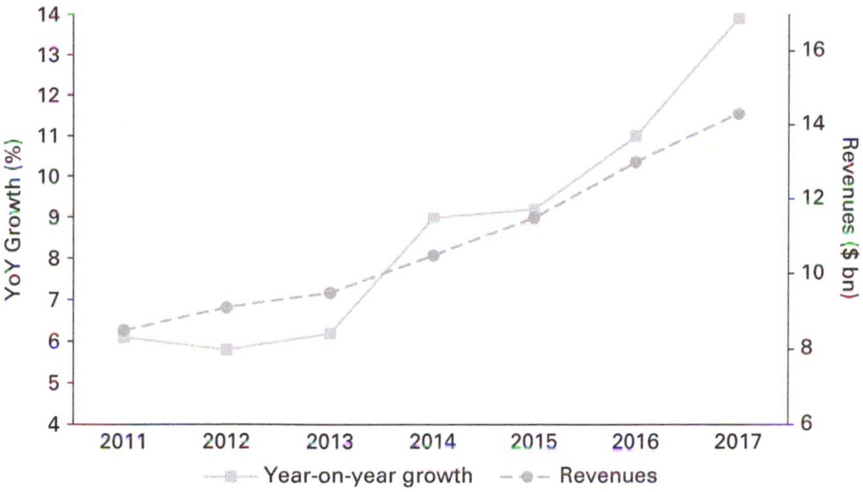

SOURCE   Based on 2018 data from Planet Retail

the United States, it is a sophisticated hard discounter with deep pockets. It carries more manufacturer brands than Aldi, something which is important in relatively more brand-conscious United States (vs Europe).

How this book can help you

The book consists of three parts. The first part reveals the secrets of hard discounter success. Chapter 2 lays out the hard discounter business model for profitability at low price points. Chapter 3 examines the strategies of four key hard discounters: Aldi, Lidl, Trader Joe's, and DIA. Chapter 4 looks at the impact of hard discounters on five key markets, each with its own characteristics – Germany, UK, Australia, Poland, and Turkey. Finally, Chapter 5 looks at the impact of hard discounters on the world's largest market: The United States. After reading Part One, you will understand the power and versatility of hard discounting in its various forms and in key markets.

The second part of the book examines what conventional retailers can do to combat the hard discounter challenge. Chapter 6 deals with the effects of hard discounter entry on conventional retailers. Who is hurt most? Who might actually gain? Chapter 7 explores strategic responses conventional retailers can employ and how the recommended response varies by retailer format. Finally, Chapter 8 outlines how conventional retailers can reduce their procurement costs from national brand manufacturers and private-label suppliers in an attempt to narrow the price gap with hard discounters. After reading Part Two, you will have acquired actionable insights and strategies to not only cope with – but prosper in – a retail environment that includes powerful hard discounters.

Part Three examines what manufacturer brands can do in a world increasingly dominated by hard discounters. Chapter 9 explains how manufacturer brands can create winning value propositions against hard discounters ('competition'). Chapter 10 explores another option, where manufacturers try to benefit from the rise of hard discounters by producing their private labels ('cooperation'). Chapter 11 introduces a third option: to sell through hard discounters. While that option is not for the faint-hearted, brands can no longer opt out of the fastest-growing retail format ('co-opetition'). After reading Part Three, you will be able to decide how to respond to the challenges posed by hard discounters by a judicious use of one or more of these strategies.

The final chapter pulls together the themes and lessons of the book and looks into the future.

Before starting Part One of the book, two comments about terminology. As per the purpose of this book, hard discounters will often be contrasted with other retailers in the market. Sometimes (especially in Part Two), we will zoom in on various formats, such as brand discounters or mainstream retailers. In other places, we will refer to the whole of other retailers by the short-cut *conventional retailers*. This is not at all to imply that these retailers are not innovative or cutting-edge in what they do; they are only conventional in the light of the retail disruption wrought by hard discounters. Further, consistent with the definition of PlanetRetail, when we talk about grocery, we use it as an overarching term to include edible grocery (foods and beverages), health and beauty products, and household and pet care.

Notes

1 GfK (2003) Markets, discounters, private labels, presentation at 22nd Kronberg Meeting, 27 March.
2 Fertel, R (2017) The American bazaar, *Wall Street Journal*, 20 May, p. C9.
3 Siegel+Gale, *Global Brand Simplicity Index, 2017*.
4 www.linkedin.com/pulse/power-brand-building-your-own-personal-corporate-world-onyebuchi?forceNoSplash=true, last accessed 2 September 2017.
5 GfK (2007) Between premium and private label – opportunities for the middle segment? Presentation at 26th Kronberg Meeting, 25 January 2007.

6 GfK (2017) Versrapport, 2010–2017.

7 *The Economist* (2015) When what comes down doesn't go up, 2 May; MacPherson, N (2018) Pay rises will not solve Britain's productivity problem, *Financial Times*, 23 March, p.10.

8 www.statista.com/statistics/416213/average-annual-wages-italy-y-on-y-in-euros/, last accessed 23 March 2018.

9 Stern quote taken from 'Markets, Discounters, Private Labels: The German Marketplace', presentation given at the annual GfK Kronberg meeting, 27 March 2003; Grey, S (2008) Aldi: A Grocer for the Recession, *Forbes*, 28 October; Iacob, M (2009) Recession-resistant retailers, *Forbes*, 2 February.

10 *The Economist* (2008) The Germans are coming, 16 August, pp. 53–54.

11 Lamey, L (2014) Hard economic times: a dream for discounters, *European Journal of Marketing*, 48 (3/4), pp. 641–56.

12 'Consumption with Pleasure Instead of Frustration', presentation at the 25th Kronberg meeting, 2006.

13 http://www.bbc.com/news/business-34315643, last accessed 2 September 2017.

14 Steenkamp, J B (2017) *Global Brand Strategy: World-wise marketing in the age of branding*, Palgrave Macmillan, London.

15 Chaudhuri, S (2015) Look out, US grocers, UK's free-for-all heads across the pond, *Wall Street Journal*, 11 September, p. A1.

16 www.thisismoney.co.uk/money/news/article-3113612/Aldi-surge-goes-snaps-heels-Britain-s-five-supermarkets.html, last accessed 2 September 2017.

17 www.independent.co.uk/news/business/news/lidl-and-aldi-pose-biggest-supermarket-threat-ever-9191275.html, last accessed 21 March 2018.

18 www.theguardian.com/business/2015/jan/13/morrisons-chief-dalton-philips-quits-supermarket; www.dailymail.co.uk/news/article-2907768/Morrisons-chief-executive-quits-Britain-s-fourth-largest-supermarket-posts-sales-drop-3-1, both last accessed 21 March 2018.

19 www.businessinsider.com/german-store-lidl-plans-us-expansion-2015-11, last accessed 2 March 2018.

20 Euromonitor International, 'Grocery Retailers in Germany 2017'.

21 Aldi's revenues in 2016 were AU $9.3 billion. If we consider the price differential and the price deflation caused by Aldi – for example, Woolworth confirmed that 'Strong competition in the grocery sector has driven 19 consecutive quarters of price deflation' – we arrive at a ballpark estimate of AU $16 billion. www.dailymail.co.uk/news/article-2695548/Australian-grocery-prices-tipped-permanently-slashed-supermarket-price-wars-increase.html, last accessed 2 September 2017.

22 Information in this paragraph is taken from Kantar Retail (www.kantarretail.com/) and Planet Retail (www.planetretail.net/).

23 Total sales of hard discounters was around US $300 billion in 2017, of which we conservatively estimate around 75 per cent is private label (cf. Aldi's private-label share is around 90 per cent and Lidl's private-label share outside of Germany is in the range of 80–90 per cent). Hard discounter private labels are around 50 per cent cheaper than manufacturer brands, and thus, if all hard discounter private-label sales come from manufacturers, this would mean about $450 billion in lost sales. However, some portion of hard discounter private-label sales comes from other retailers. But added to this amount should be the lost revenues due to other retailers expanding their own private-label assortment and the lost revenues due to manufacturer brands reducing their prices.

24 supermarketnews.com/retail-financial/lidl-confirms-us-expansion, last accessed 2 September 2016.

25 www.statista.com/statistics/612519/average-annual-real-wages-united-states/, last accessed 23 March 2018; Fleming, S and Donnan, S (2016) Household income tumbles in majority of US cities this century, *Financial Times*, 12 May, p. 1.

26 American Customer Satisfaction Index (2018) ACSI retail report 2017.

27 nrf.com/news/disruptive-discounters, last accessed 2 September 2017.

PART ONE
Hard discounter strategies

Understanding the hard discounter business model

02

How are hard discounters able to grow so fast? How are they able to make money at such low price points? Why has it proven so difficult for conventional retailers to copy elements of their model to fight them off? To answer these questions, we must take a close look at the business model that powers the hard discounter format. While different hard discounters, of course, do not follow the exact same model, there are many similarities that are brought together in Figure 2.1. The core of the business model is the virtuous cycle, in which a high volume per stock keeping unit (SKU) leads to irresistible value for money for consumers. This contributes to high profitability that funds expansion of the store network, which further increases the volume per SKU, and so on. We take up each of these in turn.

We need to point out, though, that each of these four key success factors can only be in place because of specific and crucial enabling processes, which are also outlined in Figure 2.1. In our discussion of the key success factors, we will take a look at these enabling processes as well.

High volume per SKU

High volume per SKU is not feasible in a mainstream supermarket which carries 25,000–40,000 items. There is simply not enough consumer demand to achieve high sales volume for so many SKUs. The hard discounter solves this problem by limiting the number of SKUs offered to around 1,000–2,500 items. In each category, it carefully selects only the most popular flavours, package sizes, or other types of variety. This strategy leads to high volumes per item. We illustrate this for the Netherlands, where we compare Aldi with market leader Albert Heijn (Table 2.1).[1] Aldi carries about 1,250 different items versus 27,500 items offered by Albert Heijn. Aldi generates

Figure 2.1 Hard discounter business model

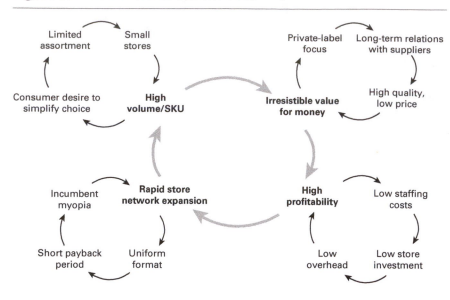

Table 2.1 Comparison of sales per SKU between Aldi and Albert Heijn in the Netherlands in 2016

	Aldi	**Albert Heijn**
Total revenues	€2.5 bn	€13 bn
Market share	7.0%	35.2%
Number of stores	500	950
Number of SKUs	1,250	27,500
Revenues per store	€5.0 mn	€13.7 mn
Revenues per SKU	€2.0 mn	€0.5 mn
Revenues per SKU per store	€4,000	€500

SOURCE Based on 2017 research from EFMI Business School

revenues of €2.5 billion per year with 500 stores, while Albert Heijn generates €13 billion per year with 950 stores.

At first sight, Albert Heijn outperforms Aldi almost by a factor of three when sales per store are compared: €13.7 million versus €5.0 million. But when we compare the sales per item, a totally different picture arises: Aldi sells €2 million per SKU per year versus €0.5 million for Albert Heijn. So, even with only one-fifth of the market share, Aldi's revenue per SKU is four times that of Albert Heijn. And Albert Heijn is the market leader! The situation for other chains is even bleaker. If we further take into account that many Aldi items are sold in other countries, the factor of four can easily become a factor of 10 or more. That is one of the amazing effects of item rationalization.

But why would consumers patronize a store that limits their freedom of choice by more than 95 per cent? Because more choice is not always preferred by shoppers.

Consumer desire for choice simplicity

It is a common supposition in Western society that choice is good, and the more choice, the better. Economic theory dictates that the greater the number of options in a product category, the higher the likelihood that consumers can find a close match to their needs. This attracts a broader, more diverse set of people to the store, as they can be more confident that they can find a suitable item in that store, facilitating one-stop shopping. Economic theory further postulates that consumers derive utility from freedom of choice and enjoyment of exploration in the store. As it turns out, this is not necessarily the case.

In one famous study conducted in an upscale grocery store in Menlo Park, California, researchers showed that consumers were more likely to make a purchase when presented with an assortment comprising of six flavours of jam than with an assortment comprising of 24 flavours (all flavours were of the same brand).[2] The difference was substantial: only 2 per cent of the consumers in the extensive-choice context made a purchase versus 12 per cent of the consumers in the limited-choice condition. This study is not an isolated instance. A stream of subsequent work has documented that consumers regularly experience choice overload, leading to less satisfaction, more post-purchase regret, and lower likelihood of purchase.[3]

Why would a large assortment lead to a lower, rather than higher, probability that a consumer makes a purchase from the assortment? Because a large assortment can be cognitively overwhelming. You need to absorb and process so much information about brands, product characteristics, and prices, that many shoppers either get confused or are simply not willing to make the effort. Sounds exaggerated? Consider this: one of us needed to purchase 13-gallon kitchen trash bags and went to the local Harris Teeter.

The choice was overwhelming. In this mundane and low-involvement category, Harris Teeter carried 49 SKUs, across four national brands (including two he had never heard of) and one private label. It took him eight minutes to process the information, to understand broadly the differences, check prices and promotions, and make his choice. And trash bags is a category with a 'small' assortment. He counted 180 SKUs of dry pasta at that same store.

When is preference for a limited assortment most likely?

A large assortment can lead to choice overload, which, in turn, leads to lower satisfaction, more regret, and greater likelihood of choice deferral. Obviously, that does not happen all the time and for everybody. So, when is choice overload more likely, and, hence, preferable to have a smaller assortment to choose from? Four conditions stand out:[4]

- *If the shopper is under time pressure.* If he or she has to make a decision fast, having too many choices becomes a burden, not a bonus. The typical grocery trip easily encompasses 20 or more items, which are often purchased after work, in between other chores, or with (bored) children in tow.

- *If the shopper is intent on buying rather than browsing.* On some occasions, consumers may go to the grocery store to learn more about the available options or just for fun. In those instances, a large assortment in any given category is pleasurable, not burdensome. But most consumers have neither the time nor the interest to constantly engage in extensive browsing.

- *If the shopper is focused on making a satisfactory decision.* Economic theory holds that consumers are utility maximizers. To achieve this, you need to evaluate the prices and characteristics of all options and then make a choice. For this, a full product assortment is needed. However, the *homo economicus* is a figment of economists' imagination. It is necessary to derive mathematical solutions to complex models. Most of the time, consumers are satisficers, not maximizers. Satisficers prefer to quickly choose the option that meets the minimum criteria (the word 'satisfice' blends 'satisfy' and 'suffice'). Do you really want to purchase paper towels that maximize your utility after extensive study, or ones that just do their basic functions satisfactorily? Satisficing behaviour is especially common if the shopper believes little is at stake. This applies to most CPG categories. Compared to durables or services, prices tend to be low and risk of nonperformance is modest.

- *If the consumer has limited brand knowledge.* Consumers who have deep knowledge of available brands and how they score on product attributes can find their way even in a large assortment with relative ease. Conversely, when you have limited knowledge, the task can be overwhelming. Let us give an example. The local Harris Teeter carries 14 brands of canned tomatoes: Hunt's, Del Monte, Vine-Ripe, Furmano's, Dei Fratelli, Rotel, Cento, Pomi, Tuttorosso, San Marzano, Rao's, and the store brands Harris Teeter, HT Traders, and Simple Truth. Across these 14 brands, the retailer's assortment comprises 103(!) SKUs across four package sizes (from 6 ounces to 28 ounces), seven levels of processing (from plum to crushed), two types of production (regular, organic), and 14 flavours, ranging from roasted garlic to Mexican style with lime juice and cilantro. One of us who regularly shops at that store was completely unaware of the existence of 10 of these brands, let alone understands (or cares about) the difference between Italian-style and Mexican-style Del Monte canned tomatoes. Most of all, he does not really want to think about all these options.

For many consumers, not just one or two, but easily three or all four of the above criteria apply. Unfortunately, in a brick-and-mortar store, the retailer cannot adapt the assortment to individual shoppers. Thus, the consumer has to choose between a store with a large assortment in all categories or a small assortment in all categories.[5] Many consumers opt for the store with the large assortment, but an ever-growing group of consumers prefers the low complexity of a limited assortment for at least some of their shopping trips.

Preference for small stores

Limited assortment goes hand in hand with small stores. You do not need 60,000–65,000 square feet – the average size of a conventional supermarket like Kroger in the United States or Asda in the UK – to display 1,000–2,000 SKUs. Their small assortment allows hard discounters to operate small stores that are generally in the range of 8,000–15,000 square feet, which reinforces their lower shopping complexity. Smaller stores are easier to navigate and find products in. Do the test yourself. How many feet or metres do you have to walk in an Asda or Kroger during your shopping trip? We bet it is at least three times as much as in a Trader Joe's or Aldi. Large stores may not only be cognitively demanding, but also physically draining.

Hard discounters understand that smaller shopping space and limited assortment allow for a much simpler – and potentially more satisfying – shopping experience. Brendan Proctor, CEO of Lidl US, explained Lidl's thinking in the *Washington Post*:

> A lot of the supermarkets are so large, it's a challenge for people to go shopping. If I wanted to go in and get a bottle of ketchup – first of all, there are probably about 24 aisles in the store. I have to find what aisle it's in. I get there, I find that there's 50 types of ketchup. Who honestly needs 50 types of ketchup? So we can streamline that.[6]

Irresistible value for money

High volume per SKU contributes to the ability of the hard discounter to offer irresistible value for money. But how is it able to offer high quality for a low price? Because it sells predominantly private labels, where it has complete control over pricing and quality. High volume per private-label SKU means that the hard discounter is in an excellent position to negotiate with its private-label suppliers. In general, there is a high degree of standardization of processes and decision making concerning sourcing of products throughout the discounters' organizations. Contracts for supply are renegotiated annually – although multi-year contracts are not uncommon – and the buying process is kept as simple as possible. Meetings with suppliers are restricted to a bare minimum, resulting in low transaction costs for both sides. Once the contract is signed, there are usually no surprises at a later stage for the manufacturer. This is in sharp contrast with the common practice of traditional retailers, who tend to continue to extract money from their suppliers even after contract negotiations are finalized.

A stable, long-term relationship with suppliers generates substantial efficiencies. Unless there are serious issues around quality, uncompetitive prices, or delivery rates, the current supplier is favoured as switching is time-consuming and adds costs. Orders and volumes from discounters are reliable and predictable due to the absence of promotions and superior planning and replenishment procedures. Furthermore, payments arrive on time and in full. Negotiations are tough and discount clients are extremely demanding. Nevertheless, private-label manufactures love to work with them for the reasons mentioned above. Table 2.2 summarizes the contrasting experiences private-label suppliers in Europe have working with hard discounters versus conventional retailers.[7]

Long-term relationships encourage suppliers to invest in high-quality products. As a consequence, hard discounters' products often exceed the

Table 2.2 How private-label suppliers in Europe experience the relationship with hard discounters and conventional retailers

	Hard discounter	**Conventional retailer**
Negotiations	Very demanding but adherence to agreements	Very demanding and prone to additional demands afterwards
Relationship with supplier	Focus on longer-term collaboration to the mutual benefit of both parties	Transactional and short term, the main concern being to have bought at the lowest price
Number of contact persons	Mostly one point of contact	Multiple points of contact, involving multiple departments
Turnover of contact persons	Low: purchase managers remain in place for longer, allowing them to build knowledge and understanding of products and markets	Frequent: resulting in loss of efficiency, expertise, and continuity in existing projects; however, it opens opportunities to educate more receptive new contact persons
Decision making	Relatively fast and transparent, aided by the purchase manager having responsibility for entire process and relationship with supplier	Long and relatively opaque due to internal politics and different departments having sometimes contradictory objectives
Private-label quality	40% of suppliers think that discounters' private-label quality is better than that of conventional retailers	0% of suppliers think that conventional retailers' private-label quality is better than that of discounters
Quality vs price	Search for the optimal tradeoff between quality and price	Quality is compromised in favour of low price

SOURCE Based on 2017 data from IPLC

quality of private labels from mainstream retailers. Table 2.3 shows some test results for the UK. As UK retailers are generally seen as the most sophisticated private-label operators in the world, meeting their exacting quality standards is as tough a test as you can get. In our comparison, we focus on the Big Four retailers – Tesco, Sainsbury's, Asda, and Morrisons.

Table 2.3 shows that Aldi and/or Lidl often offer better quality than one or more of these large, sophisticated retailers. And that does not even take price into account. Private-label products for hard discounters can be

Table 2.3 Quality rating of the private labels of Aldi, Lidl and the 'Big Four' conventional retailers in the UK, 2016–2018

Dishwasher tablets		Laundry detergent		Diapers		Orange juice		Ground coffee		Bacon	
Aldi	78	Lidl	83	Aldi	77	Sainsbury's	77	Aldi	82	Asda	83
Lidl	71	Tesco	82	Lidl	63	Lidl	76	Sainsbury's	73	Sainsbury's	80
Tesco	49	Sainsbury's	80	Tesco	61	Morrisons	75	Lidl	70	Lidl	70
Morrisons	48	Aldi	79	Asda	60	Tesco	75	Asda	70	Aldi	70
		Morrisons	60	Morrisons	52	Aldi	74	Morrisons	69	Morrisons	66
				Sainsbury's	50	Asda	74			Tesco	61

NOTE *Which?* did not always report the quality rating for every Big Four (Tesco, Sainsbury's, Asda, and Morrisons) retailer.
SOURCE Based on various issues of *Which?* (2016, 2018)

Table 2.4   Price indices of private label in conventional retailers and Lidl in 2016

Retailer	Country	Price index versus national brand (= 100)	
		Copycat private label conventional retailer	Private label Lidl
Albert Heijn	The Netherlands	69	54
Tesco	United Kingdom	51	38
Delhaize	Belgium	63	45
Carrefour	France	69	51
Edeka	Germany	81	40
Carrefour	Spain	75	56
Tesco	Poland	62	56
SPAR	Austria	65	40
COOP	Switzerland	66	37
Average		*67*	*46*

SOURCE Based on 2016 data from IPLC

manufactured at lower cost, given the large volumes involved and absence of sudden changes in product specifications. This enables the hard discounter to sell its private-label products at prices that are around 50 per cent lower than leading national brands, and around 30 per cent lower than the private-label equivalents of national brands at traditional retailers. Table 2.4 shows that this performance is found across different countries.

To sum up, because of their large volumes and long-term relationships with suppliers, hard discounters are able to deliver good-quality products for a low price. What is not to love about that?

High profitability

Irresistible value for money creates high demand for hard discounter products, but, given their low prices, how can they make money? It is not because gross margin is higher. On the contrary, while the cost of goods sold (COGS) is lower for hard discounters, their prices are so much lower that their gross margin is significantly lower than for conventional retailers. The secret is strict cost control. Based on annual reports from grocery retailers, expert

Table 2.5   Profitability of conventional grocery retailer versus hard discounter in Western Europe in 2017

	Conventional grocery retailer	Hard discounter	Hard discounter advantage
Revenues	100	100	
Cost of goods sold (including product loss)	(73)	(81)	
Gross margin	27	19	−8
Store-related operating costs	(12)	(7)	+5
– Labour	(8)	(5)	
– Other costs (rent, depreciation, utilities…)	(4)	(2)	
Operating margin (store based)	15	12	−3
Overhead (SG&A)	(11)	(6.5)	+4.5
– Central staffing	(3)	(1.5)	
– Logistical costs	(4)	(3)	
– Marketing	(4)	(2)	
Earnings before interest and taxes	4	5.5	+1.5

SOURCE Authors' estimates

opinions, and documentation from the EFMI Business School and the German EHI Retail Institute, we have developed a normative income statement of a typical conventional grocery retailer and a typical hard discounter in Western Europe (Table 2.5).

Store-related operating costs

Store-related operating costs are much lower for hard discounters. Labour costs are a major factor. Lower staffing costs are due to greater efficiency, not to lower wages. In fact, hard discounters are known for paying their employees relatively well.[8] There are few, if any, service counters. Restocking shelves is fast and easy as the assortment is limited and many items are sold in a box that does not need unpacking due to the use of shelf-ready packaging.

Hard discounters save considerably on rent and depreciation. Stores are small and often are in secondary locations. Investments in store interiors is low, generally only one-third to one-half of the investment per square foot of store space in a conventional grocery store. In the Netherlands, for example, the average investment costs for a complete store interior for a mainstream retailer are about €80–€100 per square foot; it is about half this amount for Aldi and Lidl, even when they have an in-store bakery. The most spartan hard discount stores, without any service departments, only require an investment of about €20–€30 per square foot. This leads to low depreciation costs, which, for example, for Aldi Süd in Germany, are only 1.1 per cent of revenues versus an industry average for conventional grocery retailers of almost 2 per cent.[9]

Overhead

Overhead is reduced by the absence of sumptuous offices and the lower costs of central staffing. Relatively few purchase managers are needed to buy only 1,000–2,500 SKUs. Also, hard discounters have neither intricate category plans based on expensive marketing research nor complex loyalty programmes and large customer service departments. And do you really need a public relations department? Aldi Netherlands, for example, does not have one. It is not seen as a core activity that creates consumer value, but may only invite needless inquiries consuming valuable management time.[10]

Significant money is also saved on logistics. Because of the limited assortment of goods, less warehouse space is needed and the available space can be used more efficiently. Sales volume per item is high, which makes the order-picking process simpler and faster. Conventional grocery retailers have so many slow-moving items that some have opened special warehouses that carry the items that move less than one box (often containing 6 or 12 products) per week per store, because these items make the process of picking all the needed items via a regular warehouse too complex and too slow. Transportation from the warehouse to the stores is focused on efficiency rather than to prevent stock-outs. The main objective is to supply stores with full truck loads, which might implicate that some product groups are only supplied once or twice a week.

While hard discounters employ relatively few marketers, they do spend significant amounts of money on marketing (albeit that marketing expenses vary substantially between countries). They cannot profit from heavy advertising by national brands to drive store traffic, so they have to do more of the heavy lifting themselves. Promotional activity is much lower than that of conventional retailers. These players can easily sell anywhere between

25 and 35 per cent of their weekly sales at a price discount of 25–30 per cent. This means that promotions cost 6–9 per cent of total margin. A large part of this margin loss is usually compensated by the manufacturer whose brand is being promoted, but even if the retailer pays only a quarter of the discount, it is still an important marketing expenditure for the retailer. We estimate that hard discounters spend on average two percentage points less on marketing activities than regular grocery retailers do.

To put it all together, while the gross margin of a typical hard discounter is easily eight percentage points lower than that of a typical conventional retailer, after operating costs are subtracted, the picture changes dramatically to a hard discounter profit advantage of 1.5 percentage points. While costs structures and actual profit margins do vary across retailers, countries, and time (eg price wars), the lesson is clear. Hard discounters can – and often are – actually more profitable than conventional retailers while offering their assortment at significantly lower prices. However, for this to happen, the hard discounter needs to move large volumes, which requires a large store network.

Store network expansion

Because of their smaller store format, hard discounters can build stores in relatively densely populated areas, saving travelling time for shoppers. Stores largely follow a uniform layout, saving costs and accelerating store expansion. The floor plan of Lidl stores in the United States, for example, is completely standardized – from the fresh bakery at the entrance to the location of frozen foods at the diagonally opposite corner of the store. This allowed Lidl to open 47 stores within six months of entering the market in June 2017. But how can store expansion be financed? Favourable profitability is one source, but there are more.

Investment costs

Hard discount stores can spread like wildfire because of the short payback period on store investment. Whereas a regular supermarket may need five to seven years to earn back the store investments, a hard discount store needs only half that time, freeing up capital faster to fund new stores.[11] There are examples of hard discount chains whose payback period is even shorter. Take Action, one of the fastest growing warehouse discount chains in Europe. Its CEO Sander van der Laan said that Action stores were able to earn back all the store investments within one year.[12] The low investments per store, solid profitability, and short payback period allow hard discounters to expand their store network at an unprecedented speed.

Store expansion is also funded by hard discounters' working capital management. In food retailing, suppliers are usually paid anywhere between four and eight weeks after delivery, while the retailer receives its money when the product is sold to the consumer. Now, suppose that a retailer, on average, has a product for two weeks (warehouse, transport, and store) before the product is sold to the consumer, and that the retailer, on average, pays the supplier after six weeks. In that case, the retailer has four weeks of 'free credit'.

Hard discounters are known to have a very high stock rotation, as they carry few – if any – slow-moving SKUs. Conversely, about 60 per cent of the SKUs of a conventional grocery retailer sell less than one box per week per store. Industry experts estimate that hard discounters, on average, have a one-week 'free credit' advantage compared to conventional grocery retailers. This reduces working capital requirements, freeing up resources for store expansion.

Lack of response by conventional retailers

A common thread in hard discounter success is the lack of a vigorous response by conventional retailers until it is too late. This has happened in Germany, Belgium, the Netherlands, Australia, the UK, and Poland. Signals from the United States are somewhat mixed. On the one hand, there are reactions like that of the late Jack Brown, executive chairman of Stater Bros. Markets, the market leader in Southern California. In 2016, Aldi entered the area but he was not concerned. He was confident customers would decide to stick with Stater 'because we are doing what we've done for 80 years – working to be the best full-service supermarket in the area'.[13] On the other hand, what happened in the UK appeared to have made a deep impression on retailers like Kroger and Food Lion. Wherever Lidl entered a ZIP code, they dropped prices significantly.[14] The immense publicity Lidl's entry received in the US press would have also contributed to the awareness of hard discounters.

Underestimation of a new rival, especially one that seems inferior at first sight, is common in business. Remember the first Toyotas and Hondas that were derided in Europe and the United States because they did not look nearly as impressive as Chryslers or Peugeots? Similarly, an Aldi store does not look impressive at all to executives who are used to large, well-lit supermarkets with a rich assortment of goods. Yet, this complacency has allowed hard discounters to gain a foothold in market after market and expand from there. Remember that an army is most vulnerable just after it has landed on a foreign coast. If you do not address the problem right there and then, they will set up camp, bring in more troops, and break out.

To make matters worse, complacency is overlaid with the tyranny of the quarterly regime – a necessity to meet the quarterly expectations of financial markets. Going head to head with a hard discounter, and certainly one with the deep pockets of Aldi and Lidl, costs money – a lot of it. If hard discounter market share is still small, competing by dropping prices costs conventional retailers considerably more than it costs the hard discounter because conventional retailers' sales are higher. They have to take a hit to their profits right now – when it is not strictly 'necessary' from a market share point of view. As a result, the inevitable adverse effects of dropping prices on shareholder value are felt in the short run, while the adverse effects of hard discounter growth will only show up in the long run. Indeed, incumbents may wonder whether the adverse effects will materialize at all, given that they are prone to underestimate the threat posed by these seemingly unsophisticated retail outlets. So, here is the dilemma: the CEO of an existing retailer is asked to take a certain short-term hit (and loss of bonus) to increase the likelihood of an uncertain future gain. Many rational CEOs may decide that doing nothing is the best course of action. Consequently, they allow hard discounters to build up a network, which increases their volume and allows them to negotiate even better deals with private-label suppliers, and so on.

Managerial takeaways

Hard discounters have become successful in country after country by following the same tightly integrated business model. The core of the model is a set of four key performance factors:

1 high volume per SKU;

2 irresistible value for money;

3 high profitability; and

4 rapid expansion of their store network.

These factors are interrelated and mutually support each other, creating a virtuous cycle of hard discounter success. This makes their model hard to imitate by conventional retailers, who would need to copy all elements to reap the benefits. Each of these four factors is the result of an interrelated set of supporting activities and requirements.

#1 High volume per SKU is achieved by:

☐ Deep understanding of consumers' desire to simplify their shopping task, without giving them the feeling that their choices are unduly constrained by lack of options.

☐ A limited assortment that offers more choices in the categories where it matters most while restricting choice in other categories. Fancy labels are used by leading discounters like Aldi and Lidl for their private labels to give the consumer the illusion of variety and choice.

☐ Small stores with few aisles that are easy to navigate, to reduce the complexity of shopping.

#2 Irresistible value for money is achieved by:

☐ A strong focus on private labels, which make up anywhere between 50 and 90 per cent of the assortment.

☐ Long-term relationships with suppliers, where the hard discounter promises predictable and large volumes, prompt payment, and no sudden renegotiations of terms.

☐ High functional product quality for a low price. This is possible because of the large volumes and long-term relationships with suppliers.

#3 High profitability is achieved by:

☐ The hard discounter's ability to squeeze any excess store-related and overhead costs out of the system. Thus, strict and absolute cost control is the name of the game.

☐ Keeping store-related operating costs low (compared to conventional retailers) via lower staffing and lower investment per store. Staffing costs are lower because of lower service levels and easier restocking due to the smaller assortment and leaving individual SKUs in their outer boxes.

☐ Absence of sumptuous offices and lower central staffing. An important element here is that a smaller assortment and long-term relationships with suppliers reduce the number of purchase managers needed. Having a smaller number of SKUs also reduces logistics costs.

#4 Rapid store expansion is achieved by:

☐ The use of a uniform store plan.

☐ Short payback period on store investments. To finance rapid expansion, the hard discounter leverages the fact that it needs only around three years to earn back the store investments, versus five to seven years for a conventional supermarket. Moreover, rapid shelf turnover means that the hard discounter has a considerable amount of free working capital that can be used to accelerate store expansion.

☐ Lack of vigorous response to the invasion of the hard discounter until it is too late has helped hard discounters immeasurably in country after country.

Notes

1 Data supplied by EFMI Business School (www.efmi.nl/).

2 Iyengar, S and Lepper, M R (2000) When choice is demotivating: can one desire too much of a good thing? *Journal of Personality and Social Psychology*, **79** (6), pp. 995–1006.

3 Chernev, A, Böckenholt, U, and Goodman, J (2015) Choice overload: a conceptual review and meta-analysis, *Journal of Consumer Psychology*, **25**, pp. 333–58.

4 Ibid.

5 Obviously, the absolute number of options differs between categories and astute retailers, whether they be large supermarkets or hard discounters, adapt the size of the assortment to broad needs in the marketplace. However, in almost any given category, the assortment carried by a mainstream retailer is significantly larger than that of a hard discounter.

6 Halzack, S (2017) A first look at how German grocer Lidl plans to conquer the US market, *Washington Post*, 15 February.

7 IPLC (2017) 'Driving Private Label Growth through Collaboration', Research Report. Results based on interviews with 113 senior managers from 16 European countries who work at private-label suppliers (both dedicated suppliers and dual trackers).

8 www.forbes.com/sites/derosetichy/2013/08/13/why-aldi-is-giving-walmart-a-run-for-its-money/, last accessed 2 January 2018.

9 csimarket.com/Industry/industry_Profitability_Ratios.php?ind=1305, last accessed 2 January 2018.

10 www.nrc.nl/nieuws/2015/02/18/een-vraag-voor-aldi-moest-je-faxen-nu-verandert-d-1467046-a547088, last accessed 2 January 2018.

11 Based on a situation where the retailer owns rather than rents the store.

12 www.nrc.nl/nieuws/2017/07/31/action-koerst-op-10-miljard-omzet-12320968-a1568500, last accessed 2 January 2018.

13 www.supermarketnews.com/retail-financial/gallery-most-admired-retailers-aldi-no-threat-stater-and-more-trending-stories, last accessed 12 June 2016.

14 Gielens, K (2018) The competitive price effects of Lidl's entry in the US grocery market, UNC working paper, January 2018.

Strategies of key hard discounters: Aldi, Lidl, Trader Joe's and DIA

03

Hard discounters around the world share many characteristics, most notably the limited product range, relatively small selling space, low price positioning, and the dominant role of private labels in their assortment. Yet, hard discounters do differ from each other according to the private-label strategy pursued.

Some hard discounters use the banner name as a brand for (most of their) private-label products. This is easy to implement and allows for generalization of the overall positive image of the hard discounter to individual products. Others use fancy brand names for different categories. This gives shoppers the illusion of choice and creates more variation of in-store visual stimuli.

Further, discounters differ in the importance of private labels in the total assortment – whether it is high (50–80 per cent) or overwhelming (>80 per cent). When we combine these two dimensions, this results in a two-by-two matrix (see Table 3.1) consisting of four cells, with examples in each cell for 2017. This chapter will describe the key strategies of four successful hard discounters, each belonging to a different cell. We will take a close look at Aldi, Lidl, Trader Joe's, and DIA.

Aldi – the inventor of the hard discount concept

Aldi is the retail banner of the largest global hard discount chain as of 2017. It was founded by brothers Karl and Theo Albrecht in 1946 when they

Table 3.1 Four types of hard discounters in 2017

Private-label focus	Private-label branding strategy	
	Fancy labels	**Banner brand**
Overwhelming (> 80%)	Aldi	Trader Joe's
	Lidl (US, most other countries)	Leader Price
	Norma	
	Eurospin	
High (50–80%)	Lidl (Germany)	DIA
	Biedronka	Penny
	BIM	
	Netto	

took over the family-owned grocery store Albrecht Lebensmittel in Essen, Germany. In post-World War II Germany, there was no room for bells and whistles; everybody was far too busy rebuilding the country in which 20 per cent of all homes and most industry had been destroyed. Grocery products were scarce, and GDP per capita was only one-third that of the UK, so the Albrecht brothers focused on offering an assortment of about 200 staples at the lowest possible prices. Initially, products were sold 'over the counter', but soon the self-service concept – first introduced by Piggly Wiggly in the United States – was adopted to reduce labour costs.

By 1960, the Albrecht brothers already operated 300 stores. In 1961, the brothers split the company into two legally independent operations because they could not agree on whether to sell cigarettes or not. The Ruhr River was used as a geographical separation. Karl went on with Aldi Süd, running Aldi supermarkets south of the Ruhr, while Theo formed Aldi Nord, focusing on Germany north of the Ruhr. The company assumed its current name in 1962, which is a portmanteau combining *Al*brecht and '*Di*skont', the German word for discount. Aldi Nord (headquartered in Essen) and Aldi Süd (headquartered in nearby Mülheim) both use Aldi as their banner but employ different logos.[1]

The separation did nothing to decelerate the growth of Aldi, however. Milestones in the German market were 1,000 stores in 1975, 2,000 stores in 1985, and 3,000 stores in 1995. In 2017, Aldi Süd was operating 1,883 stores in Germany, which generated €15.6 billion in revenues. Aldi Nord operated 2,300 stores, generating €12.3 billion. Aldi's global strength is still quite dependent on its home market. Here, Aldi's outstanding reputation undoubtedly owes much to the company's continuity and credibility in all its operations. It has gained consumers' confidence and, by this, has established a strong retail brand. Aldi tends to have the lowest prices per basket, and so is considered the price leader in Germany. Virtually all competitors follow Aldi's price and product changes.

In the last 10–15 years, Aldi has been moving slightly more upmarket. There is an increased focus on fresh, chilled, and frozen foods, and a growing number of convenience, ready-to-eat, speciality, and premium products, as they test new price strata.

International expansion

Grocery retailing is often regarded as an industry that does not lend itself to international expansion because of differences in shopping behaviour and consumer tastes. However, the Albrecht brothers were way ahead of their time in recognizing that there exists a global segment of people who are interested in getting best value for money, even if they have to compromise on other aspects like store experience and assortment breadth.[2] As early as 1968, Aldi Süd acquired Hofer, an Austrian discount chain. Hofer still operates under this name today, but it adopted the concept, the assortment, and look and feel of the Aldi Süd stores. Aldi Nord entered the Netherlands in 1975, then Belgium in 1976, and Denmark in 1977. In 1976, Aldi Süd opened in the United States with the Aldi concept, while Aldi Nord acquired Trader Joe's. Over the following decades, Aldi expanded to major European countries such as France (1988), the UK (1990), and Spain (2002). It also entered Eastern European countries, as well as Australia. To avoid murderous competition, the Aldi brothers agreed not to both enter any foreign country with the Aldi banner. In 2017, Aldi owned 11,210 stores, of which around 90 per cent use the Aldi banner, generating revenues of €90 billion (Table 3.2).[3]

Aldi Nord versus Aldi Süd

While it is customary to treat Aldi Nord and Aldi Süd as a single discounter, they operate largely independently of each other. Aldi Süd has been consistently quicker to innovate and move with the times.[4] In 2017, it even started selling its own-branded products via the online platform Tmall in China, using its Australian suppliers to serve the Chinese market. Aldi Süd was relatively early in expanding its product range and stores beyond its Spartan origins in line with changing customer expectations, because owner Karl Albrecht had a more flexible approach to the discount dogma than his

Table 3.2 Aldi banners worldwide in 2017

Company	Banner	Number of outlets	Revenues (€ bn)	2012–2017 CAGR (%)
Aldi Nord		5,291	34.0	4.3
	Aldi	4,796	24.4	1.9
	Trader Joe's (US)	495	9.6	12.3
Aldi Süd		5,919	56.0	9.3
	Aldi	5,161	49.5	10.0
	Hofer (Austria)	566	4.9	4.7
	Aldi Suisse (Switzerland)	192	1.6	4.6
Total Aldi		*11,210*	*90.0*	*7.2*

NOTE CAGR = compound annual growth rate. Trader Joe's five-year CAGR in dollars is 8.2 per cent. Reported are gross revenues, including VAT, because net sales were not available for all banners.
SOURCE Based on 2017 data from Planet Retail

brother Theo. This greater readiness to move with the times is reflected in sales figures. In the five years leading up to 2017, Aldi Süd revenues grew by 9.3 per cent. In contrast, Aldi Nord sales grew by only 4.3 per cent, and this performance is inflated by the stellar performance of Trader Joe's, which is operated completely independently and – as we will see later in this chapter – follows a very different strategy. Aldi Süd continues to expand, most notably in Australia, the UK, and the United States, and innovations from these countries have fed back into the stores in Germany.

Aldi Nord is largely playing catch-up with Aldi Süd; its stores and product range have been slower to modernize and remain closer to the retailer's austere origins and the founder's personality. Indeed, Theo Albrecht was legendary for his tight-fistedness. After he was kidnapped in 1971, he first haggled down the ransom and then, on his release, went to court for the right to declare the money as a tax-deductible business expense (he won). In recent years, though, Aldi Nord has started to implement a range of improvements, including new product categories and packaging designs for its private-label brands. The new, more appealing store concept – internally dubbed 'new generation' – is being rolled out across Aldi Nord's entire European network. Smaller stores of less than 7,000 square feet are being closed. Aldi Nord is expected to see a surge in growth from the roll-out of its new store concept. The investment of €5 billion is the largest spending spree in the history of the thrifty retailer. However, the banner still lags behind its sister company and its competitor Lidl.

The five pillars of the Aldi business model

Notwithstanding these differences between Aldi Nord and Aldi Süd, five common pillars continue to be the foundation of the Aldi business model. By adhering to these principles, Aldi manages to be a price-setter in almost every country it operates in.

Pillar #1: ultra-limited assortment

Limited variety is typical for any hard discounter, but with around 1,000 SKUs, Aldi has a considerably more limited assortment than some other leading chains. Trader Joe's offers about 3,500 different items, and Lidl between 1,500 and 2,000 SKUs. Over time, Aldi has expanded the assortment to between 1,200 and 1,400 products in some countries like the UK and the United States to satisfy consumer needs, but this is still lower than Lidl. One major advantage of this strategy is that Aldi is able to sell unimaginably high volumes per item and subsequently save considerably on production costs.

Aldi supplements its basic assortment with limited-time offers such as electronics, apparel, and seasonal products like camping or snow gear. Limited-time offers are sold as long as supplies last. This provides a strong inducement for shoppers to go to Aldi frequently and creates a powerful buzz. For example, the annual winter ski sale in Australia – which is Aldi's biggest day of the year – traditionally attracts thousands of shoppers across the country desperate to snap up a cool saving on snow gear.[5]

Pillar #2: unwavering focus on cost avoidance

Aldi is renowned for its extreme reluctance to add costs to the system. There are no counter service departments, shelves are basic, and store decorations are kept at an absolute minimum. Aldi sells directly from the pallet or from the master carton; it has been one of the innovators of the concept of 'shelf-ready packaging'. In many cases, only a part of the carton has to be unwrapped and consumers can easily pick the product they want.

Shopping carts can only be used when the shopper deposits a coin (a quarter in the United States, £1 in the UK). This is a widespread practice in Europe, but not in the United States. The coin is returned to the shopper when the cart is turned in after their visit. This eliminates the need for staff to wrangle shopping carts. Aldi has a bring-your-own-bag policy, which might seem a modern form of sustainability, but Aldi has had this policy for a long time. You also have to bag your own groceries – quite common in Europe, but virtually unheard of in the United States.

Historically, Aldi had a policy of no mass-media advertising, at least in Germany. As Karl Albrecht, in one of his few public statements, once said, 'Our advertisement is our low price'. However, this is changing. In 2016, a joint advertising campaign from Aldi Nord and Aldi Süd was launched on German TV, cinemas, radio, billboards, and online.[6]

Pillar #3: unique private-label strategy

About 90 per cent of Aldi's selection is private-label brands. This allows Aldi total control over the varieties and formats offered within each product group. To provide consumers with the feeling of choice, Aldi makes use of fancy labels, also called private brands. Each product group has a specific private brand, such as Tandil for detergents, Moser Roth for premium chocolate, and Almare for seafood. Few national brands have made it onto Aldi's shelves, especially in Germany, beyond Coca-Cola, Beiersdorf, Ferrero, P&G, and several spirits brands like Baileys.

Its limited number of brands and SKUs per category reduces consumers' choice complexity. Also, brands do not have to compete with each other within the store, which means that no complex promotions or in-store marketing display materials are needed. This saves labour costs and reduces the amount of items out of stock due to promotion-induced spikes in demand (except for the limited-time offers, where the possibility of out-of-stock serves to create store traffic).

Pillar #4: decentralized organization

One might think that Aldi is a company that is managed centrally, but almost the opposite is true. Its decentralized structure gives country heads and regional heads considerable flexibility when it comes to the assortment offered in their stores. Aldi believes that what it gives up in efficiency it gains back in local responsiveness. In grocery retailing, national, and even regional differences, can be significant. Aldi regards its decentralized structure as a decisive factor in shaping its national and international success. It allows Aldi to leverage its proximity to its customers and its knowledge of markets to tailor its range to the needs of local shoppers. This also applies to the area of corporate responsibility; the expectations and needs of Aldi's customers and other stakeholders differ considerably from country to country. For example, British consumers care much more about local sourcing of goods (especially foodstuffs) than Dutch shoppers.

Finding the right balance between local responsiveness and (inter)-national efficiency is always a challenge. Aldi recognizes that many issues can be addressed more efficiently and more effectively if the national organizations combine their efforts. In these cases, the exchange of experience and best practices across national borders is used to develop a coordinated approach to achieve common goals. Internationally agreed strategies form the framework and basis for realizing joint goals in the national organizations.

Pillar #5: company culture dedicated to simplicity

Aldi is famously secretive about its inner workings, and this is made easier by the fact that it is privately held. But according to Dieter Brandes, a former top manager of Aldi Germany, it is the culture of simplicity that permeates everything Aldi does. It helps employees to focus on the bare essentials: top quality for the lowest possible price. Simplicity is exemplified in Aldi's 'Doing-Without Checklist', which consists of 20 NO rules. Examples include: no external market research, no customer surveys, no budget forecasts, no public appearances, no publicity, no PR departments, no sumptuous business offices, no company cars, no gifts accepted or invitations for dinners from vendors. This list is quite similar to that of IKEA, another famous company that completely upset an entire industry by offering good quality for a low price.[7] According to Brandes, Aldi's corporate culture is a key success factor: 'As assortments, store interior and price level can be copied, culture is almost invisible to the outside world'.[8]

Lidl – the only firm Aldi fears

Lidl is owned by Schwarz Gruppe GmbH, a German family-owned retail group that also operates hypermarkets under the Kaufland banner. In 2017, Lidl had 10,697 stores – almost all in Europe – which generated €75.4 billion in revenues, making it the world's second largest hard discounter. Lidl's compound annual growth rate over the period 2012–2017 was 7.1 per cent, according to Planet Retail. Lidl's sales account for 80 per cent of the Schwarz's total turnover.

Aldi-copycat

The origin of the company goes back to 1930, when Josef Schwarz became a partner in the Südfrüchte Großhandel Lidl & Co. This company changed its name to Lidl & Schwarz KG and was turned into a general food wholesaler. For a long time, the company did not seem to be anything special until the 1970s when Dieter Schwarz, the son of Josef, started to become interested in the discount concept after witnessing the burgeoning success of Aldi. Dieter Schwarz did not want to use the name Schwarz-Markt for his discount banner, as this name literally means 'black market'.[9] The first Lidl discount store was opened in 1973 in Ludwigshafen am Rhein, just 200 miles away from Essen, the original hometown of Aldi. It was a copycat of Aldi and carried around 500 products. Dieter Schwarz rigorously removed slow-moving SKUs from the shelves, and kept costs low by keeping the size of the retail outlet as small as possible. When his father Josef died in 1977, Lidl operated 33 discount stores. By the late 1980s, Lidl was a household name in Germany, with nearly 500 stores stocking around 900 SKUs. Again following Aldi, Lidl set its sights early on international expansion, starting with France in 1989, followed by Italy (1992), and the UK (1994). In 2017, Lidl operated in 28 European countries and the United States, with international markets accounting for 70 per cent of total sales.

Similarities and differences with Aldi

Comparing Aldi and Lidl is a bit like comparing Venus and Serena Williams. Both are known to be 'power hitters' and both achieved tremendous results. Venus, the elder one, was ranked first in the world before Serena. With seven grand slam titles, she definitely ranks amongst the best tennis players in the world over the last few decades, but it was Serena who took women's tennis to another level. By 2017, she had won a record total of 23 grand slam titles, winning each grand slam at least three times. She could therefore be argued as more well-rounded, stronger, and more relentless than her older sister. Although Aldi's Nord and Süd combined still are larger, Lidl might become the Serena Williams of hard discounting.

Like Aldi, Lidl follows a no-frills approach of displaying most of its products in their original delivery cartons. Stores are generally between 10,000 and 15,000 square feet and store ambience is basic. The quality of the products is good and prices are kept very low. The large majority of the assortment consists of private labels, and Lidl supplements its assortment with limited-time offers to drive store traffic. Because the resemblance between Aldi and Lidl is so striking, they are each other's fiercest competitors. But there are also important differences that might explain why Lidl is catching up and is likely to become the world's number one hard discounter soon. These differences are centred around:

1 international expansion;

2 organizational structure;

3 assortment strategy; and

4 marketing programmes.

#1 International expansion

Lidl is more aggressive in its international ambitions than Aldi. In 2017, it was active in more European countries than Aldi (28 versus 18) and had more stores outside of Germany: 7,509 versus 5,756 under the Aldi banner. This international presence helps Lidl in several ways. First, it increases economies of scale, which helps Lidl keep operating costs as low as possible. Second, the international store presence helps Lidl in building its brand, even before it has entered a market, as many people are already familiar with the concept if they have shopped at Lidl during an overseas trip. The entry of Lidl into the United States will add plenty of growth opportunities, provided US customers embrace the Lidl concept.

#2 Organizational structure

Lidl's corporate strategy is considerably more centralized than Aldi's. Regional and national European managers have little leeway in deciding which products to include in their assortment. Most products are available on a European-wide basis with little variation across countries. Each country has but a small purchase department – mostly for produce. To illustrate the difference between Aldi and Lidl, take ambient (shelf-stable) orange juice. Lidl will choose what it deems to be the best supplier, and its product will be carried in all Lidl stores in Europe (for the United States, another supplier might be used because of transportation costs). Aldi would also have centralized purchasing, but if a regional or national manager feels the product is not suitable for their customers, they have the autonomy to purchase it elsewhere, provided this can be done at or below the target price.

Lidl's centralized structure allows it to place orders of large, guaranteed quantities of the same product from a supplier, driving down costs, while at the same time demanding high quality. It also enables Lidl to introduce new products in its international store network much faster than Aldi. On the downside, this makes Lidl more prone than Aldi to ignore idiosyncrasies in local markets, something that should not be disregarded in foods and beverages.

#3 Assortment strategy

Lidl's assortment is about one-third larger than Aldi's. Private labels are the cornerstone of its offering. Like Aldi, Lidl uses fancy brands for different product categories. Some examples are Freeway (soft drinks), Toujours (baby products), Via D'or (fats and oils), Cimarosa (wine), and W5 (cleaning products). Furthermore, they carry separate fancy brands for vegetarian products (My Best Veggie), light products (Linessa), fair-trade products (Fairglobe), and dairy products (Milbona). Lidl also carries an assortment of limited-time non-grocery offerings.

The relative focus on national brands is the main difference in assortment strategies between Aldi and Lidl. Lidl gave a bigger role to national brands after discovering that national brands could help them grow their market share. Table 3.3 shows this for the period 2005–2008.[10] Aldi's market share in Germany was stagnant over this period, while Lidl's market share grew from 8.3 to 10.9 per cent. About half of this growth was due to national brands. As a rule of thumb, wherever Aldi is stronger than Lidl, Lidl carries a larger number of national brands, offering shoppers the choice between its own private label and a leading national brand in many categories. Conversely, wherever Lidl is the leading discount operator, it offers fewer national brands.

Lidl is improving the shopper experience within specific categories, notably bakery and wine. It has rolled out in-store bakeries, enabling shoppers to see production take place. Although this can be considered as a 'frill,' adding costs to the store operation, it reinforces Lidl's credentials on fresh products, a key product category for generating store traffic. Lidl has introduced more

Table 3.3 Role of national brands in Aldi and Lidl in Germany

	2005	2006	2007	2008
Aldi				
Overall market share (%)	15.8	16.1	15.5	15.8
Private-label share (%)	*14.9*	*15.0*	*14.6*	*15.0*
National brand share (%)	*0.9*	*0.9*	*1.0*	*0.8*
Lidl				
Overall market share (%)	8.3	9.3	10.2	10.9
Private-label share (%)	*6.0*	*6.6*	*7.0*	*7.2*
National brand share (%)	*2.3*	*2.6*	*3.2*	*3.7*

SOURCE Based on Bachl (2009)

upmarket wines to make it a feature category and to appeal to affluent shoppers. This initiative has met with success. In the last few years, Lidl has won many awards for its own wines at the International Wine & Spirit Competition.

A remarkable initiative is Lidl's collaboration with fashion icon Heidi Klum. The new collection, 'Esmara by Heidi Klum', was introduced in September 2017 in over 10,000 Lidl stores, including in the United States. Klum explained, 'Lidl is known for making quality products at affordable prices and I'm proud to partner with them on this fashion collaboration. I wanted to create fashion with a wow effect that is easy to combine and makes every woman look fantastic – and all at an unbeatable price.' Consistent with Lidl's philosophy, the low price points do not mean customers will be getting low-quality materials. The line features lace, sequins, leopard print, and even a real leather jacket, which will be the most expensive piece in the collection at around $60.[11] One can wonder, though, whether there is a natural 'fit' between a glamorous model like Klum and an austere hard discounter.

#4 Marketing programmes

Lidl invests more heavily in advertising than Aldi. Although systematic data are hard to obtain, in Germany, Lidl was the largest advertiser among grocery retailers in 2017 (€279.7 million) and the sixth-largest advertiser in Germany, ahead of such companies as McDonald's, Daimler, Unilever and Samsung. Aldi was not among the top 20 German advertisers.[12] In the UK, Lidl was the largest advertiser in grocery retailing in 2015, spending £78 million on TV, radio, cinema, print, and outdoor – up from just £12 million in 2012. In this market, though, Aldi also invested heavily in advertising (£62.5 million in 2015). To compare, Asda spent £77.4 million, Tesco £64.2 million, Sainsbury's £55.7 million, and Morrisons £44.7 million.[13]

Interestingly, many consumers follow Lidl on Facebook. Based on the number of likes received, it does well on this social medium compared to conventional retailers. In the UK, by the end of 2017, Lidl had 1.7 million Facebook followers versus 2.3 million for market leader Tesco; in Germany, 2.4 million versus 1.1 million for market leader Edeka; in Spain, 2.0 million versus 500,000 for market leader Mercadona; and in the Netherlands, 700,000 versus 440,000 for market leader Albert Heijn. It shows that Lidl is not just a 'poor man's brand', but has grown towards becoming a social media champion. Not bad for a hard discounter!

Trader Joe's – the upscale hard discounter

Trader Joe's is a spectacularly successful US hard discounter, based in Monrovia, California. It is owned by Aldi Nord, but independently operated. In the period 1997–2017, Trader Joe's revenue had grown, on average, by 10.7 per cent *annually* to $9.7 billion in 2017. Growth could have been much faster if it had opened stores at a higher rate, which it purposely does not do. Trader Joe's strategy is to grow in a controlled way to maintain 'the Trader Joe's customer experience'. It sells a limited range of approximately 3,500 SKUs in stores of roughly 12,000 square feet. The company buys directly from manufacturers to eliminate the extra cost of a middleman. It features 'honest', affordable, everyday low prices. According to Trader Joe's, '"Sale" is a four-letter word to us. We have low prices, every day. No coupons, no membership cards, no discounts. You won't find any glitzy promotions or couponing wars at our stores. If it makes you feel any better, think of it as all our items are on sale, day in and day out.'[14]

Food and beverages account for 90 per cent of its revenues, with the remainder equally split between household and pet care, and health and beauty products. Private labels account for 80–85 per cent of its selection. Excluding wine, where brands are of limited importance in the first place, private labels account for over 90 per cent. Unlike Aldi or Lidl, its private-label products are largely sold under the banner name (eg Trader José's salsas, Trader Ming's fried rice, Trader Giotto's marinara sauces).

The retailer spends little on marketing. Most people hear about Trader Joe's through word of mouth. Virtually all promotion comes through its zealous fan base acting as brand promoters, often featuring their favourite snacks and experiences on their own social media. The one form of promotion is Trader Joe's Fearless Flyer ('As Always, Free, and Worth Every Penny'), a quirky bulletin with amusing stories, product information, and recipes.

With sales of $1,633 per square foot, its retail productivity is twice that of Aldi and Lidl stores, four times that of a Walmart Supercenter and eight times that of Dollar General. Trader Joe's was ranked #2 among US grocery chains on customer satisfaction by the American Customer Satisfaction Index in 2017.[15] Perhaps most amazingly, Trader Joe's may increase the value of your home! A study conducted by the online real estate database company Zillow found that homes grow more rapidly in value if they are closer to a Trader Joe's.[16] Homes near future Trader Joe's locations were appreciating at close to the same rate as other homes in the same city before the stores opened. However, two years after a Trader Joe's opened, the median home value within a mile of the store had appreciated 10 percentage points more than homes in the city as a whole. According to Zillow Group Chief Economist Stan Humphries:

> Like Starbucks, the stores have become an amenity in their own right – a signal to the home-buying public that the neighbourhood they're located in is desirable, perhaps up and coming, and definitely improving. Even if they open in neighbourhoods where home prices have lagged behind those in the wider city, they start to outperform the city overall once the stores arrive. [17]

Clearly, Trader Joe's is not your usual hard discounter. What makes it so different?

Unique positioning and assortment

Most hard discounters position themselves against mainstream grocers like Kroger, Carrefour, Tesco, and even Walmart. Not so with Trader Joe's, which is a kind of lower-end Whole Foods Market. Trader Joe's targets affluent, open-minded, educated shoppers who are interested in new and unusual experiences. The company describes itself as a 'neighbourhood grocery store with foods and beverages from the exotic to the basic'. Its assortment emphasizes imported and domestic organic and fresh grocery staples, as well as gourmet and ethnic food, with few, if any, preservatives or artificial ingredients. It has an unusually broad and deep wine selection, with prices ranging from $4 to $60 and above. In a nutshell, Trader Joe's is 'different'. It offers a treasure hunt for food with a special twist, at affordable prices. While much of this is similar to Whole Foods, they are clearly different on this last aspect. In March 2017, we compared prices for a basket of 32 items and found that Trader Joe's is 31.5 per cent cheaper than Whole Foods. Consumers are aware of this. In a *Consumer Reports* survey, Trader Joe's was rated best of all chains on prices overall, as well as for organic options, while Whole Foods rated second to last.[18] The price gap may narrow in the wake of the acquisition of Whole Foods by Amazon in September 2017, but the price gap for that same basket in December 2017 was still 30.3 per cent. It is unlikely to disappear, as Trader Joe's business model is vastly more efficient than Whole Foods'.

In-store experience

The moment you enter a Trader Joe's store, you immediately notice this is not your typical austere hard discounter. Store employees wear brightly coloured Hawaiian shirts and are called crew members (with the store manager being a 'captain'), considering themselves 'traders on the culinary seas'. Shop interiors look like the inside of a ship, featuring cedar plank walls and nautical decor. Each new store has its own artist to paint customized murals that reflect the neighbourhood history. For example, the store in Chapel Hill features the banners of UNC, Duke, and NC State – three perennial rivals in local college sports.

Personnel are upbeat and helpful – not your typical hard discount experience. If a customer asks about a product, the employee never points but instead walks them over to the location, offering to tear open a package to let the customer sample the product. As one employee said, 'We do everything here, and I mean everything. When that bell rings twice (gesturing to one of the hand-pulled bronze bells near the checkout lines) we go sprinting from the front to the back of the store for customers. We do anything we need to.'

How does the company get such engagement from its employees? One element is that Trader Joe's pays above-average wages and benefits. However, compensation is not the whole story. A team atmosphere pervades the crew. All employees, including the captain, work all aspects of the store, cooperating on myriad jobs. Trader Joe's hires a certain sort of person: one who is unabashedly engaged in what they do. It wants people working there who care about their jobs, no matter what their job is. This has not gone unnoticed. In the aforementioned *Consumer Reports* survey, Trader Joe's received the maximum rating of five on 'staff courtesy' on a five-point scale from worst to best. Whole Foods received a score of four, Aldi a score of three, and Walmart, the lowest score, one.

The combination of a unique assortment sold by friendly personnel in funky stores at discount prices, has created a retail brand with a deep personality, which allows consumers to form a relationship with their respective local store. This is what David DiSalvo, a contributor to *Forbes* magazine, wrote:

> Walking into a Trader Joe's, my demeanour is noticeably different than when I'm shopping anywhere else. Somehow I don't mind going there. At times – and it's still hard for me to believe I'd say this about shopping – I actually look forward to it. Trader Joe's (TJ's to its fans) does something pleasant for my brain, as it does for millions of others.[19]

DIA – the convenience hard discounter

Grupo Distribuidora Internacional de Alimentación, S A (DIA) is a Spanish retailer that operates mainly hard discount stores under the DIA banner in Argentina (882 stores in 2016), Brazil (1,100), China (377), and Spain (4,011), and under the Minipreço banner in Portugal (623). DIA was founded in 1979 and, from 2000–2011, it was part of the Carrefour Group. Following its spin-off, DIA became independent and debuted in Madrid's IBEX 35 stock market on 2 January 2012. DIA hard discount stores are austere and small, typically between 4,500 and 8,000 square feet. In densely populated downtown areas, stores can be as small as 2,000 square feet. Revenues in 2017 stood at $11.1 billion. Much of DIA's growth is taking place in Latin America, where it generated $2 billion in revenues in Argentina and $2.5 billion in Brazil in 2017. In that year, these two countries accounted for 43 per cent of total revenues, up from 16 per cent in 2008. In fact, the entire revenue growth in the preceding five years was due to success in Latin America and China, where DIA earned $250 million in sales in 2017.

DIA's assortment strategy

DIA was the first retailer to launch private labels in Spain in 1984. In 2017, private labels accounted for more than half of DIA's revenues. DIA's private label is a fast follower, not an innovator like Lidl. Initially, all private-label products were sold under the DIA brand name, but DIA learned that this umbrella brand strategy did not work well in high-involvement categories, as the brand was seen as cheap. In response, DIA introduced category-specific private labels: Bonté (personal care), Baby Smile and Junior Smile (infant and toddler care), Basic Cosmetics (beauty products), and AS (pet care). It also introduced the brand Delicious for gourmet foods.

In Spain, DIA's main competitor in the hard discount segment is Lidl. While DIA's private label is priced below Lidl's, the latter offers more innovation and higher quality due to its much larger scale. To counter this, DIA differentiates itself by offering three or four national brands in each category, to provide innovation and give the consumer more choice. In addition, DIA is helped by its greater flexibility in store size. Lidl's business model requires stores of 10,000 square feet or more. In downtown areas of larger cities, such a large space is hard to find. In contrast, DIA can work with 2,000 square feet, meaning that in many places, DIA can avoid head-to-head competition with Lidl.

Private label also is a key component of the assortment in DIA's overseas markets. In Argentina and Brazil, it is practically the only retailer that operates around private labels. How was DIA able to overcome the generally higher levels of distrust of private labels in these countries? As is so often the case, a recession was the trigger. The period of 2012–2016 was very difficult for Argentina, while Brazil experienced the worst recession in its history from 2015–2017.[20] But DIA quickly realized that, to win in the long term, it needed to give shoppers a positive reason to buy. It positions and communicates its private label as the choice of the smart shopper. In China, DIA overcame scepticism about private labels by emphasizing that they were sourced from Spain and Europe. This positioning caters to the widespread distrust among Chinese consumers of food products made in China in the wake of many product-harm scandals.

2PF business model

According to José Antonio Lombardía, Chief Marketing Officer of Grupo DIA, the backbone of DIA's business model comprises 1) proximity, 2) price, and 3) the franchise model (2PF).

#1 Proximity

DIA cemented its position as the category leader in neighbourhood shopping by aggressively expanding the footprint of its markets. As mentioned above, in Spain, it has over 4,000 stores, while in 2015–2016 alone, it increased its number of outlets in Argentina by 22 per cent and in Brazil by 38 per cent. Neighbourhood locations offer customers easy access to fulfil their daily purchase product requirements, saving them time. DIA regards the digital channel as another means to achieve proximity, especially in China, where e-commerce accounted for 20 per cent of grocery retailing in cities like Shanghai in 2017. In November 2015, it opened a store on Tmall, selling branded Spanish goods and DIA's private labels (especially its premium brand Delicious) to the remotest corners of China, with order fulfilment by Alibaba. It intends to leverage these learnings in Europe as well.

#2 Price

The second pillar is price. Over time, and helped by being the first to introduce private labels in Spain, DIA has been associated with low prices. Lombardía acknowledged that DIA's price image is more favourable than the actual price advantage over its competitors. The DIA Club loyalty programme, launched in 1980, is another cornerstone of the company's privileged price positioning. Club members accounted for 75 per cent of DIA's sales in 2016. They get access to exclusively priced products, receive discount coupons for national brands and DIA's private-label products, and even have the possibility of deferring payments weekly or monthly. At the same time, the programme gives the company unique insight into customer behaviour and allows for targeted promotions. For example, heavy beer drinkers receive beer coupons, while new mothers receive diaper coupons.

#3 Franchising

Franchising is the third pillar of DIA's business model and is crucial to its strategy of profitable growth underpinned by proximity and price. The rapid expansion of its store network would not be possible if DIA had to finance all the stores by itself. Its franchisees are family-owned businesses, which DIA believes is the best operating model for excelling in the highly localized neighbourhood shopping segment. For DIA, its franchisees are the brand's best ambassadors, as their commitment and local market knowledge deliver customer satisfaction. Families are very tight in Latin cultures, and a franchised store provides employment for the entire family – husband, wife, and children – who are also willing to work more than eight hours a day if required. Franchised establishments account for over 50 per cent of the DIA discount stores. The franchise model is used especially heavily in emerging markets – in 2017 the share of franchised stores ranged from 64 per cent (Brazil) to 84 per cent (China) of all DIA's outlets.

Managerial takeaways

While hard discounters around the world share a number of characteristics – small, relatively austere stores, limited assortment, low price positioning compared to full-service retailers, and the dominant role of private label – they are far from monolithic. Our analysis of four major types of hard discounters yields the following insights:

- The role of national brands ranges from minimal to substantial. There is compelling evidence that there is a clear limit to the market potential of a (near) private-label-only concept. The number of people that want to include at least some national brands in some categories in their purchase repertoire is much larger than private-label-only buyers. To continue to grow, hard discounters need to continue to fine-tune the relative emphasis on national brands versus private labels in their assortment, without losing the efficiencies and low-price image that come with the strong private-label focus.

- The hard discount concept can be positioned against mainstream retailers or upscale ones. The former is most common, but Trader Joe's proves that it is also possible to compete against upscale retailers with a concomitant less austere retail concept.

- While it is most common that the hard discounter owns its stores, DIA shows the potential of the franchise concept. This holds great promise, especially in poorer countries and in countries where family ties are strong. It allows the hard discounter to thrive in lean economic environments.

- For hard discounters to compete with juggernauts Aldi and Lidl, two strategies stand out. One strategy is to leverage proximity by developing a network of (even) smaller stores that can be established in heavily urbanized areas – or rural areas – where either the larger space required for an Aldi or Lidl is hard to find (urban) or where the density of demand is too low for such a store (rural). A second strategy is to move upwards and position yourself as a value alternative to an upscale retailer.

- Aldi (especially Aldi Süd) and Lidl are gradually moving beyond their very austere origins. Their assortment has doubled or tripled in size since they were founded, store interiors and exteriors are becoming fancier, and national brands are gaining a foothold. These upgrades have extended their appeal to new shoppers, beyond the low-income segment. In the longer run, this may undermine their unique image of unbeatable value for money, which would open the back door to lower-priced new competitors. After all, supermarkets and hypermarkets also started as new low-price concepts.

- Success in emerging markets shows that acceptance of the hard discounter concept is not restricted to developed markets. Additional guarantees or information (eg emphasizing the banner's success in Western markets) are important to allay quality concerns of shoppers in emerging markets who often equate low prices with low quality.

Notes

1 The two logos and the geographical split in Germany can be found at loveincorporated.blob.core.windows.net/contentimages/gallery/4cb3146e-cb83-4e0c-9d12-1174df4f4720-13-Courtesy-Chris828.jpg, last accessed 11 June 2018.

2 For more information on such value brands, see Steenkamp, J B (2017) *Global Brand Strategy: World-wise marketing in the age of branding*, Palgrave MacMillan, New York.

3 www.planetretail.net/, last accessed 25 September 2017.

4 Scally, D (2017) Divided it flourished, but Aldi may stand better chance if reunited, *The Irish Times*, 2 February.

5 www.news.com.au/lifestyle/fashion/fashion-trends/aldis-biggest-sale-day-of-the-year-is-back-on-may-20/news-story/1e4cbb4c7cf73444dbdef6c977b80d84, last accessed 7 September 2017.

6 Planet Retail (2017) 'Aldi in Germany'.

7 Steenkamp, J B (2017) *Global Brand Strategy: World-wise marketing in the age of branding*, Palgrave MacMillan, New York.

8 Brandes, B and Brandes, N (2012) *Bare Essentials: The Aldi way to retail success*, BoD–Books on Demand, 2012.

9 en.wikipedia.org/wiki/Lidl, last accessed 15 December 2017.

10 Bachl, Th (2009) Einfluss von Preiserhöhungen und Wirtschaftskrise auf das Konsumverhalten 2008 (presentation given at the annual GfK Kronberg meeting, Kronberg, Germany, 22 January 2009).

11 people.com/style/heidi-klum-launching-clothing-with-lidl/, last accessed 17 September 2017.

12 www.statista.com/statistics/381227/advertisers-ranked-by-ad-spending-germany/, last accessed 11 June 2018. Only the top 20 leading advertisers were reported.

13 www.campaignlive.co.uk/article/lidl-p-g-ramp-adspend-big-four-supermarkets-rein/1389841, last accessed 8 September 2017.

14 www.traderjoes.com, last accessed 15 December 2017.

15 American Customer Satisfaction Index (2017), ACSI Retail Report 2017, 28 February 2018.

16 Rascoff, S and Humphries, S (2016) *Zillow Talk: Rewriting the rules of real estate*, Grand Central Publishing, New York.

17 zillow.mediaroom.com/2016-01-25-Homes-Near-Trader-Joes-Whole-Foods-Stores-Appreciate-Faster, last accessed 16 December 2017.

18 *Consumer Reports* (2017) Faster, fresher, cheaper, July, pp. 30–43.

19 Section based on www.jeanchatzky.com/wednesday-welcome-how-to-save-money-at-trader-joes/; www.forbes.com/sites/daviddisalvo/2015/02/19/what-trader-joes-knows-about-making-your-brain-happy/#4be33e9d1213; www.consumerreports.org/cro/news/2015/04/america-s-cheapest-supermarkets/index.htm; zillow.mediaroom.com/2016-01-25-Homes-Near-Trader-Joes-Whole-Foods-Stores-Appreciate-Faster, last accessed 30 September 2017; *Consumer Reports* (2015) America's best, freshest supermarkets, May, pp. 24–27; ACSI Retail Report 2017; Planet Retail.

20 www.bloomberg.com/news/articles/2017-03-21/argentine-economy-exits-recession-easing-pressure-on-macri, last accessed 16 December 2017; Leahy, J (2017) Brazil emerges from its worst ever recession, *Financial Times*, 1 September, p. 13.

Hard discounter 04 success around the world

In this chapter, we will discuss hard discounters and their routes to success in five countries. First, we will look at Germany, the birthplace of the hard-discount concept. Here, the conventional retailers decided to join the fray by starting their own hard-discount chains. Then, we turn to the UK, the most sophisticated private-label market, dominated by huge retail chains that have built a sophisticated architecture of different private-label tiers. The UK was long thought immune to hard discounters, and Aldi and Lidl's breakout occurred after 2010. Next, we will take a look at Australia, where the grocery retail sector was dominated by two huge home-grown retailers accounting for over 80 per cent of the market. No overseas grocery chain had ever been successful in building a retail operation from scratch – until Aldi came.

Then, we turn to hard discounters in two important emerging markets: Poland and Turkey. Here, not Aldi or Lidl but local retailers, Biedronka (Poland) and BIM (Turkey), have been the most successful hard discounters, albeit that they are hard discounters very much in the mould of Aldi. Taken together, these countries highlight the strength and versatility of the hard-discount concept in the face of widely varying economic and competitive conditions.

While there are variations between countries, as we will see, hard discounter success in a country follows a fairly predictable sequence of stages. We will conclude the chapter with this hard discounter life-cycle model.

Germany – conventional retailers co-opting the hard-discount concept

Germany is the cradle of the hard-discount concept, and the world's two largest discount chains by far are German. As such, Chapter 3 provided a detailed description of Aldi and Lidl and how they rose to prominence in

Germany. But Aldi and Lidl were not the only German hard discounters. The success of Aldi did not go unnoticed and copycats soon entered the marketplace. Norma opened its first stores in the 1960s, Plus started operations in 1972, Penny was founded in 1973, and Netto (owned by Dansk Supermarked) entered Germany in 1990. Germany is also home to a large brand discounter, Netto Marken-Discount ('Marken' is German for brands), which started up in 1984.

Table 4.1 provides the market shares of the discounters and other major banners for 1997, 2007 and 2017. The market share of hard discounters increased sharply in the decade between 1997 and 2007 – from 19.2 per cent to 31.9 per cent. However, since then, the share has largely stabilized. In 2017, hard discounter share stood at 29.8 per cent, albeit this is somewhat misleading because this share is affected by the acquisition of Plus by Edeka, who folded the banner into its Netto Marken-Discount banner. The main engines powering the growth of hard discounting have started to sputter.

Table 4.1   Grocery retailers' market share in Germany

Banner	Dominant store type	Company	Market share (%)		
			1997e	2007	2017
Edeka	Supermarket	Edeka Zentrale	9.0	12.1	17.4
Aldi	Hard discounter	Aldi Group	9.9	14.1	14.3
Rewe	Supermarket	Rewe Group	5.1	4.2	10.0
Lidl	Hard discounter	Schwarz	3.0	8.3	9.6
Kaufland	Hypermarket	Schwarz	2.6	6.3	7.4
Netto Marken-Discount	Brand discounter	Edeka Zentrale	2.0	2.2	6.7
Penny	Hard discounter	Rewe	2.4	3.2	3.7
Real	Hypermarket	Metro	4.3	5.1	3.3
Marktkauf	Supermarket	Edeka Zentrale	1.7	2.2	1.8
Norma	Hard discounter	Norma Lebensmittel	1.1	1.7	1.6
Netto	Hard discounter	Dansk Supermarked	0.4	0.6	0.6
Plus	Hard discounter	Tengelmann Group	2.4	4.0	–

NOTE Except for Netto, banners with a 2016 market share below 1.5 per cent not included. Due to changes in banners and reporting, market shares for 1997 are approximate only.
SOURCE Based on 2007/2017 data from Euromonitor International, 1997/2007/2017 data from Planet Retail, and authors' own estimates

In the last decade, the combined market share of Aldi and Lidl has barely changed. What happened?

Why Aldi and Lidl's growth has levelled off

Several factors contributed significantly to the steep decline in the growth trajectory of the two prototypical hard discounters. One reason is simply saturation: Aldi and Lidl have run out of white space. By 2017, there were over 3,000 Lidl stores and over 4,000 Aldi stores in Germany. Over 90 per cent of German households live in close proximity to a Lidl and an Aldi store. Growth in market share now has to come from increased store productivity (sales per store), not by adding stores.

Moreover, three mainstream retailers co-opted the discount concept by establishing (or acquiring) their own discounter: Plus (by Tengelmann), Penny (by Rewe), and Netto Marken-Discount (by Edeka). While this did little to stop the rise of discounters per se, these retailers thus ensured that a significant portion of total grocery sales stayed within their respective companies. In 1997, their discounter banners accounted for 6.8 per cent of the market, rising to 9.4 per cent in 2007, and 10.4 per cent in 2017. Much of these sales would have flowed to Aldi and Lidl if the conventional retailers had not followed the old dictum, 'If you can't beat them, join them'. Yet, as Table 4.2 shows, these copycats lag far behind Aldi and Lidl in

Table 4.2 Retail productivity of discounters in Germany in 2017

Banner	Revenues (€ bn)	Number of stores	Selling space ('000 sq ft)	Revenue/ store (€ mn)	Revenue/ sq ft (€)
Aldi	27.0	4,167	36,888	6.5	732
Lidl	18.9	3,193	26,092	5.9	724
Netto Marken-Discount	13.1	4,221	34,950	3.1	375
Penny	7.3	2,160	16,652	3.4	438
Norma	3.1	1,305	10,010	2.4	310
Netto	1.2	353	2,884	3.4	416
Total German grocery retailing	196.4	93,268	445,238	2.1	441

NOTE Data refer to operations in Germany only.
SOURCE Based on 2018 data from Euromonitor International, and authors' own calculations

retail productivity.[1] This reinforces the incredible efficiency of these retailers. Clearly, Aldi and Lidl are making much more money on their discount operations than Penny or Netto Marken-Discount.

Finally, hard discounters in general, and Aldi and Lidl as the biggest chains in particular, benefited from the prolonged economic difficulties experienced by Germany in the aftermath of unification and the economic recession in the early 2000s. Conversely, economic conditions improved significantly after economic reforms (known to Germans as Hartz IV) were introduced in 2005 and hard-discount growth slowed down.

United Kingdom – breakout into the world's most sophisticated private-label market

The UK is arguably the most sophisticated private-label market in the world. Players in 2017 include a huge internationally operating retailer (Tesco), the largest subsidiary of the world's largest retailer (Walmart's Asda), strong local chains (Sainsbury's, Morrisons), and two upscale retailers (Waitrose and Marks & Spencer). These retailers have developed an elaborate architecture of various types of store brands, including basic, standard and premium ranges, as well as super-premium, speciality and niche brands. And they are very successful with their store brands, which account for one out of every two pounds spent on groceries in the UK in 2017. By any standard, this is a tough market to crack, and indeed, it took Aldi and Lidl a long time.

Although Aldi and Lidl entered the UK in the early 1990s, their success was modest until 2010, with a combined market share of less than 5 per cent. While respectable, this is not really the kind of threat that made the 'Big Four' (Tesco, Asda, Sainsbury's, and Morrisons) tremble. Since 2011, they have enjoyed a virtual breakout (Figure 4.1), with growth accelerating since 2013. In 2017, Aldi overtook Co-op to become the UK's fifth-largest grocer, while Lidl has surpassed Waitrose to become the seventh-largest. By April 2018, Aldi commanded 7.3 per cent of the UK grocery market, and Lidl 5.4 per cent.

To put this into perspective, from 2012 to 2017, Aldi and Lidl's combined sales grew 140 per cent, from £6.85 billion to £16.41 billion. In the same period, the number of stores increased from 461 to 735 (Aldi) and from 531 to 719 (Lidl). The increase in stores is impressive, but much lower than the revenue increases, which means that store productivity increased dramatically – from £6.9 million to £11.3 million per store. In 2017, productivity

Figure 4.1 Market share of Aldi and Lidl in the UK, 2005–2017

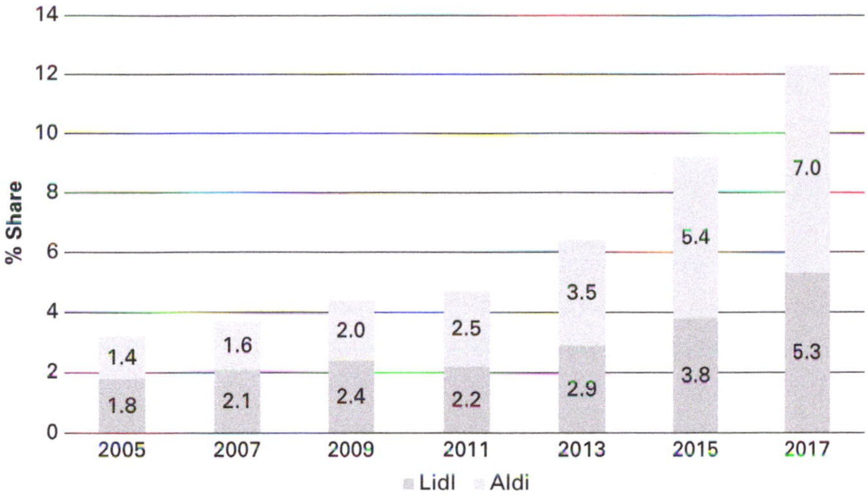

SOURCE Based on 2017 data from Kantar Worldpanel

per square foot at Aldi was the highest in the industry: £1,312 per square foot of selling space. Lidl, Tesco, Sainsbury's, and Morrisons all achieved between £900 and £1,100 per square foot.[2]

In November 2014, Aldi announced it would have 1,000 stores in the UK by 2022. Matthew Barnes, Aldi's UK & Ireland CEO, said he saw potential for at least 1,300 stores, citing a desire to have an Aldi outlet serving every 25,000–30,000 people across the UK.[3] Lidl will invest £1.5 billion over the period 2018–2020 to build 40–50 stores annually. Planet Retail projects combined sales of Aldi and Lidl as £25 billion in 2022. Aldi and Lidl are also experimenting with grocery e-commerce and home delivery, starting with wine and weekly specials (non-grocery offers that are available only for a limited time). Wine is an ideal category for such a launch – not only because discounters are increasingly using it in-store to position themselves as having a more upscale proposition, but also because it covers high-ticket items with low price transparency. Manufacturer brands barely play a role, and bottles can easily be shipped in standardized packaging.

The effect on the 'Big Four' has been brutal. In 2017, Asda posted its worst annual figures since being taken over by Walmart in 1998. Sales fell 5.7 per cent and pre-tax profits plunged 19 per cent. The others were also severely affected. Tesco's sales dropped by 5.8 per cent in 2015, and Morrisons saw its sales decline for three consecutive years: 2.3 per cent in 2013 and 5.0

per cent in both 2014 and 2015. And in April 2018, Sainsbury's and Asda announced their intention to merge.

Key factors in explaining Aldi and Lidl's success in the UK

Complacency of the 'Big Four'

For too long, the 'Big Four' ignored the discounters, focusing on competing with each other instead. For example, in 2011, Asda announced it would be 10 per cent cheaper than any other conventional supermarket or it would refund the difference. Andy Clarke, CEO of Asda, said, 'From today our price promise is backed by a copper-bottomed guarantee – if the basket of food you buy in our stores is not at least 10 per cent less than *each of our major rivals*, we'll put our hand in our pocket and give you back the difference' (emphasis added).[4] Clearly, it did not regard Aldi or Lidl a 'major rival'. Why this complacency? According to a UBS report, four misconceptions stood out:

1 The assumption among the 'Big Four' that 'our customers wouldn't shop there' misjudged shoppers' price sensitivity and willingness to split baskets between supermarkets and discounters.

2 Claims that 'our branded goods will act as a differentiator' were undermined by discounters adding national brands to ranges.

3 The conviction that 'their fancy brands cannot stand up against our store brands' was proven wrong by the many awards won by Aldi and Lidl's own-label products.

4 Their belief that 'our promotional prices are as low as theirs' ignored shoppers' increasing preference for the consistency and simplicity of everyday low pricing (EDLP).[5]

Moreover, the 'Big Four' made large investments to drive multi-channel growth (e-commerce, convenience) and diversify into non-core adjacent markets (mobile phones, financial services, restaurants). Healthy margins were needed to fund these new initiatives. Thus, they kept increasing prices rather than make pre-emptive price investments just when austerity and income stagnation hit British families in the wake of the global financial and Eurozone crises. Increased price sensitivity made (overwhelming) choice less important than great value for money. The major UK supermarkets became uncompetitive on their core range against the discounters. Anecdotal reports suggest the price gap between the discounters and mainstream UK supermarkets on comparable private-label goods exceeded 25 per cent.

Smart moves by Aldi and Lidl

While these are all important enabling factors, Aldi and Lidl grabbed the available opportunities in a smart way. They shattered perceptions that their food is of low quality by investing in new products and distinctive marketing. Aldi, for example, expanded its assortment from 800 to almost 1,500 SKUs and introduced the premium 'Specially Selected' range. The *Telegraph* wrote in 2015: 'Aldi's Specially Selected range will inspire foodies up and down the country to re-invent their recipes with exotic, exciting and organic ingredients.'[6] Upgrading their assortment has led to Aldi and Lidl winning many UK Grocer Own Label Awards. In 2017, Aldi was crowned the best supermarket for parents by the Loved by Parents Awards for the fourth time. Its own label baby and toddler range, Mamia, also won Platinum in the Best Baby Food Range and Best Organic Baby Food Range for its 100 per cent organic and sugar-free pouches, and five Platinum awards across the diaper range.[7] This is telling. Young parents are among the toughest audiences to convince. If you can convince young parents to buy your products for their children, you have won the contest. These and other kudos received wide press exposure.

Aldi and Lidl also invested in local sourcing, which showed their engagement with British society. Research found that shoppers wanted Aldi to become 'more British', so fresh meat, milk, and eggs are all now sourced from Britain. While this added some costs, the above-noted dramatic increase in store productivity more than compensated for it. Lidl signed the National Farmers' Union's 'Back British Farming' charter, which calls on the food industry to show support for British farming by strengthening its British product offerings and working in close partnership with British farmers to develop committed, fair, beneficial, and transparent relationships. Seventy per cent of Lidl's core range is sourced from British suppliers, especially in perishables, where local sourcing makes sense due to short lead times.

Lidl touts its commitment to responsible sourcing. In 2017, it won the inaugural Marketing Campaign of the Year Award at the annual MSC (Marine Stewardship Council) UK Awards. The awards recognize those retailers and suppliers working hardest to sustain the world's oceans. Lidl was the only brand to win two awards that year, and it coincided with the supermarket announcing that 100 per cent of Lidl's own brand of fresh and frozen wild-caught fish will be MSC certified sustainable by 2019.[8]

These hard discounters also invested in distinctive marketing. Aldi sponsors Team GB, who won 67 medals, including 27 gold, in the 2016 Olympic Games. One of the most innovative and eye-catching aspects of the 2016 campaign was the combination of fresh produce and the Olympic theme in its ads. One ad showed a group of athletes set against a Union Jack flag with the blue and red sections made out in blueberries and tomatoes. Even more spectacular was the dramatic image of the Rio skyline, which was made entirely out of 30 types of fruits and vegetables.

Aldi gained extensive publicity for this innovative campaign while establishing its British credentials. It extended its sponsorship for another four years leading up to the Tokyo 2020 Olympic Games, with a new TV advertising campaign highlighting its support for Team GB. Aldi's standing in the industry was further enhanced through it signing up to the NFU Fruit & Veg Pledge, as well as its commitment to making fresh fruit and vegetables more affordable through its 'Super 6' promotions.[9] Every fortnight, Aldi selects six fresh fruits and vegetables and offers them at an even lower price than usual. To help customers make great-value meals, they also showcase six meat and fish products to choose from.

Setting aside decades of football (soccer) rivalry with the Germans, the English Football Association (FA) signed a multi-million-pound deal with Lidl in 2015, making Lidl the official supermarket sponsor for England's football team. Lidl also closed deals with the Football Association of Wales and the Scottish Football Association to become a grassroots partner of all three associations, financing professional coaching opportunities for over 1 million children aged 5–11 in Great Britain. Not ignoring its core strength in providing value to British households, Lidl employs hard-hitting advertising which, every week, compares an item from another retailer against what you can buy for the same money (or less) at Lidl. One ad compared Lidl with Waitrose. It showed a picture of two sea bass fillets, for which you pay £5.49 at Waitrose, and another picture of the bass fillets, a 250-gram bag of wholegrain rice, a courgette, and a red bell pepper – together with a dish thus prepared – all for £4.34 at Lidl, with the text, 'A delicious fish dinner for two'.[10]

With all these elements in place, Aldi and Lidl are slated for further growth. At what level their market share will plateau is uncertain, but we expect it could very well go to 20 per cent in the intermediate future. That means that conventional retailers might stand to lose another £13 billion in revenues.

Australia – leveraging the opportunities offered by a cosy duopoly

Australia has the most concentrated grocery retailing market in the world. For most of its recent history, the two leading players – Woolworths and

Coles – controlled over 80 per cent of the market. IGA and a variety of other small retailers accounted for the remainder. Before Aldi entered the market, no foreign-owned retailer had ever established a successful greenfield operation. Aldi entered Australia in 2001 when it opened its first stores in New South Wales. It gradually expanded and by the end of 2017 had nearly 500 stores in almost all Australian states. Along the way, it also steadily increased its market share (Figure 4.2). In 2017, Aldi claimed a 13.2 per cent share of the country's AU $90 billion supermarket spend, while the combined share of Woolworths and Coles had slipped to 68.9 per cent. Aldi is now clearly the nation's third-biggest chain, ahead of IGA, which had 9.3 per cent.

It helps that, in the words of Megan Treston, director of Nielsen's Retail Industry Group, Australians are 'promiscuous shoppers' who tend to shop at all the major retailers. Less than 10 per cent of all households shopped in just one store in 2017. Nielsen data show that, once shoppers go into Aldi, the quality and the value works for them. A new buyer will buy low-risk staples; once they feel reassured about Aldi quality, they will add more. That is how Aldi has achieved the holy trinity of retail in Australia: more shoppers in stores, shoppers spending more, and shoppers visiting more frequently.[11] Aldi's rate of growth in these three shopper metrics is

Figure 4.2 Woolworths' operating margin and Aldi's market share in Australia, 2001–2017

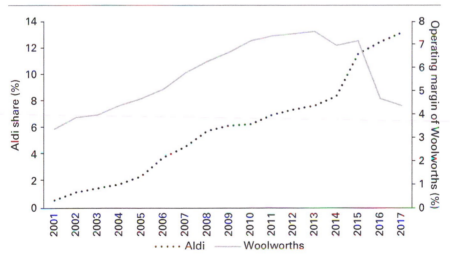

NOTE Operating margin refers to Woolworths' food and liquor operations in Australia. It is expressed as percentage of revenues.
SOURCE Based on Woolworths annual reports, 2001–2017, and research by Nielsen and Roy Morgan Research, 2001–2017

impressive. In 2014, 53 per cent of Australian households visited an Aldi store compared to just 7 per cent in 2001. In markets in which Aldi operates, two-thirds of households visited an Aldi store. Purchase trips per buyer was 19.3 – up from seven in 2001. The number of units bought per visit reached 23.2 compared to 20.5 in 2006.[12] Along the way, Aldi moved into the lives of affluent Australians. In 2006, just 26 per cent of Aldi shoppers were from high-income families. By 2014, the proportion of high-income shoppers had risen to 50 per cent.[13]

The role of the duopoly

Many elements of Aldi's strategy, including transparent pricing, offering good-quality products for a low price, and its exclusive, limited offers ('Special Buys'), appeal to Australians like they appeal to buyers in Germany, the UK, the Netherlands, and elsewhere. Like it did in the UK, Aldi also invested in local sourcing. In 2015, it started to ship fruits and vegetables directly from Australian farms to its stores, removing a key competitive advantage for Woolworths and Coles.

Aldi was helped by a prevailing sense of complacency in the Australian grocery market. Despite their rivalry, Coles and Woolworths co-existed in a highly profitable, protected market. They had dominated the market for so many years that they had difficulty even envisaging how this comfortable state of affairs could be disrupted. Australians love underdogs, or the 'little guy', but there was no David to take on Goliath. Until Aldi entered the fray.

To better understand what the duopoly meant for Australian shoppers, Figure 4.2 shows the operating margin for Woolworths' food and liquor operations since 2001, the year Aldi entered the market.[14] What can we learn from this graph?

1 Historically, Woolworths (and Coles) earned high margins relative to other developed nations, a sign of overpricing. In 2014, Woolworths' operating margin was 7.0 per cent (Coles' was 5.2 per cent) versus an average supermarket margin of 3.3 per cent in the EU.[15]

2 In the period that Aldi built its presence in Australia, Woolworths' operating margin actually increased, from 3.4 per cent to a high of 7.6 per cent in 2013. Clearly, for a long time, Woolworths did not take Aldi seriously.

3 Third, the wake-up call came when Aldi's market share grew nearly four percentage points, from 7.7 per cent in 2013 to 11.6 per cent in 2015. Woolworths and Coles greatly increased price promotion activity, which, in 2017, was increasingly replaced by a strategy of EDLP because, in

the words of Coles, 'price promotions breed distrust'. This narrowed the price gap, but it was too little too late to stop the bleeding. Aldi had achieved critical mass and Woolworths' operating margin was in free fall.

Here is how a sceptical journalist for the newspaper *The Australian* described her first experience with Aldi in 2016, wondering what all the fuss was about:

> I've just paid $50 for two bottles of wine, a bag of oranges, 12 loo rolls, a free-range chicken, a bottle of olive oil, two packets of halloumi cheese, 500g of coffee and a chiller bag. The same shop would have cost me around $75 in Woolworths or Coles. I also found myself lingering over the $60 food dehydrator in the central aisle – $100 cheaper than the one I bought recently. Am I an Aldi convert? I can't say I am. But I can feel myself teetering on the edge of that slippery slope.'[16]

While it lasted, the duopoly was great for Woolworths and Coles, and for their shareholders. Other than fighting one another, there was no real motivation to innovate or change. Unfortunately, this did nothing to prepare them to compete with one of the world's most efficient retailers. Aldi cites the Woolies–Coles duopoly as part of the reason for the German chain's success in Australia. 'There are more players and greater competition in other markets', a spokesperson told news.com.au.[17]

Hard discount in emerging markets – Biedronka and BIM

Biedronka

While Germany is generally associated with hard discounting, it is less well-known that Poland rivals Germany in hard discounters' share: 30.6 per cent in 2017, up from 15.0 per cent in 2007, according to Europanel. But in Poland, it is not Aldi or Lidl that is fuelling this growth but a local banner, Biedronka. Biedronka is owned by the Portuguese company Jerónimo Martins, and in 2017, accounted for 21.3 per cent of the Polish grocery market, far ahead of #2 Lidl with 6.6 per cent, and conventional retailer Lewiatan (5.1 per cent). By early 2018, Biedronka operated 2,820 stores, versus Lidl's 640 stores, Netto's 374, and Aldi's paltry 112.

Biedronka is a Polish success story. Founded in 1995, it generated revenues of €510 million in 1999, which, by 2017, had grown to €12.0 billion.

This is a growth of 19.2 per cent *annually*! No other discounter has achieved such success. These sales were achieved with around 1.5 billion store visits, indicating that the average basket size per trip is small, around eight euros. Biedronka is also profitable, with earnings before interest, taxes, depreciation, and amortization (EBITDA) of 7.2 per cent in 2017. For comparison, EBITDA of Britain's Sainsbury's that year was 4.8 per cent while France's Auchan achieved 4.0 per cent.

Why does Biedronka drive hard-discount success in Poland?

The Polish market has several characteristics that are very different from those of Western Europe. Despite two decades of economic growth, Poland is still a relatively poor country, its GDP per capita being only 30 per cent of Germany's. The grocery retail sector is highly fragmented, with a large number of traditional independent small grocers, which accounted for 19 per cent of the market in 2017. Most Poles, due to limited disposable incomes and lack of storage space (around 45 per cent of the population live in apartments), shop once a day, buying small amounts per trip. They prefer mostly small- and mid-sized store formats, which are considered optimal in terms of location and sales area.[18]

Thus, in many aspects, grocery retailing in Poland is more similar to other advanced emerging markets in Eastern Europe or Latin America than to neighbouring Germany. This makes Biedronka's case especially interesting as it provides a possible blueprint for hard-discount concepts in other emerging markets. Aldi and Lidl's current assortment, positioning, and store network are too advanced to grab market leadership in Poland. Biedronka's concept is more aligned with less-developed retail conditions prevalent in Poland. It sells a limited assortment of less than 1,000 SKUs in small stores (around 7,000 square feet). The stores have a look and feel reminiscent of an Aldi Nord store in the 1990s. Around 60 per cent of its assortment is private label, sold under fancy labels such as DADA diapers and Italico coffee capsules.

In the minds of consumers, Biedronka offers both the lowest prices in the marketplace and the convenience of proximity shopping. Biedronka operates a vast network of stores, with locations close to where people live. About 70 per cent of the Polish population lives in rural areas and in small cities. These areas are underserved by larger chains whose cost structure requires higher population density. This means that, in large parts of the country, Biedronka does not face stiff competition from retailers with deep pockets such as Tesco, Carrefour, Auchan, or even Lidl. Rather, it competes with traditional independent small grocery stores, which rapidly lose market share. Between 2012 and 2017, 41 per cent of all independent small grocers closed and revenues declined by 37 per cent. Much of that loss was scooped up by Biedronka.

Biedronka is running out of white space, though. Since 2016, it has shifted its focus to increasing revenues per outlet through optimization of assortment instead of store expansion. To increase revenues, it is expanding its assortment of branded products and premium goods in an attempt to upgrade consumer perceptions of the chain from a discounter to a supermarket. This seems a smart strategy. As Poland continues to develop economically, Biedronka should grow with the increased wealth of Polish shoppers. Otherwise, it will lose its edge over Lidl.

BIM in Turkey

In Turkey, the grocery retail sector is even more fragmented, with 136,000 independent small grocers accounting for 38 per cent of the market in 2017. At the opposite end of the scale, we find world-class international retailers including Carrefour, Migros, and Makro. Yet, the market leader is not one of these giants but a homegrown hard discounter, BIM, whose market share grew from 4.7 per cent in 2012 to 7.6 per cent in 2017. Organic expansion has been the driver of growth for BIM. It opened around 500 new stores annually between 2013 and 2017, and by the end of 2017, operated over 6,000 stores. Geographically, the network is concentrated in Northwestern Turkey, although there are stores nearly everywhere in the country. Given the high share of mom-and-pop stores, BIM aims to expand via franchising.[19]

BIM is clearly modelled on Aldi – not surprising since the chain was set up by a former Aldi manager and some of the management was trained in Germany. In fact, BIM makes no secret of its admiration for the German company, describing itself as the 'Turkish Aldi'. However, many BIM stores are not up to the standard of Aldi stores in Germany, often appearing to be at least a decade behind in terms of store investment and modernization, but this might be the appropriate concept for the country.

Virtually all stores are rented, which allows BIM flexibility to switch locations. BIM's strategy is to acquire sites that are small, between 2,000 and 6,500 square feet, and located on accessible secondary streets. Such sites are easier to secure and cost less than competitors' sites. Stores have minimal shelving and refrigeration, which means they have low capital expenditure requirements. The stores are easy to restock, yielding higher productivity.

BIM limits the basic product assortment to about 600 SKUs, augmented by a number of limited offers that increase footfall, again taking a leaf from Aldi's book. The 600 basic products – mainly fast-moving staples – are high-volume items that typically provide 80 per cent of a household's weekly needs. As a result, BIM's logistics and warehouse costs are significantly lower than its competition.

Prices are low, with BIM stating that it keeps the percentage of its operating costs as low as Aldi or even lower. In 2017, over 70 per cent of BIM's sales were private label, which were, on average, 30 per cent cheaper than corresponding manufacturers' branded products. Here, too, the Aldi concept is copied – a large number of different fancy labels, each covering a small group of items. Some of the products are exclusively produced for BIM by brand manufacturers. BIM plans to increase its private-label share to over 90 per cent by 2022, as it tries to become as independent as possible from manufacturer brands.[20]

Hard discounter life-cycle model

Hard discounters' entry and expansion broadly follows a sequence of four stages that is quite similar across countries (Table 4.3).[21]

- In stage 1, hard discounter(s) are entering the country and establishing a store base to support at least one distribution centre. In geographically large countries like the United States or Australia, this store base will be concentrated in one region. Customers are cautious, if not outright suspicious, of pricing, quality, and unknown fancy brands. The austere shopping environment does little to inspire trust. The primary target group is low-income shoppers – people that *have* to patronize a hard discounter, rather than people who *want* to shop there. Conventional retailers treat this interloper with benign neglect.

- Over time, as the hard discounter network expands and stories about great value – not just rock-bottom prices – spread, hard discounters are attracting more inquisitive, more well-to-do, smart shoppers, curious to check it out. After all, who doesn't like a great deal? Conventional retailers notice this and feel the need to belittle hard discounters ('Who on earth would want to shop there? Certainly not my customers.') rather than just ignore them.

- In stage 3, hard discounters have captured a share of the market that is beginning to bite. A growing number of shoppers, including smart

Table 4.3   Hard discounter life-cycle model

	Entry	**Ramp-up**	**Consolidation**	**Mature**
Target customers	Low-income shoppers: 'I can't make ends meet'	Low-income + value seekers: 'you really should try [Aldi]'	Low-income + value seekers + smart shoppers: 'I'm not stupid'	Entire market: 'why didn't you tell me about [Aldi] sooner'
Customer trust	Cautious, even suspicious	Inquisitive	Converted	Mainstream
Assortment	Dry grocery staples and some packaged fresh products	+ non-food on in-out basis (eg computers, garden sets, sportswear)	+ selection of national CPG brands	+ bake-off department + speciality labels (organic, exclusive)
Use of brands	Limited	Traffic drivers	Peak	Drop-off
Shopping trip type	Fill-in shopping trip	Fill-in shopping trip and treasure hunt trip	Stock-up grocery trip	Main grocery trip
Response of conventional retailers	Neglect	Derogation	Panic	Coordinated response
Time period (indicative)	5–7 years	7–10 years	10–15 years	15+ years
Combined market share of hard discounters	<1%	1–5%	6–10%	10–25%

SOURCE Based on Powers *et al* (2017)

shoppers, use the hard discounter for stock-up grocery trips. Hard discounters expand the assortment of national brands and their fresh foods. Full panic sets in among conventional retailers. Profit margins among conventional retailers start to decline substantially, caused by loss of market share and the need to cut prices.

- In the fourth stage, hard discounters have become acceptable to virtually all shoppers. For many, they have become their main retailer with top-ups at conventional retailers. Hard discounters have added limited service departments and organic products. Conventional retailers start to develop coordinated response strategies. They initiate heavy cost-cutting, expand their private-label share, and exert pressure on national brands to drop their prices.

Managerial takeaways

The success of hard discounters in countries differing widely in competitive structure, economic conditions, and geographical size, attests to the power and attraction of the concept. Several elements of the hard-discount concept are key success factors across these markets:

- attractiveness of offering high-quality products at a low price;
- reduced shopping complexity by offering a limited assortment of mostly private labels at constant prices (EDLP versus HiLo);
- convenience of proximity shopping.

The country case studies revealed a number of other insights:

- Hard discounters benefit from embedding themselves firmly in local society through various activities, including sourcing locally and sponsoring local events and causes.
- Bad economic times are good news for hard discounters. They grow disproportionately in recessions and do not give their gains back in good times. To paraphrase Rahm Emanuel, President Obama's first chief of staff, they 'never let a crisis go to waste'.
- Oligopolistic retail structures where a few retailers completely dominate the retailscape can actually benefit courageous and persistent hard discounters. Incumbents either deride the hard discounter newcomer or are loath to respond in fear of starting a price war where they have much more to lose. The hard discounter can also tap into latent discontent among shoppers who have been overcharged for a long time, the natural consequence of oligopolistic conditions.
- In developed markets, the original hard-discount proposition of being the cheapest in town fails to resonate with all but the low-income segment of the population. It is essentially a negative proposition as cheapest is also often seen as nastiest. You go there because you have to, not because you

want to. Emphasizing great quality for a sharp price, and thus appealing to motives of being a smart shopper rather than a cheapskate, is key to breaking out into the mainstream market.

- In emerging markets – characterized by a highly fragmented retailscape, lower incomes, lower car ownership, smaller dwellings (in cities), and frequent shopping trips – the original austere store concept pioneered by Aldi in the 1950s and 1960s is still viable. It underpins a widespread network of small stores that sell products at rock-bottom prices. But as these markets evolve, the hard discounter needs to gradually upgrade as well, lest it lose out to Aldi and Lidl. They can use Aldi's development trajectory in Germany or the UK as an example of what to do when.

- Conventional retailers can counter dedicated hard discounters by developing their own discount banner. This can stunt the rise of dedicated hard discounters, but evidence suggests that conventional retailers' discount banners have difficulty even coming close to dedicated hard discounters on store productivity.

Notes

1 Authors' calculations based on data reported in the series of reports on the German grocery sector, published by Euromonitor International, January 2018.

2 Authors' calculations based on data reported in the series of reports on the UK grocery sector, published by Euromonitor International, March 2018.

3 https://www.theguardian.com/business/2017/may/11/aldi-plans-uk-supermarket-for-every-30000-people, last accessed 17 December 2017.

4 www.dailymail.co.uk/money/bills/article-1710498/Asda-well-be-10-cheaper-or-money-back.html, last accessed 17 December 2017.

5 Powers, S *et al* (2017) Global Consumer: Will private label swallow up $48 billion of branded US consumables value? UBS report, 11 July.

6 www.telegraph.co.uk/sponsored/foodanddrink/fabulous-foodie/11362798/specially-selected-aldi-range.html, last accessed 4 September 2017.

7 www.express.co.uk/life-style/food/832228/aldi-supermarket-offers-uk, last accessed 4 September 2017.

8 www.lidl.co.uk/en/Lidl-wins-two-MSC-UK-awards-7348.htm, last accessed 24 August 2017.

9 Youngman, A (2016) Aldi strikes gold with Team GB sponsorship, *Produce Business UK*, 30 August.

10 For the ad, see www.lidl.co.uk/en/A-delicious-fish-dinner-for-two-8081.htm, last accessed 4 September 2017.

11 Barrawclough, A (2016) How Aldi supermarkets created converts in Australia, *The Australian*, 16 January.

12 Dring, G (2014) Discount discovery: how Australians have embraced Aldi, *Nielsen Australia*.

13 Barrawclough, A (2016) How Aldi supermarkets created converts in Australia, *The Australian*, 16 January.

14 We report operating margin before significant items such as divestitures to more accurately reflect profitability of continuing operations.

15 Mortimer, G (2017) Why Australian supermarkets continue to look to the UK for leadership, *The Conversation*, 22 January.

16 Barrawclough, A (2016) How Aldi supermarkets created converts in Australia, *The Australian*, 16 January.

17 www.news.com.au/lifestyle/food/why-do-australians-love-aldi-the-secrets-to-the-supermarkets-phenomenal-success/news-story/fb4c5e30228f5f23b-720f7b0caee3018, last accessed 29 December 2017.

18 Data on Biedronka and other retailers in Poland are taken from the Euromonitor International series of reports on grocery retailing in Poland, January 2018.

19 Data on the Turkish grocery market are taken from Euromonitor International (2016), Grocery Retailers in Turkey, December.

20 Analysis of BIM's strategy draws heavily on BIM in Turkey, Planet Retail, 2017.

21 The hard discounter life-cycle model was introduced by Powers, S *et al* (2017) Global Consumer: Will private label swallow up $48 billion of branded US consumables value? UBS report, 11 July.

The next frontier – dissecting the US grocery retailscape

05

With annual sales of over US $1.15 trillion in 2017, the United States is the world's largest grocery market.[1] It is also a fiercely competitive market with 300,000 outlets – comprising a bewildering variety of retail formats, from traditional independent small grocers to giant hypermarkets – battling for the favour of 330 million consumers. The US market is dominated by Walmart Inc., a hyper-efficient, everyday low price (EDLP) retailer with total US sales of $398.7 billion in 2017, of which around 56 per cent is groceries. Although it operates multiple formats, big-box retailing is what it does best, and this will remain its most significant channel by far for the foreseeable future. However, the age of the relentless physical expansion of its hypermarkets is ending. A slowdown was inevitable: there is a limit to the number of large-scale outlets even a country as vast as the United States can support. Just 57 new hypermarkets were opened in 2016, and only 35 in 2017, compared to a historic rate of 120–130 new stores per year.

Despite Walmart's huge size, the US grocery retailscape is quite framented for a developed market (Table 5.1). The top five companies accounted for around 40 per cent of total grocery expenditures in 2017, versus 70–90 per cent in Australia, Germany, France and the UK.[2] Another remarkable feature of the US market is the large difference in size between Walmart Inc. and the runner-up, Kroger Co. Walmart's market share in groceries is more than twice that of Kroger. The degree of fragmentation is tellingly illustrated by the fact that a retailer with a mere 4.4 per cent of the market is the country's fourth-largest retailer. The number four retailer in the UK (Morrisons) had a market share of 10.4 per cent, and the number four in France (Casino) had 11.5 per cent in 2016.

Table 5.1 Market share of US grocery retailers in 2017

Company	Major banners	Dominant store type	Market share in grocery (%)
Walmart Inc.	Walmart, Walmart Neighborhood Market, Sam's Club	Hypermarket	19.6
Kroger Co.	Kroger, Fred Meyer Stores, Harris Teeter, Pick 'n Save	Supermarket	8.8
Costco Wholesale Corp.	Costco	Wholesale club	4.7
Albertsons Inc.	Albertsons, Safeway, Shaw's, Jewel-Osco, Vons, Acme	Supermarket	4.4
Ahold Delhaize N.V.	Food Lion, Stop & Shop, Hannaford, Giant, Martin's	Supermarket	3.3
Public Super Markets Inc.	Publix	Supermarket	2.7
Walgreens Boots Alliance	Walgreens, Duane Reade	Drug store	2.4
Target Corp.	Target	Hypermarket	2.2
Aldi	Aldi, Trader Joe's	Hard discounter	2.1
CVS	CVS	Drug store	1.8
HE Butt Grocery Co.	H-E-B	Supermarket	1.5
Amazon	Whole Foods Market	Supermarket	1.3
Dollar General Inc.	Dollar General	Brand discounter	1.3
Dollar Tree Inc.	Dollar Tree, Family Dollar	Brand discounter	1.2
Meijer Inc.	Meijer	Hypermarket	1.1

NOTE Market share refers to share of the grocery market. Some companies (eg, Walmart, Costco, dollar stores) have significant (30 per cent or more) non-grocery sales. The large majority of Walgreens Boots Alliance and CVS sales are in non-grocery.
SOURCE Based on 2018 data from Euromonitor International and Planet Retail

Developments in the US market

#1 Disruption

Until recently, the US grocery market was fairly predictable. For conventional retailers, this comfortable state of affairs was ripped apart in the span of a few days in mid-June 2017 by three important developments. First, Lidl opened its first stores in Virginia and the Carolinas. Second, in response, Aldi announced a dramatic acceleration of its previously cautious expansion plans; it will open 900 new stores by 2022, bringing its total to 2,500 – the same as Kroger currently has. Third, Amazon entered the grocery market in full force by announcing it would acquire Whole Foods.

David Ciancio, a former Kroger executive, expressed the prevailing feeling in the industry succinctly when he commented in the *Wall Street Journal*, 'This is the most disruption the grocery industry has seen in the last half-century'.[3] He was not exaggerating. Kroger Co.'s share price fell from $30.28 on June 14, 2017 to $22.29 on June 16, a whopping 26 per cent decline. Netherlands-based Ahold Delhaize's share price fell 17 per cent in that period. Even mighty Walmart was not immune to the anticipated disruption – its share price fell 6 per cent.

#2 Increasing consolidation

Grocery retailing in the United States is becoming increasingly consolidated – albeit from a relatively low level – as large companies continue to acquire local and regional chains. Between 2012 and 2016 the number of major grocery banners decreased from 44 to 37. For example, Kroger Co. acquired Harris Teeter for $2.5 billion in 2014, and in 2015 it paid $800 million for Roundy (parent of Pick 'n Save). In that same year, Albertsons Inc. acquired Safeway Inc. for $9.2 billion giving it control of the Safeway Inc.'s store banners. It also bought part of the bankrupt Great Atlantic & Pacific Tea Company. In July 2016, global giants Royal Ahold and Delhaize Group completed their merger, to become the fifth-largest retailer in the United States. Ahold Delhaize also owns the leading grocery chains in the Netherlands (Albert Heijn, with a market share of 35.4 per cent in 2017) and Belgium (Delhaize, 22.0 per cent).

#3 Growing popularity of smaller formats

A growing number of retailers are shifting away from large to smaller store formats in order to meet the needs of an increasingly urbanized population.

One such example is regional supermarket operator Hy-Vee (2017 revenues: $9.8 billion). In trade magazine *Supermarket News*, Tina Potthoff, Hy-Vee's VP of communications said, 'After evaluating recent changes in consumer shopping and lifestyle behaviours, we are adjusting our growth strategy to best meet our customers' changing wants and needs. Over the next several years, we will continue to expand our offerings across the Midwest by constructing new, smaller-format stores.'[4]

As sales at its hypermarket outlets were slowing, Walmart increased the number of Walmart Neighborhood Market stores. These stores average about 42,000 square feet, about a fifth of the size of a Walmart Supercenter (while this is small for Walmart, it is not small in a general sense, given that the average US supermarket is 45,000 square feet). In 2017, there were 700 Walmart Neighborhood Markets. Target was following suit. It operated around 30 small(er)-format stores in 2017, including a new 45,000-square-foot store in Manhattan's hip Tribeca neighbourhood, where the retailer hopes to glean lessons it can apply to future stores.

Target and Walmart face significant hurdles in transitioning to smaller stores, as their core competency is in operating hypermarkets. That this transition is not easy is evidenced by Walmart's failure to make a success of Walmart Express stores (12,000–15,000 square feet). According to industry expert Jeremy Bowman, Walmart made the mistake of shrinking its proven Supercenter format to fit into a much smaller size instead of developing a concept around the small format.[5] The Express stores were too small to fill customers' food shopping needs and carried products like stationery and toys. Most also included a pharmacy. It stocked multiple brands of the same item, costing space. Consumers often felt the product selection was not right. Instead of targeting urban areas as its dollar store and convenience store rivals were doing, Walmart opened Express stores in the rural Southern areas it already dominated, with the majority located within 10 miles of a Supercenter.[6] In 2016, Walmart closed all its 102 Walmart Express stores. In contrast, its Neighborhood Markets have been more successful because they are almost entirely grocery stores.

#4 Shift to organic, fresh, and local

Ever more US consumers are shifting away from traditional, processed foods to organic, healthy, local, and fresh foods. In response, the race has begun among grocery retailers to offer more low-cost organic, local, and unprocessed products. This trend offers a unique opportunity for retailers to differentiate themselves. Many retailers have expanded their assortment of locally sourced products, especially in fresh foods. They also started developing their own lines of organic products. Historically, national brands have a weak presence in fresh and organics, and purchase behaviour is fluid – it is a new category for many consumers without firmly established brand loyalties. Retailers from Trader Joe's and Aldi to Kroger and Walmart are all jumping on the healthy bandwagon with their own private-label lines. For example, Kroger offers Simple Truth Organic branded products ranging from paper towels to tomato bisque, Albertsons offers O Organics, and H-E-B offers H-E-B Organics, to name but a few.

#5 Value consciousness

US consumers have become more value-conscious, fuelled by prolonged slow income growth. Real median household income peaked in 1999 and this level was surpassed only in 2016.[7] According to a 2017 IRI survey, 31 per cent of US households, including 36 per cent of the key millennials segment, are struggling to afford groceries, despite the economy doing well.[8] An entire generation of shoppers entered adulthood in a period of little sustained income growth, while healthcare costs and college tuition increased dramatically. To make ends meet, these new consumers shift more of their purchases to lower-priced goods.

Industry analysts expect value-seeking behaviour at the consumer level to continue into the future, especially if/when the economy turns sour.[9] According to Benno Dorer, CEO of Clorox, affordability is one of four megatrends that are here to stay, along with health and wellness, sustainability, and fragmentation.[10] A study conducted in 2017 revealed that when it comes to selecting which retailer to patronize, 95 per cent of all shoppers prioritize low price points, and 82 per cent say a store's selection of private labels is important.[11] This offers prospects for sustained private-label growth.

#6 Attitudes towards private labels

In 2017, private-label share in the United States stood at 21.2 per cent versus 36.5 per cent in Western Europe. This large difference reflects the fact that, historically, private labels have been less dominant in the United States. It had few nationally operating retailers, while many brand manufacturers were available across the entire country. Further, US retailers regarded themselves as a house of brands, rather than a (store) branded house. Walmart was a good example of this. Despite its massive size, and hence its ability to persuade brand manufacturers to produce high-quality private-label products for them, private labels accounted for only 17.5 per cent of Walmart's grocery revenues in 2017.[12]

However, the times are changing, fuelled by the increasing value orientation of US households. In the period 2007–2017, private-label share grew 31 per cent, from 16.2 per cent to 21.2 per cent, while private-label share in Europe grew 'only' 19 per cent. We expect this trend to continue. According to Kantar Retail's director Diana Sheehan, private-label items do not carry the same stigma for millennials as they do for the baby boomer generation. Millennials entered adulthood when private labels had already taken off – a far cry from the cheap and nasty generics of their parents' generation.[13] In the aforementioned IRI study, 85 per cent of millennials felt that store brands are equal in quality to their national competitors, while 76 per cent believe that the private labels are better value. If you have retailers doing private label well and you have shoppers open to those products, it is a perfect situation in which to see a jump in growth.

Brand discounters

An interesting feature of the US market is the size and success of two large brand discounters, Dollar General Inc. and Dollar Tree Inc. While total revenues (grocery and non-grocery) of these two companies combined were an impressive $47.5 billion in 2017, this is achieved with a very large number of stores (see Table 5.2). Dollar stores are much smaller (around 8,000 square feet) than the average supermarket in the United States, let alone a Walmart Supercenter. Their smaller size enables them to take their low prices where Walmart cannot easily go – right into the heart of residential neighbourhoods. Dollar stores sell a combination of basic staples such as rice, beans, and toilet paper, often in smaller package sizes, along with 'treasure hunt' products like party decorations and children's toys. In 2017, Dollar Tree's eponymous stores sold all items for a unit price of $1.00 or less. Dollar General is a dollar store in name only. Its merchandise is generally low-priced – 75 per cent of all merchandise retailed at $5 or less in 2017 – but it does not necessarily have to be $1 or less. Despite low prices, dollar stores' profitability is good. The operating margin of both Dollar General and Dollar Tree was around 8 per cent in 2017, twice as much as Walmart.[14]

Low absolute prices make dollar stores very attractive to low-income shoppers: their customers typically come from households earning roughly $40,000 per year. A 2017 survey by GlobalData Retail found that 73 per cent

Table 5.2   Brand discounters vs hard discounters in the United States in 2017

	Dollar Tree	Dollar General	Aldi	Trader Joe's
Revenues (groceries and non-groceries)	$22.5 bn	$25.0 bn	$14.3 bn	$9.7 bn
CAGR 2012–2017 (%)	7.2	8.3	10.5	8.3
Grocery share of total revenues (%)	60	60	> 95	> 95
Private-label share (%)	< 20	< 20	> 90	> 80
Number of stores	14,599	14,609	1,752	487
Average store size (sq ft)	7,718	7,427	10,333	12,000
Sales per store	$1.54 mn	$1.71 mn	$8.16 mn	$19.60 mn
Sales per sq ft	$200	$230	$790	$1,633

NOTE CAGR = compound annual growth rate; CAGR for Dollar Tree is corrected for acquisition of Family Dollar in 2015.
SOURCE Authors' calculations based on 2017 data from Planet Retail

of dollar store customers shop there to make ends meet. However, a growing number of higher-income shoppers patronize these stores because of their convenient location, and even the well-heeled are not above appreciating a good deal. Neil Saunders, managing director of GlobalData Retail explained, 'These more affluent shoppers like the idea of being savvy and getting a bargain on everyday goods. Since the financial crisis, many households are more cost-conscious and much more attuned to getting good value for money than they once were.'[15]

Brand discounters complement their branded assortment with private labels, which are seen as differentiators and margin enhancers. Common practices employed by Dollar General are 'switch and save' messaging and point-of-sale signage that encourage shoppers to compare the price and quality of its DG store brand with those of (alleged) national brand equivalents.

The dollar stores are aware of the threat posed by hard discounters, especially by Aldi. And for good reason, as there is considerable overlap in their value proposition and target segments. They share a low price positioning, operate smaller stores with a limited assortment, over-index on lower-income shoppers, and appeal to people looking for deals and specials ('treasure hunt'). In an effort to pre-empt Aldi, Dollar General is ramping up the number of its stores and renovating existing ones. In 2017, it installed over 18,000 coolers in its existing stores. For 2018 alone, it plans to open

900 new stores, renovate 1,000 old stores, and relocate 100 stores.[16] It is also expanding its selection of groceries and health and beauty care. By the end of 2018, 450 stores will offer fresh produce.[17] To reach metropolitan shoppers, Dollar General has begun experimenting with a smaller (less than 5,000 square feet) store called DGX, which carries more grocery items at the expense of the home goods carried by the regular stores.

Yet, dollar stores have significant vulnerabilities. Their private-label programme remains unsophisticated compared to those of Aldi and Lidl. The small size of the stores complicates a strong push into perishables, which drives store traffic. The amount spent on a shopping trip was, on average, $12 versus $27 dollars at hard discounters in 2016. Fewer trips per household (13 times versus 15 times per year for hard discounters), combined with smaller amounts spent, depresses store productivity. Brand discounters' sales per square foot in 2017 were around $200–$230, significantly below the industry average of $454, and less than one-third of Aldi's (Table 5.2).[18] One reason they can survive on such low productivity is that the startup costs are very low. Dollar General spends as little as $250,000 on a new store, but this gives store interiors and exteriors a rather cheap look and feel. Brand discounters also lack the massive global scale and deep pockets of the hard discounters.

Hard discounters in the United States

After Lidl opened its first stores in June 2017, there were four main hard discounters in the United States: Aldi, Lidl, Trader Joe's, and Save-A-Lot. Store productivity at Trader Joe's is phenomenal, roughly twice as high as Aldi's (Table 5.2), which already runs a very efficient operation. This was discussed in detail in Chapter 3. Save-A-Lot closely resembles Aldi and, with sales of $4.6 billion in 2017 according to PlanetRetail, is much smaller than either Aldi or Trader Joe's. In this chapter, we will focus on the activities of Aldi and Lidl in the United States.

Aldi – from going slow to rapid acceleration

Aldi entered the United States in 1976. Since then, it has expanded slowly and without fanfare, building around 25–30 new stores annually, primarily in Eastern and Midwestern states. Only in 2009 did it pass the 1,000-store mark. Unlike Walmart, Aldi has faced little opposition when it wants to build a store, and is not seen as threatening to the local ecosystem. The stores are small-format and they usually get space from an existing landowner who is part of the community rather than from a large real estate developer.[19]

After 2010, Aldi accelerated its expansion programme, opening new stores at a rate of 80–100 per year, and entered new regions such as California and Texas. In 2017, it announced it would invest $5 billion to add 900 new stores by 2022 and remodel 1,300 existing stores. This should put them on a trajectory to grab 4–5 per cent of the market in five years, taking into account both strong organic growth (9.1 per cent annually in 2012–2017) and store expansion. According to industry experts, this indicates that Aldi is not only concerned about the potential market effects of Lidl, but, importantly, that it is also convinced that its model is really starting to resonate with consumers.[20] The remodelling initiative features open ceilings, natural lighting, and environmentally friendly building materials, such as recycled materials, energy-saving refrigeration, and LED lighting. As part of this refurbishment activity, it added more national brands to its assortment and expanded its offering of perishables (produce, fresh meat, etc).

In 2018, Aldi and Kohl's announced an experimental partnership where Aldi would offer its private-label groceries next door to Kohl's apparel and home goods. The retailers have similar brand identities and cater to the same value-focused shopper.[21] Aldi also started to experiment with online shopping and home delivery via Instacart. In March 2018, it offered this service in Los Angeles, Dallas, Atlanta, and Chicago.[22]

Back in the 1990s, Aldi's assortment was basic staples. It sold no fresh meat and hardly any produce. Its reputation was that of a store where one buys ultra-cheap groceries, appealing mainly to the lowest-income groups. Now, it sells organic ground beef and refrigerated produce. Its store-brand foods no longer contain synthetic dyes, added transfat, or added monosodium glutamate (MSG). 'Simply Nature', an organic and natural line, has become one of Aldi's fastest-growing brands. Under this label, it sells cage-free eggs, grass-fed ground beef, and spices, to name a few. In Europe, Aldi already carried a premium private-label brand, 'Specially Selected', and in 2013, it introduced it in the United States. Items range from blue cheese-stuffed green olives and Anise Pizzelle cookies to Black Forest ham and Ahi tuna steaks. This is no longer the stuff of subsistence living. Along with the growing sophistication of its assortment, most of Aldi's new stores are in middle-income suburban neighbourhoods. But shoppers still have to bring their own grocery bags (or buy them in-store), bag their own groceries, and pay a refundable 25 cents to use a shopping cart, which many US shoppers find annoying.

Notwithstanding these upgrades in the assortment, Aldi retained its low price position. While prices vary substantially across regions in the United

States and, over time, in response to competitive conditions, in 2017 a basket of like-for-like private-label products was anywhere between 5 per cent and 20 per cent cheaper at Aldi than at Walmart, around 20 per cent below Dollar General, and 20–50 per cent cheaper than Food Lion, Kroger, and Publix. According to industry experts, like-for-like comparisons may be generous to most conventional retailers because they believe Aldi's private-label quality is higher.[23]

Lidl – 'Rethink grocery'

In June 2017, Lidl opened its first stores in the Carolinas and Virginia. By the end of 2017, it had already opened nearly 50 stores. Its gleaming 36,000-square-foot stores had 21,000 square feet of selling space, which was twice the size of Aldi stores in the United States and 35 per cent larger than Lidl's biggest outlets in Europe. Their distinct appearance, made of red brick with arching walls of floor-to-ceiling glazed glass, reflected learnings from focus groups with US consumers who told Lidl executives its European stores with exterior aluminium panels more closely resembled a car dealership than a supermarket. Unlike Aldi, it does not use coin-released shopping carts.

While private labels constitute the backbone of its assortment, Lidl carries a relatively large number of leading national brands, ranging from Red Bull, Coca-Cola, Budweiser, and Folgers coffee to Utz potato chips, Jif peanut butter, Pampers, and Sensodyne toothpaste in 2017. There is also a strong selection of organics and an excellent wine selection, including Lidl-exclusive wines, far beyond what Aldi offers in the United States. Stores have a bakery positioned near the entrance where workers finish parbaked items several times a day. Private-label packaging has been designed specifically for the US market, in many cases to leave customers with little doubt as to the national brand counterparts they should mentally compare them to. Lidl complements its grocery assortment with general merchandise, called 'Surprises'. These items change twice a week to encourage repeat visits and underpin its value credentials.

To reassure US consumers of the quality of Lidl's private-label products, they are marked with the 'Lidl Love It' guarantee: if customers do not love what they have bought, they get a refund for the item and a replacement. It carries a premium private label called 'Preferred Selection', which includes about 160 SKUs, across a number of categories including fresh and packaged meats, charcuterie, cheeses, chocolates, snacks, and more. The Preferred Selection range received the 2017 Top Innovation Award from industry magazine *Store Brands*.[24]

Lidl sources approximately 85 per cent of its products from the United States. According to one private-label supplier, Lidl appears more concerned with quality than some conventional retailers he does business with. The supplier also said that faith in the financial strength of Lidl and its owner, the Schwarz Group, made a long-term bet on volume more acceptable than with most other retail customers.[25]

Lidl's prices are at parity with Aldi's, at least at the timing of writing. We conducted a store check in June 2017 and found that a basket of private-label products cost $64.88 at Lidl versus $65.74 at Aldi. Other research found that Lidl's prices were between 6 and 10 per cent cheaper than neighbouring Walmart stores and around 15 per cent lower than Kroger stores. Lidl's price advantage was generally greater for staples than for fresh foods.[26]

Lidl's entire strategy is summarized in its slogan, 'Rethink Grocery'. What does that mean? US CEO Brendan Proctor explained:

> The feedback we got from customers in the US was very clear. People feel they've been compromised… People want a good-quality product, they want it at a good price and they don't want to spend all day in a store – they want to get back to living. That's what our model is about.[27]

Initial response to Lidl was enthusiastic. In June, Lidl was drawing 11 per cent of consumer visits to traditional grocers in nine markets in Virginia, North Carolina and South Carolina. However, by August, Lidl's share of that traffic had fallen below 8 per cent.[28] What was going on?

Lidl had made some missteps.[29] Despite meticulous preparation, some store locations were ill-chosen. According to Jeffrey Metzger, publisher of trade journal *Food World*, the company has been 'all over the place' with its store selection. According to him, the only consistent criteria seemed to be the stores' proximity to Walmart and Aldi locations.[30] A related problem was that the stores cost too much to build, which was a function of size and store design.[31] The German trade magazine *Lebensmittel Zeitung* reported that in March 2017, Schwarz's CEO, Klaus Gehrig was already expressing concerns over the cost of the 'glass palaces'.[32] This required a dense population area within a three-mile radius, while many (planned) stores were in smaller markets that did not meet this criterion.[33]

Turning to the assortment, produce selection was rather low on conventional items while (over?) emphasizing organic offerings. The emphasis on wine was not always in line with local tastes focused on beer, according to Ali Dibadj, Senior Vice President at investment management firm Sanford Bernstein. A recurring comment we heard when talking with industry experts was that Lidl tried to do too many things on its own – with significant direction from Germany – without involving local experts.

Yet, many shoppers liked what they saw. A survey conducted by consulting firm Oliver Wyman in October 2017 in the Carolinas and Virginia revealed that two-thirds of Lidl shoppers thought its store brands provided very good value for money and that freshness and quality of produce and bakery were great. An equal proportion liked the shopping experience, versus 27 per cent who were disappointed with the store. Lidl did not mainly appeal to the low-income shopper, indicating the broad appeal of the concept. Oliver Wyman also surveyed consumers in these three states who had not shopped at Lidl yet. The main reason (63 per cent) was that there was no Lidl close by. One-quarter were not aware of the existence of Lidl.[34]

Late 2017, in a sign it realized more time was needed to get a good handle on the US market, Lidl scaled back its initial expansion plans.[35] In December, Lidl announced it was interested in leasing opportunities along the East Coast for existing properties between 15,000 and 25,000 square feet that would only draw customers from a two-mile radius.[36] In March 2018, it launched its first multimedia campaign highlighting what it calls the 'bloated supermarket shopping experience' facing most US consumers. The ads debuted on March 15 in six states, and the marketing blitz includes TV and radio commercials, billboards and truck wraps.[37] In May 2018, Brendon Proctor was replaced by Johannes Fieber as US CEO.

At the time of writing, the jury is still out on how successful Lidl will be in the United States. We note, though, that Lidl has deep pockets, a long history of learning from its mistakes, is not subject to quarterly earnings reports, and is in it for the long haul. A better real estate plan could improve overall store volumes and store economics. The Oliver Wyman study indicates that shoppers are loyal to the format once they overcome their initial hesitation. If Lidl is willing to give greater decision autonomy to its US management and can improve its assortment, it increases its chances of converting curious shoppers into regular customers. Conventional retailers in other countries such as Germany, the Netherlands and the UK have underestimated Lidl's determination to succeed, to their own detriment.

Online retailing

Online retailing in 2017 accounted for only 2 per cent of total US food sales, and was heavily concentrated in cities and their surrounding suburbs. Nevertheless, it is one of the fastest-growing segments in grocery retailing. Any prediction about the future evolution of online grocery retailing is fraught with uncertainty, but the consensus is that it will continue to grow strongly in the next decade. The biggest challenge in online grocery retailing is the 'last mile': how to get the grocery order from a central point to the customer's home. There are two dominant solutions to this challenge.

The first option is *click-and-collect*, where customers pick up the order themselves. Many retailers offer this service. Click-and-collect uses the banner's brick-and-mortar stores for order fulfilment and as delivery points. In 2017, Walmart started to experiment with an automated kiosk where online shoppers can pick up their groceries at any time of the day or week. The kiosk is a 20-by-80-foot building in the parking lot of the local Walmart Supercenter. Instead of parking and waiting for a staffer to bring out the groceries, the customer enters a pickup code and waits for the kiosk to automatically fetch the order from bins inside. Walmart was also trying out vending machine-like 'Pickup Towers' in five cities across the United States that streamlined the process of retrieving non-food orders. Undoubtedly, other click-and-collect options will be developed in upcoming years.

The second option is *home delivery* of the order. Meijer and Wegmans, among others, offered this service in 2017, and in March 2018, Walmart announced it would expand its grocery delivery service to 100 metro areas by the end of the year.[38] Home delivery is logistically complex. Fresh produce is fragile. Retailers need to be able to transport their orders throughout the fulfilment journey at three different temperatures: ambient (eg packaged foods), chilled (eg butter, fresh meat), and frozen (eg ice cream, frozen vegetables). Orders might be fulfilled at a local store and delivery can be outsourced to a third party like Instacart. Instacart also functions as a shopper service, allowing the customer to order from affiliated retailers. Walmart started tests where it uses store employees to drop off online orders at customers' homes on their way home from work. According to Walmart.com CEO Marc Lore, the test takes advantage of the unique assets of Walmart – 1 million employees across the country working in stores located within 10 miles of 90 per cent of the US population, and trucks full of merchandise bound for those stores every day – and uses them to reduce costs inherent in home delivery.[39]

There are also pure online players, like Peapod. Peapod is owned by Ahold Delhaize and delivers from that company's stores as well as from its own Chicago-area warehouses. In 2017, Peapod had operations in 23 US urban markets and, with sales of around $800 million, it was the largest online grocery delivery store in the United States.

Most retailers are still struggling to make online grocery shopping economically feasible. In the UK, for each £80 basket the retailer incurs £5 in labour costs for someone to pick the items off the shelf and £5-8 for someone to deliver it.[40] While costs may be somewhat different in the United States, it illustrates the economic challenge. Delivery costs could easily be higher given the geographical size and relatively low population density in many parts of the country. With razor-thin margins on groceries, consumers expecting the same prices online and offline, and little willingness to pay for home delivery, firms struggle to make comparable money in the online channel.

While retailers have no choice to offer online options, by 2018, they were still searching for the best process to put this in to practice. The need to accomplish this has received greater urgency than ever with Amazon's push into grocery retailing.

Amazon

Amazon has made no secret of its ambition to become the world's biggest retailer, and this ambition is difficult to achieve without a significant footprint in grocery retailing. However, Amazon's success in this market has been uncharacteristically modest. In 2017, AmazonFresh, a 10-year-old grocery delivery service was still only in 20-odd cities, and Prime Now, a two-hour delivery service, was in 31 cities. Amazon Go was introduced in 2016 in Seattle. It is partially automated, with customers able to purchase products without using a cashier or checkout station. The future of these initiatives is difficult to predict, but many have lost when betting against Amazon. This being said, Amazon's acquisition of Whole Foods for $13.7 billion in August 2017 was widely regarded as the true game changer. What rendered this move so different from others?

It gave Amazon more than 450 stores, primarily in high-density, high-income metro areas in coastal states. Amazon gained an established perishable supply chain and sourcing operation, something its AmazonFresh grocery division had struggled with. The digital innovations of Amazon Go could be rolled out in Whole Foods stores. Amazon acquired a highly regarded store brand – 365 – that it subsequently introduced online. Amazon would also be able to expand into the payments business by enabling Whole Foods shoppers to pay via their Prime accounts – something already employed at the Amazon Go test location. Last but not least, by the end of 2017, Amazon had started using the store network stores as delivery points for click-and-collect orders.

Amazon is expected to integrate its intelligent personal assistant Alexa with grocery shopping. Gary Hawkins, CEO of the Center for Advancing Retail & Technology, predicted:

> I can start my shopping list as I have coffee at home in the morning, add some things to it I think of while I'm driving to work, and then ask Alexa to have my order ready to pick up at the Whole Foods I drive by on my way home later that day. What conventional retailer is even close to this capability?[41]

Amazon also got access to data. While it had virtually limitless data on shoppers' online behaviour, it lacked deep insight into their offline behaviour. Importantly, there is significant overlap between the companies' traditionally loyal customer bases. Over 60 per cent of Whole Foods' shoppers were members of Amazon's Prime service in 2017, opening the door for cross-sell promotions to entice customers who shop at both to spend more.[42] On 20 February 2018, Amazon announced that Prime members get 5 per cent back on every dollar spent at Whole Foods when they pay with the Amazon Prime Rewards Visa Card. In June 2018, it launched an in-store price promotion program tied to Prime membership.

Implications for the grocery industry

Changing consumer attitudes, expansion of hard discounters, and entry of Amazon into grocery retailing set in motion a chain of events that has had profoundly disrupting effects on the US grocery retailscape (Figure 5.1). One consequence is increasing price competition. For example, Aldi entered Southern California in March 2016. An epic price war ensued and, by September 2017, grocery prices dropped an unprecedented 3 per cent (this applies to the total grocery market; the price drop for items sold by Aldi was much higher). 'Southern California has moved from one of the highest-priced markets in the country to the most competitively priced market', said supermarket analyst Burt Flickinger, managing director of New York-based Strategic Resource Group.[43]

While Lidl's market share is still small, its effect is nevertheless significant. According to Chris Mandeville, an analyst at Jeffries, retailers in the Midwest already feel Lidl's pricing pressure despite the fact Lidl is not even in that geography. 'Lidl is affecting the pricing of Walmart and Aldi. In turn, they're impacting these retailers', said Mandeville.

Whole Foods was not much of a price competitor in the past – its nickname Whole Paycheck said it all – but that was changing too. Immediately after the acquisition became formal on 28 August 2017, Amazon started to

Figure 5.1 Disruption in US grocery retailing

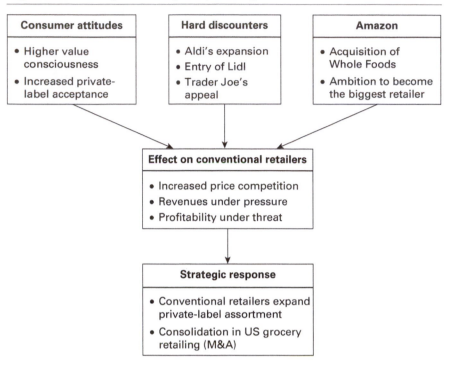

Consumer attitudes	Hard discounters	Amazon
• Higher value consciousness • Increased private-label acceptance	• Aldi's expansion • Entry of Lidl • Trader Joe's appeal	• Acquisition of Whole Foods • Ambition to become the biggest retailer

Effect on conventional retailers

- Increased price competition
- Revenues under pressure
- Profitability under threat

Strategic response

- Conventional retailers expand private-label assortment
- Consolidation in US grocery retailing (M&A)

slash prices. We conducted a store check in Whole Foods, Chapel Hill, NC in March and December of 2017 for the same basket of 31 products. The price of the total basket was 5.2 per cent lower in December. For example, it cut the price of a pound of organic ground beef from $5.99 to $4.99, organic bananas were cut from $0.89/lb to $0.69/lb, and organic spring mix from $3.99/5 oz to $3.49/5 oz. The actual price cuts and the buzz they received in the media increased foot traffic.[44] Chris McCabe, a former Amazon executive, explained Amazon's take-no-prisoners strategy: 'Amazon's using the same playbook they always have when competing with booksellers and other retailers. They take out their revenue stream by killing them slowly on price.'[45]

Conventional retailers might also see a decline in revenues. If they drop prices, dollar revenues will suffer unless they can make it up by selling a larger volume, which is difficult in saturated markets. If they do not regain price competitiveness, they will lose entire shopping baskets to competitors. Even a modest sales decline can push a retailer into the red. The extremely competitive food retail business demands high capital investments for low net margins. The average gross margin in US grocery retailing in 2017 was 12.4 per cent, while the operating margin was a meagre 0.7 per cent,

Table 5.3 Consequences of operating leverage for average US grocery retailer

| Financials | % | Before entry | Scenarios after entry of Aldi or Lidl | |
			5% decline in sales	10% decline in sales
Revenues	100	$10 bn	$9.5 bn	$9.0 bn
Cost of goods sold	87.6	$8.76 bn	$8.32 bn	$7.88 bn
Fixed costs (store, utilities, labour, overhead)	11.7	$1.17 bn	$1.17 bn	$1.17 bn
Operating profit	0.7	$70 mn	$10 mn	–$50 mn
Decline in profit under two scenarios			–86%	–171%

the lowest since the global financial crisis.[46] This means that every 1 per cent lost in sales leads to a loss in operating profit of 17 per cent for the average US grocery retailer. Table 5.3 illustrates this for an 'average' grocer with $10 billion in annual revenues. If sales decline 5 per cent, 86 per cent of operating profits are lost. If sales decline by 10 per cent, the average retailer is deep in the red. An unlikely scenario? Not if the UK points the way. In 2015–2016, while the sales of Aldi and Lidl surged, Walmart's subsidiary Asda's revenues dropped 8.0 per cent. Morrisons' plight was even worse – its revenues declined by 12.0 per cent between 2012 and 2015.[47]

How can conventional retailers respond to pressure on their profits?

Whether it is through increased price competition, lower revenues, or both, the profitability of conventional retailers will be under pressure. How can they respond? First, they should work hard to grow private labels as a proportion of their revenues. Margins on private labels are higher, so an increase in the share of private labels in one's revenues can go some way to compensate for profit losses. At a conference in March 2017, Doug McMillon, CEO of Walmart, presented the retailer's thinking on the topic: 'Having a private brand from a margin mix point of view has always been important, but it is even more important now.'[48] He added that Walmart is increasingly looking for its store brands like Great Value to drive loyalty.

This represents a significant change in thinking for Walmart, which has long relied on offering 'name brands for less'. A shift towards private label is facilitated by the fact that millennials and Generation X have a much more positive attitude towards private labels than older generations.

There is a lot of upward potential for conventional retailers' private labels. Wegmans and H-E-B had the highest private-label share among major retailers in 2017, but private labels nevertheless accounted for only 30–33 per cent of total sales. Kroger (27 per cent), Albertsons (22 per cent), Costco (21 per cent), Target (16 per cent), and Whole Foods (15 per cent) were even lower.[49] To compare, private-label share in leading European banners like Tesco, Carrefour, Albert Heijn, and Edeka exceeds 40 per cent, if not 50 per cent. In October 2017, Kroger launched Restock Kroger. As part of this plan, Kroger said it would 'aggressively grow' its 'Big 3' store brands – Kroger, Private Selection, and Simple Truth.[50] Costco announced in 2017 its goal to drive private-label share to 37 per cent of sales.[51]

Another response to the pressure on profitability is consolidation in grocery retailing to achieve scale. Weaker chains will be pushed out, either through bankruptcy or, more likely, by being acquired by a stronger rival. Which conventional retailers are most vulnerable? Walmart and the dollar stores are directly in the expansion path of Aldi and Lidl, while upscale retailers like Wegmans are in the expansion path of Whole Foods. Yet Wegmans has stellar customer satisfaction, Walmart significant financial resources and clout with suppliers, and the dollar chains can make money in environments where nobody else can. We believe that smaller, weaker regional grocery chains that lack scale and are low on customer satisfaction are most vulnerable to the disruption in the US grocery industry. Table 5.4 shows shopper satisfaction with select grocery chains in 2016.[52] We can see that a large number of regional chains, from Food Lion and Bi-Lo to Shaw's and Tops Friendly Market rated below average on overall satisfaction – and much lower than Aldi or Trader Joe's.

Ideally, conventional retailers pursue both options – increasing private label and increasing scale through acquisitions – in tandem. After all, the larger you are, the stronger your negotiating position is with private-label suppliers to get high-quality products for a sharp price.

Implications for national brands

As a result of these developments in the US grocery retail sector, we expect that private labels will breach the 25 per cent mark in the next few years. The consequences are enormous. National brands stand to lose up to $40–50

Table 5.4   Shoppers' satisfaction with select US grocery retailers in 2016

Retailer	Shopper satisfaction	Retailer	Shopper satisfaction
Above average		*Below average*	
Wegmans	89	Sam's Club	76
Trader Joe's	86	Target	75
Publix	86	Food Lion	74
Costco	85	Bi-Lo	74
H-E-B	84	Albertsons	73
Aldi	83	Giant Eagle	73
Sprouts Farmers Market	83	Jewel-Osco	72
Hy-Vee	82	Pick 'n Save	71
Harris Teeter	81	Safeway	71
Lowes Foods	79	Acme	70
Hannaford	78	Stop & Shop	69
Whole Foods	78	Shaw's	68
Kroger	78	Tops Friendly Market	68
BJ Wholesale Club	78	Walmart Supercenter	66

NOTE Satisfaction is measured on a scale from 0 to 100; mean satisfaction score across 62 grocery retailers was 77.9.
SOURCE Based on *Consumer Reports* (2017) Faster, fresher, cheaper, July, pp. 30–43.

billion in sales *per year*. But not every brand is equally vulnerable. The experience in Germany has shown that middle brands, rather than the market leader or premium brands, are the most likely to be squeezed by the march of private labels in general, and of hard discounters in particular.[53] Between 2001 and 2014, private-label share in Germany grew 55 per cent, from 24.4 per cent to 37.8 per cent, according to market research company GfK. In that period, the share of market leaders and premium brands actually increased 3.2 per cent. The big losers were the middle brands, whose market share declined by 32 per cent.[54] They lack strong marketing support and brand awareness, and are often struggling to keep up with the continuous quality improvements of hard discounters' private labels, let alone staying ahead of them.

Managerial takeaways

The US grocery market has several characteristics in which it differs sharply from Australia and Europe in 2017:

- It is more fragmented. This makes it easier for new entrants to gain a foothold.
- It is characterized by extreme differences in size. There is one giant retailer (Walmart), one runner-up, and a large number of smaller regional players.
- Two brand discounters have popularized the concept of no-frills, small-store shopping.
- It is the home market of Amazon, the world's most fearsome online retailer.
- Private-label share is significantly below that of Europe: 21.2 per cent vs 36.5 per cent.

But trends indicate major shifts in consumer attitudes and behaviour that bode well for private label. There is a strong shift away from traditional, processed foods dominated by big national brands, to organic, fresh, and healthy products, where brands traditionally have been weaker. The new generation of US consumers is more value-conscious and has a more positive attitude towards private labels than their parents and grandparents. Moreover, Amazon is heavily pushing private label. As a result, we expect private label to pass the 25 per cent mark in the near future. Hard discounters will benefit disproportionately from the shift to private labels as they run the best and most efficient private-label operations in town.

At the same time, online grocery retailing is rapidly growing. Existing grocers are experimenting with click-and-collect and home delivery, yet struggle to make it truly profitable. Hard discounters are not particularly well placed to capitalize on the growth of online shopping, but Amazon is, especially since it acquired Whole Foods.

Hence, the triple whammy of the acquisition of Whole Foods by Amazon, acceleration of Aldi's expansion, and the entry of Lidl are game changers. These developments will increase price competition and put heavy pressure on the revenues and profits of conventional retailers. To counter this, these retailers need to shift more of their emphasis towards private labels. Consolidation to achieve scale is another required strategic response. Smaller, weaker conventional grocery chains that lack scale, are low on customer satisfaction, and have an unfavourable price image are most vulnerable. Many regional stores fit that bill (Table 5.4). On the brands' side, middle brands with a lower market share that lack strong marketing support are the most likely to be squeezed.

Notes

1 Data in this section taken from PlanetRetail (2018) and Euromonitor International (2018) Retailing in the US, March. The total size of the US grocery market is surprisingly difficult to determine, as different data providers use different definitions. Recall that we use the definition used by PlanetRetail and define grocery as edible grocery, health and beauty products, and house-hold and pet care. According to Euromonitor International, total revenue of grocery retailers in 2017 was $1.12 trillion. However, almost all grocery retailers also sell non-grocery, which, by looking at PlanetRetail we estimate at 15 per cent of total revenues. On the other hand, Euromonitor does not include drug stores, warehouse clubs, and dollar stores as grocery retailers. We obtained the grocery sales of these 'non-traditional' retailers and added them to the Euromonitor sales data, which yields our estimate of $1.15 trillion in 2017.

2 http://iplc-europe.com/wp-content/uploads/2017/09/IPLC-Research-Report-2016-FINAL.pdf, last accessed 1 January 2018.

3 Gasparro, A (2017) Kroger rattles nerves in grocery section, *Wall Street Journal*, 16 June, p. B1.

4 Hamstra, M (2017) Hy-Vee adjusts growth strategy, *Supermarket News*, 7 November.

5 Bowman, J (2016) Why Walmart Express failed, *The Motley Fool*, 24 January.

6 Ibid.

7 Data from the Federal Reserve Bank of St. Louis; https://fred.stlouisfed.org/series/MEHOINUSA672N, last accessed 1 January 2018.

8 www.snackandbakery.com/articles/90831-iri-finds-consumers-still-turning-to-private-labels-in-stable-economy, last accessed 17 December 2017.

9 Stephen Powers *et al* (2017) Global consumer: will private label swallow up $48 billion of branded US consumables value? UBS report, 11 July.

10 'Accelerating Profitable Growth', Presentation at the Clorox Company Analyst Day 2015.

11 Orlando, D (2017) Frugality hangover gives private labels staying power, study finds, *Supermarket News*, 8 August.

12 Powers, S *et al* (2017) Global consumer: will private label swallow up $48 billion of branded US consumables value? UBS report, 11 July.

13 www.fooddive.com/news/grocery--growth-in-private-store-brands-poised-to-accelerate-through-2022//, last accessed 21 November 2017.

14 www.fool.com/investing/2017/12/15/dollar-general-dreams-big-with-2000-store-growth-p.aspx, last accessed 1 January 2018; see also *Bloomberg Businessweek* (2017) After the Walmart is gone, 16 October, pp. 57–61.

15 Jones, C (2017) Dollar stores buck the trend, rake in cash, *USA Today*, 21 June, p. 2B.

16 www.fool.com/investing/2017/12/15/dollar-general-dreams-big-with-2000-store-growth-p.aspx, last accessed 1 January 2018.

17 www.fooddive.com/news/grocery--dollar-general-will-carry-fresh-produce-in-450-stores-by-the-end-of-2018/, last accessed 22 March 2018.

18 Productivity in grocery retailing in 2017 was calculated based on total revenues of grocery retailers ($1,116 billion) divided by their total selling space (2,460 million square feet) using data from Euromonitor International (2018) Retailing in the US, March.

19 Clifford, S (2011) Where Wal-Mart failed, Aldi succeeds, *New York Times*, 29 March.

20 Springer, J (2017) A tidal wave of change in food retailing, *Supermarket News*, 15 November.

21 www.fooddive.com/news/grocery--could-the-aldi-kohls-partnership-be-a-model-for-supermarket-growth/, last accessed 20 March 2018.

22 www.fooddive.com/news/grocery--aldi-expands-same-day-delivery-to-chicago/, last accessed 20 March 2018.

23 Pricing data obtained from various sources, including Peterson, H (2016) Aldi is shockingly cheaper than Dollar General, *Business Insider*, 4 April. finance.yahoo.com/news/aldi-cheaper-wal-mart-deutsche-140839521.html; last accessed 1 January 2018; Gielens, K (2018) The Competitive Price Effects of Lidl's Entry in the US Grocery Market, White paper, Kenan-Flagler Business School, UNC-Chapel Hill, 2018; www.wolferesearch.com/research-library?keywords=Lidl&page=1; last accessed 1 January 2018; Powers, S *et al* (2017) Global Consumer: Will private label swallow up $48 billion of branded US consumables value? UBS report, 11 July.

24 https://storebrands.com/store-brands-names-winners-2017-best-ofawards?, last accessed 16 November 2017.

25 Springer, J (2017) Lidl opens first U.S. stores as new era in food retail begins, *Supermarket News*, 15 June.

26 www.thepacker.com/news/study-finds-new-lidl-stores-run-even-aldi-price, last accessed 11 August 2017.

27 Springer, J (2017) Lidl: First U.S. stores opening June 15, *Supermarket News*, 17 May.

28 Haddon, H (2017) Lidl stores gain little traction so far in the U.S., *Wall Street Journal*, 8 October, p. A1.

29 Ibid

30 www.fooddive.com/news/grocery--lidl-halts-construction-on-new-jersey-store/, last accessed 1 January 2018.

31 For example, Lidl purchased a 4.8 acre spot in Manuta Township, NJ in August 2017 for $3.25 million. Add construction costs and their operating costs are substantial.

32 www.lebensmittelzeitung.net/european-view/Schwarz-Group-Lidl-Rethinks-Posh-Stores, last accessed 1 January 2018.

33 www.fooddive.com/news/grocery--lidl-adjusts-real-estate-strategy-to-reach-more-customers/, last accessed 18 December 2017.

34 Oliver Wyman (2017) US consumers rethink grocery, November.

35 Sams, D and Wenk, A (2017) Lidl scaling back expansion in Georgia, *Atlanta Business Chronicle*, 27 October, p. 1A.

36 www.winsightgrocerybusiness.com/retailers/wgb-exclusive-lidl-pursuing-smaller-sites, last accessed 1 January 2018.

37 www.fooddive.com/news/grocery--lidl-goes-for-the-wallet-in-new-ad-campaign-aimed-at-grocery-competitors/; www.supermarketnews.com/marketing/lidl-launches-ads-targeting-traditional-grocery, last accessed 22 March 2018. This also contains a link to Lidl's first TV ad, called 'The Apple Pyramid'.

38 Hamstra, M (2018) Walmart to expand grocery delivery with in-house pickers, *Supermarket News*, 14 March.

39 Springer, J (2017) Walmart testing associate home delivery, *Supermarket News*, 1 June.

40 McKinsey (2017) The future of grocery – in store and online, June.

41 www.progressivegrocer.com/departments/technology/amazon-whole-foods-and-new-world-supermarketing, last accessed 1 January 2018.

42 Stevens, L and Haddon, H (2017) Big prize for Amazon: shopper data, *Wall Street Journal*, 2 June, p. B5.

43 www.ocregister.com/2017/10/23/prices-drop-in-southern-california-as-aldis-march-west-is-causing-upheaval/, last accessed 1 January 2018.

44 www.cnbc.com/2017/09/12/whole-foods-foot-traffic-surges-over-25-percent-post-amazon-discounts.html, last accessed 1 January 2018.

45 Haddon, H and Stevens, L (2017) Amazon rewrites rule book for grocers, *Wall Street Journal*, 28 August, p. B1.

46 https://csimarket.com/Industry/industry_Profitability_Ratios.php?ind=1305, last accessed 5 February 2018. Percentages refer to the last quarter of 2017 on a trailing 12-month (TTM) basis. TTM refers to the last 12-month period for a selected financial metric. Thus, here, the percentages refer to January–December 2017. TTM makes figures comparable across companies as different companies use different fiscal years.

47 Revenue data taken from PlanetRetail.

48 www.supermarketnews.com/walmart/walmart-ceo-cites-growing-importance-private-label, last accessed 19 December 2017.

49 Powers, S *et al* (2017) Global Consumer: Will private label swallow up $48 billion of branded US consumables value? UBS report, 11 July.

50 *Store Brands* (2017) Kroger strategy plays up private brands, 11 October.

51 www.iriworldwide.com/IRI/media/Q3-PL-Trends_Key-Trends.pdf, last accessed 16 December 2017.

52 *Consumer Reports* (2017) Faster, fresher, cheaper, July, pp. 30–43.

53 Kumar, N and Steenkamp, J B (2007) *Private Label Strategy: How to beat the store brand challenge*, Harvard Business School Press, Boston, MA.

54 Results derived from various GfK Kronberg reports.

PART TWO
Competitive counterstrategies for conventional retailers

How are conventional retailers being impacted by discounter entry?

06

What happens to the competitive field when hard discounters enter the market? Will all grocery retailers experience fiercer competition? Or does this depend on the specific positioning of the incumbent grocery retailer? Is Asda, with its EDLP pricing tactic, as vulnerable as Tesco with its HiLo pricing? Are there retail formats that might benefit from hard discounter entry in their area? This chapter will discuss the implications of hard discounter entry on different types of conventional retailers. This sets the stage for counterstrategies, which will be discussed in Chapter 7.

Positioning of conventional retailers

In developed markets consumers can choose from a wide variety of conventional retail formats. We distinguish five types: premium retailers, mainstream retailers, warehouse clubs, brand discounters, and proximity retailers. They each occupy a unique position in the retail market space.

Premium retailers

Premium retailers carry a wide and deep assortment of SKUs and offer all kinds of additional services to consumers, such as in-store restaurants, catering services, sushi bars, and home delivery services. Their staff are well trained and customer friendly, and shoppers love their fresh produce and ready-to-eat assortment. Premium retailers are masters in seducing the customer. They offer a mouthwatering shopping experience. Examples of this type of retailers are Wegmans and Whole Foods in the United States, Waitrose and Marks & Spencer in the UK, and El Corte Inglés in Spain. Price level is, in general, (much) higher than average, but more affluent consumers are particularly willing to pay this premium because of the superior added value provided by these retailers in terms of assortment, quality, service and convenience. Often, these chains prosper in larger cities given the density of high-income households.

Mainstream retailers

Mainstream retailers constitute the backbone of modern grocery retailing and account for the largest share of the grocery market in terms of sales in almost all developed countries. They are perceived as modest to good (there is quite some heterogeneity within this group) on assortment breadth and depth, quality of fresh produce, quality of private-label products, and service. Mainstream retailers almost never lead the market when it comes to implementing retail innovations or the development of new assortment. Instead, they offer a decent price-quality ratio; their stores are nice and relatively spacious, and accessibility is generally good. Many mainstream retailers also offer online shopping services.

A key distinction within this group is pricing and promotions. Some follow an (EDLP) approach. EDLP retailers offer a relatively low price level combined with few promotions. Examples in 2017 are Jumbo in the Netherlands, Asda in the UK, Coles in Australia, and Walmart in the United States. However, most mainstream retailers follow a HiLo strategy. They frequently run promotions, and sales of items on promotion in any given week can easily account for 20–35 per cent of total revenues in that week. To compensate for lower margins on promotional discounts, non-promoted prices are generally a bit above market average. Examples of mainstream retailers that follow a HiLo strategy in 2017 are Kroger and Albertsons in the United States, Rewe and Edeka in Germany, Loblaws in Canada, Leclerc in France, Tesco in the UK, Woolworths in Australia, and Albert Heijn in the Netherlands.[1]

Warehouse clubs

The origin of the warehouse club format dates back to the 1970s. There are few of them, but they are large. In the United States especially, this retail format has exhibited strong sales growth over recent decades. Leading the pack is Costco. In 2017, its revenues were $124 billion (grocery and non-grocery), and it had about 750 stores in North America, Europe, Australia, Japan, and Eastern Asia. Other prominent players are Sam's Club (a subsidiary of Walmart) and BJ's Wholesale Club in the United States, and Makro in Europe, Latin America, and Thailand.

Stores are generally the size of an American football field, and have the look and feel of a regular warehouse, with high ceilings and inventory stacked high in steel racks. They sell items ranging from grocery staples and fresh produce to furniture and diamond rings. However, the total number of SKUs offered is quite small. A typical Costco warehouse store stocks only 4,000 SKUs versus 25,000–45,000 SKUs for an average mainstream retailer. Package sizes are typically large. They are relatively low on convenience because store density is low, in-store shopping takes effort because of their huge size, and checkout lines are long. But because of their low prices, especially per ounce, customers are willing to accept these inconveniences. Warehouse clubs are most attractive for big shopping trips made with low frequency. Customers usually visit these stores once or twice per month and can easily spend $200 or more per store visit.

Customers need a membership card to be able to shop at a warehouse club. A card costs up to $120 per year at Costco in 2018, and offers various benefits, such as cash-back on purchases. Membership fees feed directly into the firm's bottom line, allowing warehouse clubs to sell their goods and services at a low mark-up. In 2016 alone, Costco's 86.7 million members worldwide brought in $2.6 billion in membership fees. When you consider that, in that same year, Costco's operating income was $3.6 billion, you can see that it is crucial for warehouse clubs to entice people to stay or join the club.

Brand discounters

These retailers are known for their low prices. They carry a limited assortment (usually between 3,500 and 10,000 SKUs), but leading national brands are available. They generally lack a strong performance in perishables. Typically less than 10,000 square feet in size, brand discount stores are small compared to the stores of mainstream retailers. Examples are Netto Marken-Discount in Germany, Dollar General in the United States, Iceland in the UK, and Dollar King in Australia.

Proximity retailers

Proximity retailers, also called convenience stores, are small outlets (typically 5,000 square feet or less) that offer a limited variety of grocery products at relatively high prices. In this segment we still have independent mom-and-pop shops with a small assortment of traditional grocery products, as well as modern, convenience-oriented, neighbourhood stores from large retailers such as Tesco Express in the UK, Spar City stores in Europe, and, the biggest of them all, 7-Eleven, with a total of almost 60,000 stores worldwide in 2017. These modern convenience stores carry a small assortment of staple products as well as various ready-to-eat products such as sandwiches, wraps and chilled drinks. The stores are thus very suitable for small fill-in shopping trips. Proximity is their main weapon.

Retail market space map

Figure 6.1 shows the location of these generic retail formats on perceived price (regular price, promotions, low-priced product lines) and perceived

Figure 6.1   Retail market space map before entry of hard discounters

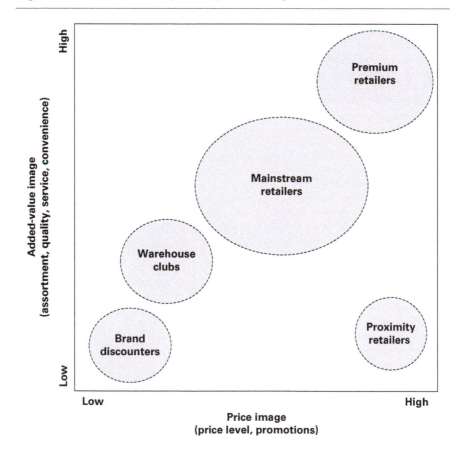

added value (assortment breadth and depth, quality, service, convenience). These two dimensions capture the two factors involved in any economic exchange: what you get (value) versus what you give (price). As one can see, the retail market space is quite well covered by conventional retail formats. Thus, consumers have plenty of choices and they generally visit several retail formats on a weekly or monthly basis. Consumers who are 100 per cent loyal to just one retailer are the exception in grocery retailing. Most consumers patronize three to five grocery banners on a monthly basis. This is also a major reason why so many grocery retailer banners still exist. A household can easily go to a warehouse club every three to four weeks and make a weekly trip to a mainstream or premium retailer. For daily trips or fill-in shopping trips, grocery shoppers may end up at a brand discounter or a proximity retailer.

How hard discounters create their blue ocean

Figure 6.1 shows no obvious gap in the market for a new retail format. Why then can hard discounters be so successful? How can they disrupt the industry? Because they create their own 'blue ocean'. Rather than competing in the existing retail market space, they create their own market space. The theory of blue ocean strategy holds that industry disruptors succeed by creating 'blue oceans' of uncontested market space, as opposed to 'red oceans' where competitors fight for dominance, the analogy being that an ocean full of vicious competition turns red with blood.[2] In red oceans, industry boundaries are defined and accepted, and the competitive rules of the game are known. Figure 6.1 represents the red ocean – the known retail market space. Conventional retailers try to outperform their rivals to grab a greater share of total grocery sales, leading to cutthroat competition that turns the ocean bloody.

Hard discounters do not compete in this red ocean. They create their own market space by breaking the boundaries of the existing retail market space. They do this by extending the price dimension downward to a level thought economically impossible. In this blue ocean, they reign supreme because they can thrive in this space while conventional retailers cannot. Figure 6.2 shows the retail market space map after the entry of hard discounters. The grey area indicates the newly created hard discounter blue ocean.

Figure 6.2 Retail market space map after entry of hard discounters

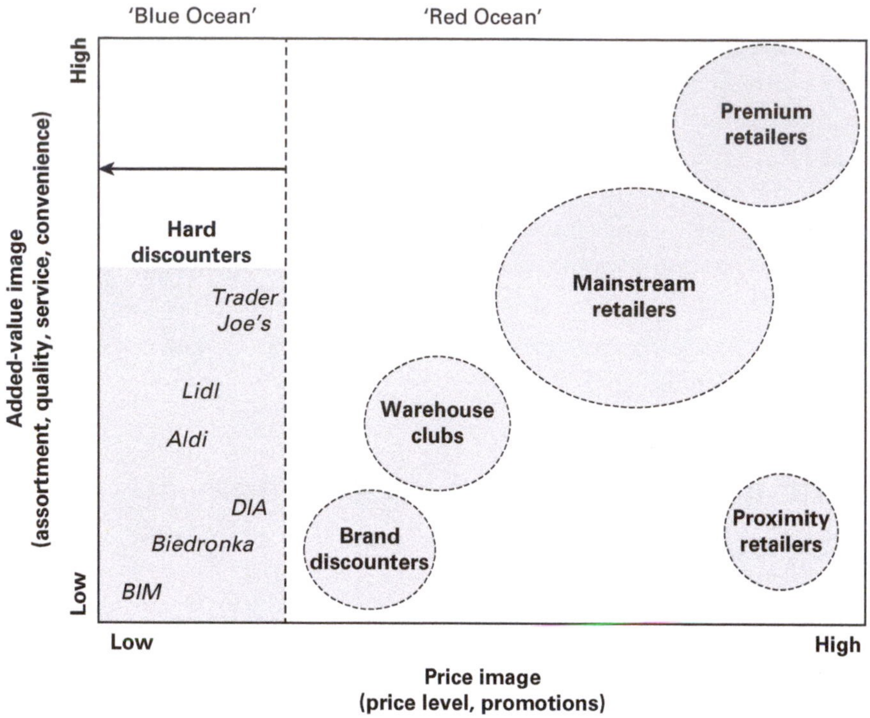

As we have seen in the previous two chapters, hard discounters are seen as the cheapest players in the market. In terms of added-value perception, consumers recognize that assortment variety is limited and additional services are mediocre at best. The shopping experience is utilitarian. But more and more consumers recognize that the quality of the assortment is generally good and that hard discounters offer some unique convenience aspects, most importantly their low choice complexity. Accessibility is getting ever better as their store network continues to expand, something we have seen in markets ranging from Poland to the UK.

Within the hard discounter blue ocean, various players occupy different locations; see Figure 6.2 for locations in 2017. BIM, Biedronka, and DIA are examples of hard discounters that rate relatively low on the added-value dimension, given their small assortment, low service, and quality perception that are lower than those offered by Aldi and Lidl. DIA is also more expensive than Aldi or Lidl, though it does a good job on proximity. Aldi scores somewhat lower than Lidl on the added-value dimension because its assortment is smaller, its stores are generally a little more austere, and its fresh foods assortment is generally perceived to be below

Lidl's. At the top of the discounter space, we find Trader Joe's: the most upscale of all hard discounters.

Impact of hard discounter entry on the shopper's mindset

Change in reference price

Hard discounters change the reference price of grocery items. If one pint of blueberries cost $3.99 at Kroger and $4.99 at Whole Foods and consumers have to pay only $1.49 at Aldi, they start to wonder why Whole Foods and Kroger are so expensive. The pricing strategy of Aldi in this case leads to a lower reference price, eg the price that consumers consider as reasonable or what they expect to pay for a certain product. This results in greater reluctance among consumers to pay a price premium at conventional retailers for products that are also sold by hard discounters. For example, when Lidl introduced the popular energy drink Red Bull at €1.49 per 0.33-litre can in Germany, it set off competition that brought the price down to €0.95 just a short time later.[3] It will be hard for a conventional retailer to charge the regular price (around two euros) again.

Change in importance of store choice attributes

The entry of a hard discounter in a local area changes the importance that consumers attach to price versus value-related store attributes when selecting which retailers to patronize. Table 6.1 illustrates this for Dutch shoppers.[4] We can see that when hard discounters become accessible to shoppers in an area, price-related attributes become more important when choosing where to shop, while value-related attributes such as service level, large assortments, and well-trained store employees become less important. We call this the hard discounter devaluation process.

The hard discounter devaluation process is reinforced by the all-too-common reaction of conventional retailers to start emphasizing price in their marketing strategy and communications with consumers. For example, in response to Aldi's success in Australia, mainstream retailer Coles started a TV campaign, 'Down, down, prices are down', using commonly purchased items to demonstrate price leadership.[5] Such campaigns encourage consumers to look for savings rather than added value, and thus plays to the unique strengths of hard discounters.

Table 6.1   Change in attribute importance for store choice when hard discounters are in catchment area

Store choice attribute	Store choice attribute importance (Scale: 1 (lowest) to 10 (highest))		
	No hard discounter present	**Aldi and Lidl present**	**Direction**
Price-related attributes:			
• Low prices	7.7	8.4	↑
• Attractive promotions	7.9	8.3	↑
• Large selection of low-priced alternatives	7.6	8.1	↑
Added-value attributes:			
• Large assortment	8.1	8.0	↓
• Store interior	7.1	6.7	↓
• Well-trained staff	7.3	7.2	↓

NOTE Data pertain to the Netherlands and span the period 2008–2016.
SOURCE Based on EFMI Shopper Monitor (2017)

Change in satisfaction with conventional retailers on store choice attributes

Hard discounter entry affects consumer satisfaction with conventional retailers on price and added-value attributes. The underlying mechanism is a well-known psychological phenomenon called the contrast effect. The contrast effect holds that if a stimulus is paired with a stimulus of significantly greater or lesser value on the same dimension(s), the difference between the two is enhanced. For example, a neutral grey target will appear lighter than it does in isolation when it is compared to a dark grey target, while it will appear darker when it is compared to a light grey target.

In the retail context, if a conventional retailer (original stimulus) is paired with a hard discounter (new stimulus that enters the perceptual field of the shopper) that scores significantly better on price-related attributes and significantly worse on added-value attributes, the difference between the two is enhanced in the mind of the consumer. As a consequence, the price image of the conventional retailer declines once hard discounters become accessible to the shopper, while its added-value image improves.

Table 6.2 Change in evaluation of Albert Heijn when hard discounters are in catchment area

Store choice attribute	Evaluation of Albert Heijn on store choice attributes (Scale: 1 (least positive) to 10 (most positive))		
	No hard discounter present	Aldi and Lidl present	Direction
Price-related attributes:			
• Low prices	6.6	6.2	↓
• Attractive promotions	7.4	7.4	0
• Large selection of low-priced alternatives	7.0	6.9	↓
Added-value attributes:			
• Large assortment	7.8	8.2	↑
• Store interior	7.7	8.0	↑
• Well-trained staff	7.1	7.4	↑

NOTE Data pertain to the Netherlands and span the period 2008–2016.
SOURCE Based on EFMI Shopper Monitor (2017)

Table 6.2 shows the contrast effect for Albert Heijn, the leading Dutch (upscale) mainstream retailer that follows a HiLo strategy with a relatively strong emphasis on added value as opposed to price. When both Aldi and Lidl become accessible to consumers in an area, price-related scores decline and scores on added-value attributes increase.

Table 6.3 shows the results for Nettorama, a mainstream retailer that positions itself strongly on price in that it claims to be the Netherlands' lowest-priced supermarket chain. We see the same phenomenon occurring: when hard discounters enter a shopping area, Nettorama's score on price attributes declines, albeit that added-value scores show little consistent movement.

When we compare the magnitude of change on these attributes between Albert Heijn and Nettorama, we find that a downscale price-oriented mainstream retailer is affected more negatively than an upscale

Table 6.3   Change in evaluation of Nettorama when hard discounters are in catchment area

Store choice attribute	Evaluation of Nettorama on store choice attributes (Scale: 1 (least positive) to 10 (most positive))		
	No hard discounter present	**Aldi and Lidl present**	**Direction**
Price-related attributes:			
• Low prices	8.2	7.6	↓
• Attractive promotions	7.8	7.5	↓
• Large selection of low-priced alternatives	8.2	7.7	↓
Added-value attributes:			
• Large assortment	7.0	7.2	↑
• Store interior	6.9	6.7	↓
• Well-trained staff	6.9	6.9	0

NOTE Data pertain to the Netherlands and span the period 2008–2016.
SOURCE Based on EFMI Shopper Monitor (2017)

added-value-oriented mainstream retailer (Table 6.4). The price-oriented player is hurt substantially more on price attributes, and benefits less on the added-value attributes.

The hard discounter devaluation process, combined with the contrast effect, creates a double jeopardy for conventional retailers. After hard discounters enter the area, the average shopper becomes more price sensitive and conventional retailers are evaluated less positively on price attributes. On the positive side, conventional retailers are perceived more positively on added-value attributes. Consumers become more appreciative of the larger assortment and better service level offered by conventional retailers. Unfortunately for conventional retailers, though, the average consumer attaches less importance to these attributes. However, as the results for Nettorama and Albert Heijn show, these effects play out differently for different types of retailers, to which we now turn.

Table 6.4   Comparison of change in evaluation of Albert Heijn and Nettorama when hard discounters are in catchment area

| | Change in evaluation when both Aldi and Lidl are in catchment area | |
Store choice attribute	Albert Heijn	Nettorama
Price-related attributes:		
• Low prices	−0.4	−0.6
• Attractive promotions	0	−0.3
• Large selection of low-priced alternatives	−0.1	−0.5
Added-value attributes:		
• Large assortment	+0.4	+0.2
• Store interior	+0.3	+0.2
• Well-trained staff	+0.3	0

NOTE Data pertain to the Netherlands and span the period 2008–2016.
SOURCE Based on EFMI Shopper Monitor (2017)

Impact of hard discounter entry on various retail formats

What we learn from what happened in the UK

To get an idea of which retailers are most vulnerable to the emergence of hard discounters, we turn to the UK. Table 6.5 shows the market share of seven leading conventional retailers, as well as Aldi and Lidl, for 2012 and 2017 – the period of hard discounter breakout. What does the UK experience show?

- Waitrose, the leading premium retailer in the UK that excels in almost every aspect of added value (assortment, quality, service, store ambience), experienced 15.6 per cent *growth* in market share. In a survey among UK consumers in 2017, Waitrose was among the top five UK brands in terms of customer service, receiving maximum ratings for 'making you feel valued', 'helpfulness of the staff', and 'resolving complaints'.[6]

- 'Premium-lite' retailer Sainsbury's was negatively affected but, compared to mainstream retailers, the decline was modest.

Table 6.5 Impact of hard discounter success of Aldi and Lidl on market share of conventional retailers in the UK in 2012–2017

Retailer	Dominant type[1]	Market share (%)		Change in market share 2012–2017	
		2012	2017	Absolute change (%)	Relative change (%)
Waitrose	Premium retailer	4.5	5.2	+0.7	+15.6
Sainsbury's	Premium-lite retailer	16.6	16.1	−0.5	−3.0
Tesco	HiLo mainstream retailer	30.7	27.5	−3.2	−10.4
Asda	EDLP mainstream retailer	17.6	15.6	−2.0	−11.4
Morrisons	HiLo mainstream retailer	11.9	10.4	−1.5	−12.6
Co-op	Proximity retailer	6.5	6.1	−0.4	−6.1
Iceland	Brand discounter	2.0	2.2	+0.2	+10.0
Aldi	Hard discounter	2.8	7.0	+4.2	+150.0
Lidl	Hard discounter	2.8	5.1	+2.3	+82.1

NOTE 1) For example, several retailers also have proximity stores.
SOURCE Based on 2017 data from Kantar Worldpanel

- Mainstream retailers were hurt the most. Tesco, Asda, and Morrisons each lost more than 10 per cent of their market share.

- There was no appreciable difference in market share loss between HiLo and EDLP mainstream retailers. In terms of relative market share decline, Asda was right between Morrisons and Tesco. However, the two mainstream chains that focused relatively more on price (Morrisons, Asda) lost more than Tesco.

- Proximity retailers were less affected by the hard discounters than mainstream retailers. While Co-op lost market share, this occurred in the early years when it was still primarily a mainstream retailer. In 2013, it initiated a shift towards becoming a proximity retailer, focusing on the convenience channel. Since its new strategy gathered steam in 2014, its market share has largely held steady.

- Brand discounter Iceland was not negatively affected by hard discounters. In fact, its market share increased somewhat (albeit from a small base).

Why might premium retailers actually benefit from the spread of hard discounter stores? Because these two formats may complement each other.[7] Before hard discounter entry, the mainstream retailer was a compromise between price and added value. Now, the consumer can go to the hard discounter to stock up on staples, and to the premium retailer to spend the money thus saved on unique offerings and speciality products. We ourselves exhibit this behaviour; we buy staples at Aldi, Lidl, and Trader Joe's, and then go on to purchase finer wares at Whole Foods or Albert Heijn. We are not alone. A store manager at Albert Heijn who was confronted with the replacement of a competing mainstream retail store by a Lidl store told us, 'I expected a sales loss of 10–15 per cent, but instead our revenues increased by about 15 per cent! The shopping area has become more attractive and many customers visit the Lidl stores as well as my store on the same shopping trip. In my case it is actually a win–win situation.'

Impact per retail format

The UK experience is instructive but, of course, performance of any individual retailer is affected by specific circumstances. For example, Morrisons' succession of strategic U-turns in 2012–2017 hurt its performance.[8] Iceland's focus on frozen products and being ranked among 'The Best Big Companies to Work For' are not necessarily descriptive of other brand discounters.[9] We conclude this chapter by taking together all insights to outline the expected impact of hard discounter entry in the catchment area on each type of conventional retailer (Table 6.6). Of course, there is variation around this general expectation, but this should give you a benchmark.

We see potential for symbiosis with premium retailers and expected limited impact on brand discounters and proximity retailers. Warehouse clubs can expect some negative fallout, but the ones who will bear the brunt of hard discounter success are mainstream retailers. This is hardly comforting given the dominance of this retail format in grocery retailing.

Table 6.6   Impact of hard discounter entry on conventional retailers

Retail format	Effect on shoppers' mindset	Effect on shopper behaviour	Expected effect on revenues
Premium retailers	Limited impact.	Positive impact.	0/+
	Consumers become more price-oriented. However, premium retailers are somewhat protected from price pressure because they excel on added value, which is the prime reason people shop there. Moreover, satisfaction with their unique assortment will increase.	If a hard discounter opens new stores, incumbent premium retailers will lose some sales, especially on comparable items. However, money saved on hard-discount purchases is likely to be spent on superior offerings of premium retailers. Availability of a hard discounter nearby might improve overall foot traffic to the area.	
Mainstream retailers	Strong negative impact.	Strong negative impact.	–
	The same reasoning as for premium retailers, but the impact will be stronger as mainstream retailers are stuck in the middle on price and added value, often not excelling on either aspect. EDLP and price-oriented HiLo players are most at risk. The lowered reference price causes margin erosion.	Many of their price-sensitive customers will switch to the hard discounter. EDLP retailers are most at risk because of easy comparison on price. Deep promotions at HiLo retailers can undercut prices at hard discounters, attracting customers who then load up on other products.	

(*continued*)

Table 6.6 (Continued)

Retail format	Effect on shoppers' mindset	Effect on shopper behaviour	Expected effect on revenues
Warehouse clubs	Slightly negative impact. Increased price orientation and reduced added-value orientation is positive for warehouse clubs. However, they are attacked on their strongest point and experience of price-oriented mainstream retailers suggests that a contrast effect can weaken their price image.	Negative impact. Warehouse clubs attract big-basket shopper groups. Hard discounters are very appealing to these shoppers and are often in closer proximity than the warehouse club. Some households might discontinue their costly membership.	–
Brand discounters	Slightly positive impact. Consumers become more price-oriented. This increases the attractiveness of brand discounters among consumers who prefer national brands.	Slightly negative impact. Brand discounters are attacked on their main positioning element: low prices. They may lose part of their sales as price-oriented shoppers now go to the hard discounter. However, the availability of a hard discounter nearby may also improve overall area attraction and lead to extra shoppers.	0/-
Proximity retailers	Limited impact. Consumers become more price-oriented. But as proximity retailers are already very expensive the overall impact will be low.	Limited impact. Shoppers go to proximity retailers for fill-in trips and urgent needs. Unless there is a hard discounter store nearby, impact will be minor.	0

Managerial takeaways

- Hard discounters do not compete within the existing boundaries of price and added value ('red ocean') defined by conventional retailers. Rather, they create their own 'blue ocean' by extending the price dimension downward while still delivering on added value.

- The entry of hard discounters has profound effects on the mindset of shoppers:

  - It pushes down the reference price.

  - It triggers the hard discounter devaluation process where price attributes become more important and added-value attributes less important in shoppers' store choice.

  - Shoppers evaluate existing retailers as more expensive than before. This, together with the increased importance of price in store choice, is the 'double jeopardy price effect'.

  - Shoppers become more satisfied with the performance of conventional retailers on added-value attributes.

- The impact of the emergence of hard discounters on the sales of conventional retailers varies by store format. Premium retailers might actually benefit from this development as there is potential for symbiosis between the two formats. Consumers purchase staples at the hard discounter and exotic, speciality, culinary, ready-to-eat, and other high-margin products at the premium retailer. Brand discounters and proximity retailers are likely to experience limited impact. Warehouse clubs are negatively affected since they charge a membership fee and their key strength is price; this plays directly into the hands of hard discounters.

- Mainstream retailers will be most negatively affected by hard discounter entry. They are stuck in the middle on price and added value. Within this large category, EDLP and price-oriented HiLo mainstream retailers are most vulnerable.

Notes

1 We note that both Coles and Woolworths follow something akin to a hybrid strategy. We classify them according to the dominant element in their pricing strategy.

2 Kim, W C and Mauborgne, R A (2014) *Blue Ocean Strategy: How to create uncontested market space and make the competition irrelevant*, Harvard Business Review Press, Cambridge, MA, 2nd edn.

3 Kimball S, Roth, T, and Underhill, W (2017) The unstoppable rise of Aldi and Lidl, *Handelsblatt Global*, Fall.

4 www.efmi.nl/. Results are based on EFMI Shopper Monitor, database 2008–2016, n = 20,245.

5 For an example, see www.youtube.com/watch?v=rPkD6rIH2MM, last accessed 5 January 2018.

6 *Which?* (2017) The heroes and villains of customer service, September, pp. 34–35.

7 Vroegrijk, M, Gijsbrechts, E and Campo, K (2013) Close encounter with the hard discounter: a multiple-store shopping perspective on the impact of local hard-discounter entry, *Journal of Marketing Research*, 50 (October), pp. 606–26.

8 Fedor, L (2016), Morrisons rapidly consolidates position amid big four UK grocers, *Financial Times*, 28 November, p. 11.

9 www.retailgazette.co.uk/blog/2014/03/34103-iceland-voted-best-big-company-to-work-for/; www.employeebenefits.co.uk/issues/february-online-2016/american-express-ey-and-nationwide-are-among-the-25-best-big-companies-to-work-for-2016/, last accessed 5 January 2018.

How conventional retailers can compete with hard discounters

07

To make money in an industry that is known for its razor-thin margins, you need to do many things right. Strategy, tactics and operations should be perfectly aligned. And even then, hard discounters might have a strong impact on your business. Reacting to the rise of hard discounters by lowering prices might seem a logical thing to do. But does it really make sense if your operation is by no means as efficient as that of hard discounters? Can you handle a 5 per cent price roll-back if your operating margin is currently just 3 per cent? These are questions conventional retailers need to consider when deciding how to compete with hard discounters. Competitive reactions, especially lowering prices, should fit into a long-term game plan. In this chapter, we will discuss strategies that conventional grocery retailers can adopt to compete with hard discounters.

Initial reactions towards hard discounters

When conventional grocery retailers are confronted with the entry and rise of hard discounters, they often go through several phases. The first phase is neglect. Conventional retailers are not particularly worried about hard discounter entrance. An example is the Finnish grocery retail market in 2002. At that time, two large chains, K-group and S-group, controlled 70 per cent of the market. Industry experts did not consider it likely that a hard discounter would enter this sparsely populated country. In the unlikely event that a hard discounter would enter Finland, it was expected to open stores only in the densely populated cities. Imagine the surprise when Lidl, upon entering the Finnish market in August 2002, built a network of stores covering the whole country. Initially, the Finnish competitors publicly stated that Lidl was not seen as a serious threat,[1] and that neglect did nothing to stop Lidl's success. The initial 10 stores in 2002 grew to a network of 160 stores by 2017, and Lidl's market share increased from less than 1 per cent in 2003 to 9 per cent in 2017. Lidl's revenues exceeded $1.6 billion in 2017 and its operating margin stood at 4.6 per cent.

The second phase conventional grocery retailers usually go through is the 'derogation' stage. This stage occurs when hard discounters' market share is increasing and more and more consumers start to embrace the hard-discount concept. In the derogation phase, conventional grocery retailers publicly downplay the hard discounters. Former marketing manager Matthijs Moeken of Dutch mainstream retailer Jumbo responded to a question during a retail conference in 2013 about the growth of hard discounters as follows: 'Consumers nowadays go more often to hard discounters due to the recession, but to be honest the stores of Aldi and Lidl are just rubbish.'[2] However, in that year, Lidl was voted 'best vegetable and fruit' supermarket in the Netherlands, a prize it has won repeatedly since.[3] The newly refurbished Lidl store in Tilburg won a prize for the Netherlands' most beautiful new supermarket.[4] Awards translated into success. In 2017, Lidl's revenues in the Netherlands exceeded $4 billion, for a market share of 10.3 per cent.

When it dawns upon conventional retailers that hard discounters are taking a significant portion of the market, they enter the third 'panic' phase. Conventional retailers try to win back customers by cutting prices and increasing promotion pressure almost indiscriminately. Gross margins go down, shareholders start to complain, and it becomes clear that a more reasoned response is called for if the retailer is to survive. This sets the stage for the fourth phase, which we call 'coordinated response'. Conventional retailers acknowledge that hard discounters are there to stay and they must develop a balanced strategy that plays to their strengths if they are to thrive in this new retail world. This chapter will be devoted to coordinated response strategies. Conventional retailers are better off skipping the first three stages and moving directly to a coordinated response strategy.

Four strategic reactions to hard discounter encroachment

In our research and consulting, we have observed four dominant strategic reactions in response to hard discounter success, two of which can be classified as defensive and two as offensive (Figure 7.1). *Defensive strategies* focus mainly on preventing the existing customer base from shopping more often at hard-discount stores by improving the retailer's price image. We distinguish between 'fight-back strategy' and 'downgrading strategy'. Retailers that follow a defensive approach are pragmatic and exhibit a 'go with the flow' attitude: 'If consumers want low prices, give them to them.' Of course, this might further increase the price sensitivity of grocery shoppers.

Offensive strategies are about moving away from hard discounters by offering more added value, where we distinguish between 'value-improvement strategy' and 'value-redefinition strategy'. The basic idea behind these offensive strategies is to avoid going head to head with hard discounters on their main strength: low prices. Retailers who follow an offensive approach say, 'Why should I get on the ice rink oval with Eric Heiden (the best speed skater of all time) if I am a figure skater?'[5] Rather they prefer to let Heiden beat

Figure 7.1   Strategic response options for conventional retailers towards hard discounter entry

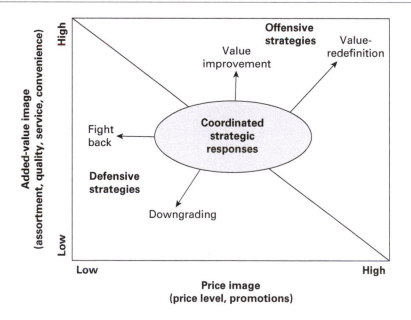

other speed skaters while they compete on the figure skating rink. Retailers following this approach work hard to improve their standing by adding more value to their retail proposition. Offensive strategies educate grocery shoppers to look for assortment, service, quality and convenience instead of affordability. In doing so, conventional retailers try to compete with hard discounters on store attributes that are more aligned with their DNA.

Fight-back strategy

The most common defensive reaction we have observed among conventional grocery retailers is the *fight-back strategy*: they go head to head with hard discounters by reducing the price of their shopping basket. This is the dominant approach in the panic phase, but it also plays a key role in the coordinated response phase. Cutting the price of shoppers' grocery carts can be achieved by lowering the prices of the existing assortment or by introducing a range of low-priced options.

Reducing prices on existing assortment

The most straightforward way for conventional retailers to compete with hard discounters is to reduce the prices of their assortment. This can be achieved by either reducing the regular price – something that is common among EDLP retailers – or by running more promotions – a route more common among HiLo retailers. In 2017, Walmart launched a full-on challenge to Aldi, slashing prices at 1,200 stores in 11 states in the Midwest and Southeast, regions where Aldi was strong. This followed surveys suggesting that prices at Aldi were around 20 per cent below those at its market-leading rival. Analysts estimated Walmart spent around $6 billion to regain its title as the low-price leader.[6]

In November 2017, we conducted a store check for 42 national brand SKUs that were sold by Aldi, Walmart and Kroger in Durham, NC. For 16 SKUs, the price was exactly the same at Aldi and Walmart. This would be extremely unlikely if they had set prices independently. The total costs of this basket of 42 national brand SKUs at Walmart was 1.6 per cent lower than at Aldi. At Kroger – a HiLo retailer – the regular price was often more expensive, but nearly half of the brand SKUs also sold at Aldi were in promotion. This indicates that Kroger responds to the presence of Aldi. As a result, the basket of national brands at Kroger was only 3.8 per cent more expensive than at Aldi.

In Australia in early 2015, a basket of Aldi private-label products was 19 per cent cheaper than Coles' standard private label and 28 per cent below Woolworths'. In the branded goods segment, Aldi was 6 per cent cheaper than Coles and 14 per cent cheaper than Woolworths.[7] In response, Woolworths and Coles cut prices significantly and, in 2017, the price difference on the private-label basket had shrunk to 10 per cent for both chains, according to consumer magazine *Choice*.

There is burgeoning evidence that US retailers have learned from what happened in the UK and Australia, and are aggressively responding to Lidl's entry into their local area. One study conducted at the end of 2017 found that the price of a basket of private-label products was, on average, 9 per cent cheaper in areas where Lidl had opened a store in the preceding six months compared to similar areas where Lidl had not opened a store (yet). The strongest reactions were observed for Food Lion, Kroger and, interestingly, Aldi (Figure 7.2). Whether the price cuts by players like Food Lion or Kroger are truly a coordinated strategy or a panic reaction is an open question. In Aldi's case, we can be confident it is part of a well-thought-out coordinated response. Aldi is more aware than any other retailer about the threat posed by Lidl, and it competes with Lidl on an international scale for dominance in hard discounting.

The main advantages of using price reductions as fight-back strategy are that they can be implemented quickly and that consumers respond strongly to price reductions; that is, grocery demand is price-elastic. However, they can be easily copied by competitors. Target, for example, also started a price roll-back campaign on thousands of grocery items in response to Walmart's

Figure 7.2 Price reduction in response to entry of Lidl in Virginia and the Carolinas in 2017

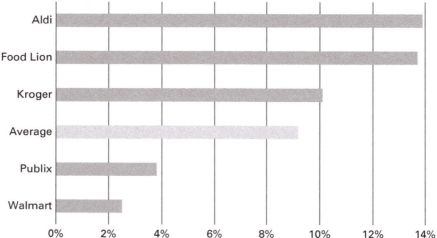

SOURCE Based on Gielens, K (2018) The competitive price effects of Lidl's entry in the US grocery market, UNC working paper, January 2018

price roll-back in 2017.[8] If everybody starts lowering prices, it quickly becomes a game of perseverance: who can endure the most pain? Ultimately, the financially weakest players will be pushed out. An alternative strategy is to keep the price architecture of your national brands and standard private label intact, and then introduce a line of economy private label.

Introduction of economy private-label range

To improve their price image, many conventional retailers have introduced an assortment of products under an economy private label. For example, Tesco carries the economy label Tesco Everyday Value, Delhaize has 365, Albert Heijn AH Basic, Woolworths carries Essentials, and Kroger p$$t. In 2009, France's Carrefour introduced Carrefour Discount, a low-cost line of 400 items. Carrefour's executive director Gilles Petit was quite clear about the reason for this move: 'Carrefour's problem remains our bad pricing image. However, Carrefour Discount should help to improve this.'[9]

Table 7.1 shows that economy private-label lines are indeed able to undercut hard discounters on price. Introducing an economy line gives shoppers a very low-priced option in categories where they buy on price, yet can still opt for more expensive options (standard or premium private label, or

Table 7.1   Price of Lidl private label versus economy private label of conventional grocery retailers in 2016

Conventional retailer	Country	Price index (National brand = 100)	
		Private label Lidl	Economy private label
Albert Heijn	The Netherlands	54	45
Tesco	United Kingdom	38	15
Delhaize	Belgium	45	35
Carrefour	France	51	49
Edeka	Germany	40	40
Carrefour	Spain	56	48
Tesco	Poland	56	41
SPAR	Austria	40	41
COOP	Switzerland	37	31
Average		*46*	*38*

SOURCE Based on 2016 data from IPLC

a national brand) in categories where quality or brand image are driving choices. That is why economy options are much more common in staples like dry pasta or canned vegetables than in shampoo or baby food. If the conventional retailer does not carry an economy line, they risk losing not only the sales in 'unimportant' categories but an entire shopping basket, as consumers will likely purchase much more at the hard discounter than only these economy SKUs.

However, economy lines are no free lunch. Conventional retailers' business models and economy private-label volumes do not allow them to offer the same quality as hard discounters. In order to offer them at a low price, they have to compromise on quality. Table 7.2 shows some interesting examples. Operating profit per unit sold is also considerably lower than is earned by the conventional retailer on its standard private-label range, a combination of lower price and lower gross margin. Research based on category sales data of Asda and Sainsbury in the UK shows that economy lines cannibalize on the sales of the conventional retailer's more profitable standard private label.[10] But at least the conventional retailer can advertise the same low prices as hard discounters.

Table 7.2 Quality comparison between national brands, Lidl's private label, and economy private label in 2016

Product	National Brand	Lidl	Economy private label
Fruit Muesli	45% fruit	50% fruit	7–10% fruit
Pasta Penne	Durum wheat semolina	Durum wheat semolina	Soft wheat flour
Tomato ketchup	148g tomatoes/100g	185g tomatoes/100g	81g tomatoes/100g
Cornflakes	Traditional flakes	Traditional flakes	Extruded flakes
Fruit biscuits	Sultanas/raisins: 31%/6%	Sultanas/raisins: 31%/6%	Sultanas/raisins: 20%/7%
Hazelnut spread	13% hazelnut	13% hazelnut	1.5–2% hazelnut
Chips	Long fries, few defects	Long fries, few defects	Short fries, more defects
Cat litter	Bentonite clay	White bentonite clay	Attapulgite

SOURCE Based on 2016 data from IPLC

Introduction of phantom brands

Economy private labels look and feel cheap. This is very different from the fancy brands carried by Aldi and Lidl, which in many respects look and feel more like national brands than private labels, let alone the economy version. Moreover, older consumers in particular still harbour some reservations about buying products that are clearly identifiable as private labels. With this in mind, Australia's mainstream retailer Woolworths initiated a new strategy in 2016. While it retained its economy private label, Housebrand, which it relaunched as Essential, it replaced its standard private label Select with so-called phantom brands that are category specific. Examples include Balnea (soap, body wash, etc), First Choice (insecticides), Strike (household cleaners), Voeu (skin care), Herbal Sensations (shampoo), Smitten (pet food), Little Ones (diapers), and Chevron (batteries). Any reference to Woolworths was dropped except in the small print on the back of a product.

The phantom brand is positioned as another leading brand, not a discount line. There are no line references between products. Each brand is totally stand-alone. Pricing is broadly on a par with Aldi and typically below the Select SKU it replaced. For example, a 700g pack of Woolworths' (new phantom brand) Hillview shredded tasty cheese cost AU $5 compared to AU $6.29 for a smaller 500g pack of Woolworths' Select cheese.[11]

Tesco tried something similar in 2008, with three important differences. First, Tesco added the phantom brands to its private-label architecture rather than replacing its standard private label, simply called Tesco. Second, there were clear line references between products because all phantom-branded products shared the tag 'Discount Brands', which was prominent on the packaging. Third, the phantom brands were not presented as brands but as a discount line. These factors contributed to Tesco discontinuing its phantom brands a few years later because they largely cannibalized the higher-priced Tesco standard, whose packaging looked staid compared to the phantom brands. Woolworths did not make these mistakes. This may not be surprising, as Woolworths' Managing Director, Claire Peters, worked previously at Tesco.

CASE STUDY   Albert Heijn initiates a price war
                 in the Netherlands

An interesting case of a fight-back strategy is the price war initiated in 2003 by mainstream retailer Albert Heijn in the Netherlands. In the preceding years, it had lost market share to Aldi and Lidl, as well as to mainstream price fighters

Dirk van den Broek, Hoogvliet, and Nettorama. In its 2003 annual report, Ahold identified the causes: 'This decline was primarily due to lower consumer spending and a negative market sentiment towards Albert Heijn mainly due to its perceived high price level.' To stem the loss in market share, Albert Heijn initiated massive price cuts in October 2003.

The ensuing price war was ruthless. Most competitors followed and, within one year, the overall grocery price level was down by almost 5 per cent. Retailers put heavy pressure on suppliers (including delisting) to reduce their prices to offset declining gross margins. Yet it paid off, at least for Albert Heijn. While its revenues were down by almost 3 per cent on a like-for-like basis in 2003, in 2004 revenues grew by 2.2 per cent, and in 2008 annual like-for-like revenue growth was 6.3 per cent (see Table 7.3). In this period, Albert Heijn outperformed the market by 3–5 percentage points annually on a like-for-like basis. Its market share increased from 25 per cent to 31 per cent, while its operating income almost tripled from €225 million to €647 million.

Table 7.3   Market performance Albert Heijn in the price war, 2003–2008

Year	Price distance on national brands with price fighters (%)	Overall market growth (%)	Like-for-like growth Albert Heijn (%)	Performance Albert Heijn compared to overall market (%)	Operating income Albert Heijn (€ mn)
2003	+15	+4.6	−2.7	−7.3	225
2004	+14	−0.6	+2.2	+2.8	288
2005	+8	−1.1	+4.2	+5.3	317
2006	+10	+3.9	+6.7	+2.8	411
2007	+9	+3.7	+7.9	+4.2	573
2008	+7	+2.8	+6.3	+3.5	647

SOURCE   Ahold annual reports and price measurements from Consumentenbond

The price war stopped the fast growth of hard discounters – at least temporarily. The combined market share of Aldi and Lidl had increased from 9 per cent to 13 per cent between 2000 and 2003, but in 2008, it was still 13 per cent. However, while Albert Heijn did well in the price war, conventional Dutch retailers without deep pockets were less fortunate. One example, Laurus, had to sell off two of its main retail banners – Edah and Konmar – in 2006 in a restructuring process to avoid bankruptcy. The move was triggered by demands from the company's lenders. Laurus said its banks had agreed to extend a waiver regarding certain loan covenants, but had demanded that it cut its net debt to €200 million by the end of 2007, from €370 million at the end of 2005.[12] This attempt to become financially healthy again only worked temporarily. In 2009, Laurus sold its remaining chain Super de Boer to competitor Jumbo.[13]

Downgrading strategy

A second defensive strategy is the *downgrading strategy*. In this strategy, the conventional grocery retailer follows a coordinated strategy of lowering its overall price level while at the same time drastically cutting operating costs, for example by reducing assortment breadth, staff levels, service counters, online services, etc. Compared to the fight-back strategy, this strategy is economically more robust as gross margin losses move in tandem with reductions in operating costs. Mainstream retailer Vomar in the Netherlands provides an example of the downgrading strategy. Consumers perceived this chain as 'middle of the road' in the Dutch competitive field. About 80 per cent of its 64 stores competed with Aldi and/or Lidl. Revenue growth was under pressure for many years before new management decided to radically transform Vomar's retail format in 2016. Vomar reduced the assortment from 12,000 SKUs to 8,000 SKUs, replaced service departments for fresh produce with self-service departments, and lowered its private-label price range to match those of hard discounters. This strategy resulted in a gross margin loss of 2.5 percentage points. Operating costs were cut significantly, but to fully compensate for lost margins, revenues would have to increase by 15 per cent. It seems Vomar made a good start. In 2017, it outperformed the average market growth by 4 per cent on a like-for-like basis.[14]

Conventional retailers can also apply the downgrading strategy at company level (as opposed to banner level) by either acquiring or starting a price-oriented banner. Penny is an example of the former strategy. Founded in 1973 as an independent German hard discounter, it was acquired by the Rewe Group in 1992 for €3.2 billion. France's Ed (pronounced E-D, for 'Europa Discount') is an example of the latter strategy. It was founded by Carrefour as a hard-discount banner in 1978. The British newspaper the *Guardian* reported in February 2018 that Tesco was working on a secret plan to develop a new discount grocery chain to take on Aldi and Lidl. The new chain would offer a far more limited range of products than the average Tesco store, around 3,000 compared with the 25,000 different items often available in a Tesco Extra.[15]

Although this idea is interesting, it has proven difficult for companies to operate a world-class hard discounter if they do not have the DNA of a dedicated hard discounter. Revenues per square foot are typically much lower than those achieved by Aldi or Lidl, something we discussed in Chapter 4 (see Table 4.2). It might easily lead to a concept that, at best, is a surrogate of 'the real hard-discount thing'. In some ways it is comparable to a national brand manufacturer that also wants to become a top player in the private-label domain, an issue we will discuss in Chapter 10. Indeed, in 2011 Carrefour sold its Ed banner, consisting of over 900 stores and with revenues of over $2 billion, to Spain's DIA. In an unexpected turn of events, though, Carrefour bought back the French stores in 2014, only to close many stores afterwards.

Value-improvement strategy

The value-improvement strategy is an offensive strategy in which the retailer tries to counter the appeal of hard discounters by offering more value to its shoppers. Some ways they can do this are by adding extra services, improving the assortment of goods, providing more convenience, or by delivering better quality. Retailers that follow this strategy are generally not innovators, but rather early adopters of innovations and concept improvements pioneered by premium retailers such as Wegmans, Whole Foods, and Hieber. The best of them are fast followers. They scan markets for trends, study initiatives of competing retailers, and improve their own concept by adopting good ideas that have proven to be successful, for example, adding lines of organic and local products that have already been successfully introduced by other retailers. Or working together with a third party that has special competencies, such as the cooperation between Morrisons and pure online player Ocado, who joined forces in the UK in 2013.

Developing a new convenience format may also be part of a value-improvement strategy. With growing urbanization and increased time pressure, proximity has become an increasingly important factor in the consumer decision-making process. In response, conventional retailers have introduced small, convenience retail formats in medium and large cities. Examples are Sainsbury Local, Tesco Express, and Albert Heijn to Go. Kroger had convenience stores under the banner names Kwikshop, Tom Thumb, Loaf N' Jug, and Quickstop, but sold these in 2018 to the UK-based EG Group. These stores might also be used for click-and-collect or home delivery for the fast-growing online shopping channel.

Value-redefinition strategy

The value-redefinition strategy is a more aggressive offensive strategy. Here, the retailer tries to lead the field by redefining what is great value. It does this by expanding the market space map outward in terms of price and value. This creates another 'blue ocean' (see Figure 7.3). Rather than focusing on low price, the retailer is dedicated to improving assortment completeness and quality, while at the same time improving customer service by offering various ancillary services, such as home catering services, personal shopping assistants, in-store restaurants, sushi bars, etc. Such retailers understand the art of seducing the customer.

Figure 7.3   Market space map after creation of new premium segment

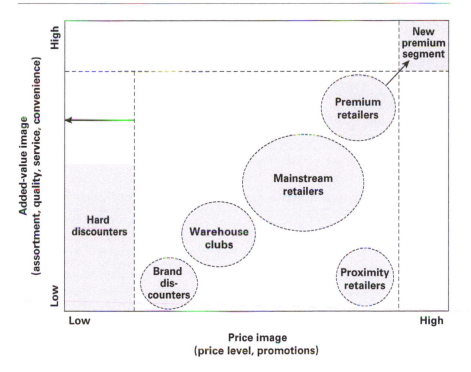

Wegmans in the United States is one of the best examples of retailers following a value-redefinition strategy. Again and again its stores surprise customers with excellent service and overwhelming choice. Their fresh departments are mouth-watering and their employees are well trained and customer friendly. It has a cult-like following who are very loyal to the store. *BuzzFeed* staff writer Rachel Sanders wrote in 2013, 'Shopping at Wegmans is essentially a journey through a small, beautifully maintained, self-sustaining city. Not an exaggeration to say that this grocery chain is the single most compelling reason to live somewhere in the Mid-Atlantic US.'[16]

Wegmans invests heavily in scholarships for its employees and sends its staff around the world to learn everything there is to know about food. In 2017, *Fortune* magazine ranked Wegmans the second-best company to work for in the United States. In 2018, Wegmans pioneered a new store concept in Natick, MA: a two-level store with direct access to the Natick shopping mall. The 134,000-square-foot store is located in a building that formerly housed one of the mall's anchors, J.C. Penney. It devoted 12,500 square feet on the second floor to two restaurant concepts.[17] Wegmans is privately held and expands much more slowly than shoppers around the country have demanded. We eagerly anticipate its scheduled arrival in Chapel Hill in 2020, one of the first Wegmans stores in North Carolina.

Another example of a retailer that follows a value-redefinition strategy is Hieber's Frische Center. Started by Jörg Hieber in 1966, Hieber operated 12 large stores in southern Germany in 2017.[18] Hieber supermarkets carry about 45,000 items, of which over 50 per cent are locally or regionally sourced. They are famous for their wine assortment, which consists of over 3,000 items. Each store has its own style. Some stores display various kinds of art. For example, one store features a drinking man made out of thousands of beer caps. Hieber stores are also famous for their fresh departments and for the quality of their employees, amongst them former top chefs. Also noticeable is that Hieber has a house brewery in its Lörrach store, brewing the brand Markt Bier, which is exclusively sold in Hieber stores. In 2013, its supermarket in Bad Krozingen won an award for the 'Most Beautiful Supermarket in the World'.

Some grocery chains are adding value by recognizing that traditional gathering spots, such as shopping malls, continue to shrink from their peaks of decades ago. They are redefining themselves as social hubs – places where parents bring their children to play, retirees gather for Bingo, and singles find romance. In Chapel Hill, Whole Foods added an entire bar and dining area. Market of Choice, an Oregon chain of 11 supermarkets, has reduced space for centre-store aisles by 22 per cent in recent years and devoted more room to couches, fireplaces with seating areas, and restaurant-like services. Lowes Foods, a Carolina-based, regional supermarket chain, redesigned its stores into a 'village concept' of shops around the perimeter with giant birthday-candle lights. At the heart of each store is a large rectangular communal table that can seat 10 to 15 people. By offering space for people to hang out and play, grocery stores are making a calculation that customers will stay loyal, shop longer, come back more often, and purchase more high-margin items like in-house prepared foods, coffee, a glass of wine, or a pint of craft beer.[19]

Examples of value-redefinition strategies are not limited to developed markets. Alibaba's 'New Retail Strategy' is among the most innovative ideas we have seen in years.[20] In 2017, Alibaba opened its first Hema stores in Beijing and Shanghai, offering consumers a stellar experience in fresh foods, an almost artistic in-store environment, ready-to-eat foodservice departments, in-store dining, augmented reality in combination with smartphones, and various online services. Payments are made automatically via Alipay. This concept blends the online and offline worlds and creates a 'blue ocean' at the top of the market space map.

Choosing a strategy

How should a conventional retailer respond to the entry of a hard discounter in its local market? The right strategy depends on the type of retailer, the expected impact on its customers, and the competitive situation. The strategy to be chosen by the conventional retailer should be in line with its DNA and should build on its own core competences. With these caveats in mind, Figure 7.4 presents a decision tree that we have found to be useful in our work with retailers. We also indicate which types of conventional retailers tend to fall into each impact category.

The defensive strategies, especially the fight-back strategy, are most applicable for price-focused/EDLP mainstream retailers such as Walmart (US), Asda (UK), or Hoogvliet (Netherlands), as well as for warehouse clubs. As customers expect the lowest prices at these formats, price-focused/EDLP mainstream retailers have an obligation to match the price levels of hard discounters. Although this strategy is costly due to lower gross margins, it can be effective as it may prevent customer loss.

For more service-focused/HiLo mainstream retailers such as Carrefour (France), Edeka (Germany), or Kroger (US), value improvement is a potentially viable alternative to the fight-back strategy. Offensive strategies – value-redefinition strategy in particular – are most applicable to premium retailers. They are already positioned as quality and service leaders in most of the markets they operate in and customers expect innovations and a 'Wow' experience.

Figure 7.4 How to respond when a hard discounter enters the market

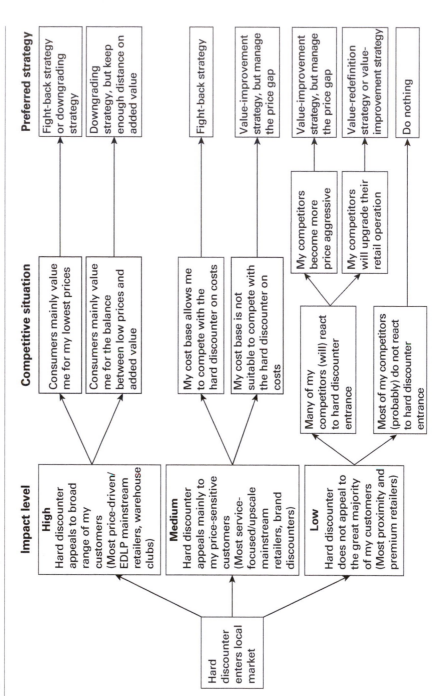

Impact level

High
Hard discounter appeals to broad range of my customers
(Most price-driven/ EDLP mainstream retailers, warehouse clubs)

Medium
Hard discounter appeals mainly to my price-sensitive customers
(Most service-focused/upscale mainstream retailers, brand discounters)

Low
Hard discounter does not appeal to the great majority of my customers
(Most proximity and premium retailers)

Hard discounter enters local market

Competitive situation

Consumers mainly value me for my lowest prices

Consumers mainly value me for the balance between prices and added value

My cost base allows me to compete with the hard discounter on costs

My cost base is not suitable to compete with the hard discounter on costs

Many of my competitors (will) react to hard discounter entrance

Most of my competitors (probably) do not react to hard discounter entrance

My competitors become more price aggressive

My competitors will upgrade their retail operation

Preferred strategy

Fight-back strategy or downgrading strategy

Downgrading strategy, but keep enough distance on added value

Fight-back strategy

Value-improvement strategy, but manage the price gap

Value-improvement strategy, but manage the price gap

Value-redefinition strategy or value-improvement strategy

Do nothing

Implementing the response strategy

The store choice model

By implementing a particular response strategy, the retailer's goal is to change the image current and potential shoppers have of one or more store image attributes. In our research and consulting experience, we have identified six generic store attributes, which we have already encountered earlier in this chapter: price level, promotions, assortment, quality, service and convenience. Here, we discuss them in more detail (Table 7.4).

Each of these store attributes provides unique benefits to the shopper. The retailer can influence consumers' perceptions of each attribute through a variety of retail-mix instruments. By employing these retail-mix instruments as part of a particular response strategy, the retailer can shift its position in the market space map in the desired direction, as indicated in Figure 7.1.

Table 7.4   Relationship between store attributes, shopper benefits, and retail-mix instruments

Store attribute	Specific shopper benefit provided	Examples of retail-mix instruments
Price	'I save money'	• Price level of private label • Price level of national brands • Economy lines • Phantom brands • Pricing strategy (EDLP/HiLo)
Promotions	'I am a smart shopper'	• Frequency and depth of promotions • Breadth of promotions • Promotion mix (monetary, non-monetary) • Loyalty programmes
Assortment	'I can buy everything I need and want'	• Breadth and depth of assortment • National brands' selection • Private label presence across categories • Produce assortment • Local products • Healthy and organic options • Store-prepared foods • New products

(continued)

Table 7.4   *(Continued)*

Store attribute	Specific shopper benefit provided	Examples of retail-mix instruments
Quality	'I can buy good products'	• Private label quality • Premium private label • Quality of fresh meat, poultry, fish • Produce quality
Service	'I like to shop at that store'	• Store interior/exterior • Service departments • Store employees • Personalized services • Store cleanliness • Return policy and complaint resolution • Dedicated space for shoppers to socialize • In-store bar and dining areas
Convenience	'Shopping is no hassle'	• Store proximity • Availability of parking space • In-store navigation • Assortment complexity • Out-of-stock frequency • Opening hours • Checkout speed • Online ordering and delivery options

- *Price level*: The main benefit the retailer offers with overall price level is that consumers can save money; they can stretch their budget a little further. Does the store offer lower prices than the competition on comparable items or is it more expensive? Does it offer a wide selection of cheaper items, such as economy private labels? Does the retailer follow an EDLP strategy with generally low prices or a HiLo-strategy with more variation in prices?

- *Promotions*: By running promotions, the retailer not only gives consumers opportunities to save money, but it also creates feelings of being a smart shopper because the consumer might be lying in wait for their favourite brands to be on promotion and then stocking up. This creates positive excitement and makes going to the store a bit like going on a treasure hunt. Which products can I acquire on the cheap this time? Retailers can improve their standing in this attribute by offering great and surprising monetary and non-monetary promotions, by expanding the number of SKUs on promotion at least sometimes, by having limited-time offers, and by offering a rewarding loyalty programme.

- *Assortment*: The main consumer benefit the retailer offers with assortment is whether the consumer can buy everything they need and want. Does the store provide a large assortment, covering foods, beverages, household items and personal care? Does it offer a wide variety of local, exotic, organic, and store-prepared foods? What is the breadth of the fresh produce assortment? Does the retailer offer its own private label in most categories? How many national brands does it carry in various categories – only the big ones, or also smaller brands that may offer excitement and surprise? Does it regularly introduce new products into its assortment?

- *Quality*: Product quality is a key purchase criterion for most consumers. Special markers are the quality of produce and fresh meats; another is the quality of the retailer's private-label products. How does it compare to other conventional retailers and to hard discounters? Does the retailer also carry premium private labels that are leading the category in terms of quality?

- *Service*: 'The customer is king' might be an old aphorism, but it nevertheless has not lost any of its relevance. During the course of a year, a shopper spends many hours in grocery stores, and that can be a source of pleasure and enjoyment. Almost half of US consumers who chose not to shop for groceries online in 2017 did so because they enjoy shopping in a brick-and-mortar store.[21] Offering great service is key to the shopper enjoying being in the store and feeling that they are welcome. Offering service departments, staffed by knowledgeable and friendly employees, contributes to the consumer liking, perhaps even looking forward to, going to that store. A nice in-store ambience and store exterior, dedicated places to socialize, and an in-store bar or dining area also contribute to retailers being able to fulfil service needs, as do return policies.

- *Convenience*: Shopping can be a hassle, and anything the store does to reduce that hassle generates benefits for shoppers. To what extent is shopping at this store simple and easy? What is the proximity of the store? Are there other stores nearby that I also need to visit? Do they have enough parking places? Is it easy to navigate through the store without missing important product groups? How long does it take to check out? Does the store offer a smooth online shopping service, including pick-up points and home delivery services?

Together, these six image attributes drive store choice (Figure 7.5). Price level and promotions affect store choice through the price image of the retailer, while the other four are drivers of store choice via the retailer's added-value image.

Figure 7.5   Store choice model

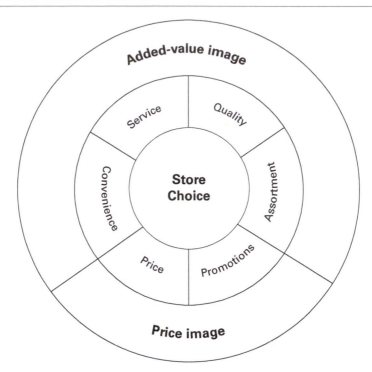

Store choice model applied to the US grocery market

The store choice model can be used to analyse where you stand in the minds of consumers versus your competition. Table 7.5 shows shoppers' perceptions of leading players for four types of grocery retailers in the United States in 2016 – premium, mainstream (national and regional), warehouse clubs, and hard discounters – based on a survey among subscribers to *Consumer Reports*.[22] Grocery retailing is a game of compromises. Almost no retailer can excel in all store attributes. Whole Foods rates highly on most value-added attributes but has a bad price image (something Amazon is trying to change). The image of Walmart is exactly the reverse. Kroger scores in the middle of the road for everything.

Table 7.5 reveals that Wegmans is an exception to the game of compromises. Wegmans receives the maximum score on 9 out of 10 value-added attributes included in the survey *and* has a favourable price image. Wegmans truly redefines the value map upward, and consumers vote with their feet. Its compound annual growth rate in the period 2002–2017 was 7.1 per cent, and its revenues per store exceeded $100 million per year in 2017.

Store attributes

Grocery banner	Retailer Type	Price	Assortment				Quality			Convenience and service		
		Competitive prices	Produce variety	Fresh store-prepared food	Local produce quantity	Selection of healthy options	Meats/poultry quality	Store brand quality	Produce quality	Staff courtesy	Checkout speed	Store cleanliness
Wegmans	Premium	+	++	++	++	++	++	+	++	++	++	++
Whole Foods	Premium	--	+	+	+	++	++	+	+	+	0	+
Kroger	Mainstream (National)	0	0	0	--	0	0	0	0	0	0	0
Walmart Supercenter	Mainstream (National)	+	--	-	--	--	--	-	--	--	--	--
Food Lion	Mainstream (Regional)	0	-	-	--	--	-	0	-	0	0	0
Jewel-Osco	Mainstream (Regional)	--	0	0	--	0	-	0	0	0	-	0
Pick 'n Save	Mainstream (Regional)	-	0	0	-	0	0	0	-	0	-	0
ShopRite	Mainstream (Regional)	+	0	0	0	0	0	0	-	0	0	0
Costco	Warehouse club	++	0	++	--	0	+	+	0	0	-	+
Sam's Club	Warehouse club	+	-	+	--	--	0	0	-	-	--	0
Aldi	Hard discounter	++	-	--	--	0	-	0	-	0	0	0
Trader Joe's	Hard discounter	++	-	0	-	++	0	++	0	++	+	++

NOTE Scale ranges from -- (= worse) to ++ (= better). Food Lion is owned by Ahold Delhaize, Jewel-Osco by Albertsons, and Pick 'n Save by Kroger. ShopRite is a retailers' cooperative.

SOURCE Based on *Consumer Reports* (2017)

Table 7.5 also highlights the strong position of the hard discounters in the United States, especially vis-à-vis regional mainstream retailers. While they excel, not surprisingly, on price, the performance of Aldi on quality, service, and convenience differs little from that of Food Lion, Jewel-Osco, Pick 'n Save, or ShopRite (or Kroger, for that matter). Only on assortment do these retailers generally score better than Aldi. That is a wobbly basis for continued success. And Trader Joe's does even better than Aldi vis-à-vis regional mainstream retailers. Indeed, if there is a second exception to the game of compromises in the United States, it is definitely Trader Joe's.

Store choice model applied to the UK grocery market

A 2017 survey among UK shoppers conducted by the consumer magazine *Which?* showed that UK mainstream retailers tend to perform better on value-added attributes versus Aldi and Lidl than most of their US counterparts (Table 7.6).[23] Yet Aldi received the highest overall score of all brick-and-mortar retailers, while Lidl ranked third. This indicates that the advantage of added-value attributes for the mainstream retailers was not sufficient enough to compensate for their significantly less favourable price image. It is remarkable that HiLo retailers Tesco and Morrisons did not rate higher on promotions than Aldi and Lidl (or EDLP Asda). Although the price image of Marks & Spencer (M&S) and Waitrose was even less favourable, they scored so much better on all added-value attributes that their overall customer score was high (worryingly this did not apply to Sainsbury's, which could be a harbinger of tough times). Interestingly, customer satisfaction with pure online retailer Ocado was very high. Along with Aldi and Lidl, it was Britain's fastest-growing grocery retailer in the preceding years.

What matters more: price or added value?

While the answer to this question of course differs between consumers in terms of income, time pressure, and other factors, can we say something at the aggregate level? For this, we used the aforementioned *Consumer Reports* survey data, which was collected for 62 grocery retailers. Shoppers also scored retailers on overall satisfaction. Satisfaction is a good proxy for store choice. We find that, for the average shopper, added value weighs more heavily than price: 64 per cent versus 36 per cent.[24] But subscribers to *Consumer Reports* probably have, on average, higher incomes and hence may be a bit less price-sensitive than the general population. If we account

Table 7.6 Perception of UK grocery retailers' store attributes in 2017

Grocery banner	Retailer type	Overall score	Price and promotions		Assortment	Quality		Service			Convenience		
			Value for money	Offers	Range of products	Store brand quality	Quality of fresh products	Staff availability and helpfulness	Store tidiness	Store appearance	Products being in stock	Ease of finding products	Checkout time
M&S	Premium	73	0	0	+	++	++	+	++	++	+	+	+
Waitrose	Premium	68	−	0	+	++	++	++	++	++	+	+	+
Sainsbury's	Premium lite	62	0	0	+	+	+	+	+	+	+	+	+
Tesco	Mainstream	64	0	+	++	0	+	+	+	+	+	+	+
Morrisons	Mainstream	63	0	+	+	0	+	0	+	+	0	+	+
Asda	Mainstream	63	+	+	+	0	+	0	+	+	0	+	0
Co-op	Proximity	50	0	0	0	+	+	0	0	+	0	+	0
Iceland	Brand discounter	65	+	+	0	0	0	−	+	+	0	+	0
Aldi	Hard discounter	74	++	+	0	+	+	−	0	0	0	+	0
Lidl	Hard discounter	69	++	+	−	0	+	−	0	0	−	0	−
Ocado	Online retailer	74	0	0	++	+	++	n.a.	n.a.	n.a.	+	+	n.a.

NOTE Scale ranges from − − (= lowest) to ++ (= highest). Tesco and Morrisons are HiLo retailers and Asda is an EDLP retailer. A supermarket's overall score is a combination of shoppers' satisfaction with the supermarket and the likelihood they would recommend it to a friend. n.a. = not applicable.

SOURCE Based on *Which?* (2018)

for this, we estimate that, for the average US consumer, added value weighs 55–60 per cent versus price at 40–45 per cent. This indicates that offensive, value-adding strategies are indeed a viable option to respond to discounter success.

Which store attributes are affected?

How does each of the four response strategies affect a retailer's standing on the store attributes that underpin store choice? Retailers that opt for the fight-back strategy will mainly focus on improving the price level and promotions attributes by lowering prices, extending the number of budget items, and intensifying promotional discounts and/or introducing reward programmes (Table 7.7). Retailers that follow a downgrading strategy will see their standing on added-value attributes (especially assortment and service) deteriorate, while at the same time improving their standing on price-related attributes. The value-improvement strategy might focus on improving convenience level, eg by adding city stores, offering online food retailing services, or extending opening hours. Also, more attention may be paid to the other added-value components by copying successful examples of other retailers. Finally, retailers that choose to adopt a value-redefinition strategy have to go full force on the store attributes that create a whole new dimension of value, but can expect their standing on price level to decrease because of the higher prices to be paid for these unique experiences.

Table 7.7   Effect of strategic response to hard discounter entry on conventional retailers' standing on store attributes

Strategic response	Price	Promotions	Assortment	Quality	Service	Convenience
Fight back	+	+	0	0	0	0
Downgrade	+	+	–	0	–	0
Value-improvement	0	0	0/+	0/+	0/+	0/+
Value-redefinition	–	0	+	+	+	+

NOTE - = deterioration, 0 = no effect, + = improvement

CASE STUDY Carrefour's response to the rise of hard discounters in France

In the period from 2002 to 2008, the market share of the hard discounters in France (Aldi, Lidl, Leader Price, DIA, Netto) grew from 11 per cent to 14 per cent, according to Kantar Worldpanel. How did market leader Carrefour react to this threat? It followed a combination of value-improvement strategy and fight-back strategy. Services were added with a big roll-out of convenience stores as well as investments in e-commerce and new pick-up points. However, Carrefour's biggest efforts were in narrowing the price gap with the hard discounters. In May 2009, it launched its economy private label, Carrefour Discount, aiming to 'improve Carrefour's image as a competitive brand among customers'.[25] Its very name signals who it intended to compete against. Carrefour Discount was, on average, 2 per cent cheaper than the Lidl brand (Table 7.1). Carrefour also put heavy pressure on national brands to slash their prices. Price reductions of up to 10 per cent on a broad range of SKUs were not uncommon. As a result, by 2014, a basket of branded goods was only 5 per cent more expensive at Carrefour than at Lidl and 6 per cent more expensive than at Leader Price.[26]

By and large, Carrefour's aggressive response to the rise of the hard discounters was successful. Its decline in market share was arrested. In the period 2013–2017, Carrefour's market share crept up slightly from 21.5 per cent to 21.7 per cent, according to Euromonitor International.[27] However, it came at a high cost (Table 7.8). Its operating margin declined from 4.0 per cent in 2008 to a low of 2.4 per cent in 2011, a reflection of the costs of its fight-back strategy but also of the declining popularity of the hypermarket format. Recovery on both metrics has occurred since then, but it has been sluggish and uneven, with 2017 being again a difficult year, reflecting the tough conditions in the French market.

Carrefour was not the only French retailer that responded to the growth of hard discounters. If anything, Leclerc pursued an even more aggressive fight-back strategy. By 2014, it had achieved price parity with Lidl on a basket of branded goods, while a basket of economy private-label goods was around 10 per cent cheaper. Its revenues grew by, on average, 2.9 per cent per year over the period 2008–2017 and, by 2017, it had captured 16.1 per cent of the market, up from 15.2 per cent in 2013.[28]

The efforts of Carrefour, Leclerc, and other conventional retailers were effective in reversing the upward trend of hard discounter success. Total hard discounter revenues fell between 2012 and 2017 from €17.1 billion to €16.2 billion. In 2014, Spanish discounter DIA sold its loss-making namesake chain in France

Table 7.8   Performance of Carrefour France, 2008–2017

Year	Net sales (€ bn)	Operating margin (%)
2008	38.0	4.0
2009	37.0	3.2
2010	34.9	3.7
2011	35.2	2.4
2012	35.3	2.6
2013	35.4	3.4
2014	35.3	3.6
2015	36.3	3.3
2016	35.9	2.9
2017	35.8	1.9

NOTE Data refer to Carrefour's operations in France only.
SOURCE Based on Carrefour Annual Reports, 2008–2017

to Carrefour, which by 2017 had closed most ex-DIA stores. The only hard discounter holding its own in France is Lidl, which saw its market share grow from 4.0 per cent in 2014 to 4.9 per cent in 2017.

Managerial takeaways

Conventional grocery retailers often go through several stages when they are confronted with competition from hard discounters. Initially, the impact of hard discounters is often underestimated, leading to costly panic reactions at later stages when it becomes clear that hard discounters are a permanent and prominent force in the grocery retailscape.

Conventional retailers should develop a coordinated strategic response in a timely manner. We distinguish four strategic responses conventional retailers can choose:

- The *fight-back strategy* and the *downgrade strategy* are both defensive strategies and focus on winning back price-sensitive customers by investing in a better price image. The main positional disadvantage of defensive strategies is that customers become even more price sensitive. And although defensive strategies might win back customers, as was shown by Albert Heijn and Carrefour, it is a painstaking effort and, as the Carrefour example shows, can cut significantly into operating profits.

- Conventional retailers can also play more offensively towards hard discounters by following a *value-improvement strategy* or a *value-redefinition strategy*. Both strategies are directed at making shoppers more oriented towards added value. By following these strategies, retailers try to compete on store attributes at which the hard discounters do not excel, such as a large assortment, extra services, and superior in-store experiences.

Figure 7.4 provides guidance as to which strategy is recommended under which conditions. But no matter what strategy is chosen, all conventional retailers should manage the price gap on comparable items. Even affluent customers of upscale retailers simply do not like paying hefty price premiums for comparable items. We consider a price premium of 5–10 per cent on national brands and 10–15 per cent on comparable store brand items to be the maximum. Higher price premiums can only be demanded for items that are truly different and unique.

To assess hard discounters' vulnerabilities, conventional grocery retailers can use the store choice model (Figure 7.5), which shows the following:

- Experience from various countries shows that hard discounters excel on price, private-label quality, and increasingly on convenience, but rate low on assortment and service.

- Conventional retailers can focus on improving these benefits to enlarge the experiential benefit gap with hard discounters, provided the price gap remains reasonable. Experience in the UK and the United States shows that mainstream retailers need to up their game considerably on these aspects. Their added-value advantage is often not sufficiently large to compensate for the large difference in price image.

Notes

1 Uusitalo, O and Rökman, M (2007) The impact of competitive entry on pricing in the Finnish retail grocery market, *International Journal of Retail & Distribution Management*, **35** (2), pp. 120–35.

2 *Food Personality* (2013) September, p. 13.

3 www.agf.nl/artikel/163308/GfK-Lidl-heeft-de-best-gewaardeerde-AGF-afdeling, last accessed 4 January 2018.

4 www.distrifood.nl/branche-bedrijf/nieuws/2017/11/lild-tilburg-mooiste-supermarkt-101113409, last accessed 4 January 2018.

5 Eric Heiden won an unprecedented five individual gold medals at the 1980 Winter Olympic Games in Lake Placid, New York. He is also – to the best of our knowledge – the only male who has won both the sprint and all-round speed skating world championship in the same year in recent times, and multiple times for that matter. Source: en.wikipedia.org/wiki/Eric_Heiden, last accessed 4 January 2018. We can remember his accomplishments vividly – the only non-Dutchman for whom we rooted in speed skating contests.

6 https://www.reuters.com/article/us-aldi-walmart-pricing-exclusive-idUSKBN1870EN, last accessed 4 January 2018.

7 Mehra, P (2006) Aldi's private labels hurt Woolworths, Coles the most, *The Australian Business Review*, 22 January.

8 www.cnbc.com/2017/09/08/target-shares-tumble-following-retailers-promise-to-slash-prices.html, last accessed 6 December 2017.

9 www.chainstoreage.com/article/carrefour-launches-low-cost-private-label-brand, last accessed 6 December 2017.

10 Geyskens, I, Gielens, K, and Gijsbrechts, E (2010) Proliferating private-label portfolios: How introducing economy and premium private labels influences brand choice, *Journal of Marketing Research,* **47** (October), pp. 791–807.

11 http://www.news.com.au/finance/business/retail/woolworths-introduces-new-range-of-phantom-brand-private-label-products/news-story/86d3039995f6a5 58e63c4d5840843837, last accessed 2 January 2018.

12 www.planetretail.net/NewsAndInsight/Article/16458, last accessed 23 March 2018.

13 https://www.nrc.nl/nieuws/2006/02/04/foutenfestival-nekt-ambities-laurus-definitief-11078711-a1296214, last accessed 23 March 2018.

14 Presentation of Vomar CEO Aart van Haren at EFMI Food Retail Outlook conference, 6 September 2017.

15 www.theguardian.com/business/2018/feb/11/tesco-planning-discount-chain-to-take-on-aldi-and-lidl, last accessed 15 February 2018.

16 www.buzzfeed.com/rachelysanders/why-wegmans-is-the-greatest-supermarket-ever?utm_term=.xhWyPEZng#.th239L1qG, last accessed 4 January 2018. The article contains a photo essay.

17 www.drugstorenews.com/article/wegmans-open-new-store-concept, last accessed 23 December 2017.

18 For more information and a visual tour of the stores, see www.hieber.de, last accessed 4 January 2018.

19 This paragraph is based on Chaker, A M (2018) Finding love in the frozen-food aisle, *Wall Street Journal*, 12 March, p. A12.

20 www.cnbc.com/2017/07/18/alibaba-hema-stores-blend-online-and-offline-retail.html; www.alizila.com/video/take-tour-hema-supermarket-experience-new-retail/, last accessed 4 January 2018.

21 Hamstra, M (2017) Consumers enjoy in-store experience, *Supermarket News*, December, p. 20.

22 *Consumer Reports* (2017) Faster, fresher, cheaper, July, pp. 30–43. Ratings are based on 50,218 respondents who rated one or two banners between July 2015 and September 2016. The survey reflects 93,447 visits to supermarkets, supercentres and warehouse clubs.

23 *Which?* (2018) Best and worst supermarkets, March, pp. 3035.

24 We averaged the scores of each retailer on the 10 added–value attributes and on the two price attributes (price of organics was also included in the survey). We then regressed retailers' overall satisfaction on price and added-value image. Model fit was excellent: R^2 = 92.6 per cent. We used the relative magnitude of the regression coefficients as measure of relative importance of price versus added value.

25 Carrefour's Annual Report, 2009.

26 www.lek.com/sites/default/files/LEK_1635_DiscountRetailers_Web.pdf, last accessed 4 January 2018.

27 Euromonitor International reports on grocery retailers in France, January 2018.

28 www.lek.com/sites/default/files/LEK_1635_DiscountRetailers_Web.pdf, last accessed 4 January 2018. Sales data from Planet Retail, market share from Euromonitor International.

Strategies to reduce procurement costs

08

In the last chapter, we discussed retailer strategies to compete with hard discounters. Retailers that serve a large base of price-oriented customers should be extremely careful in managing the price gap with hard discounters on items that are more or less the same. Neglecting the price issue can be a costly mistake in a world where hard discounters are present. When asked about his vision on competing with hard discounters, Dick Boer, CEO of Ahold Delhaize responded as follows: 'We have learned a lot from the rise of Lidl in the Netherlands. We have given them too much space and should have managed the price gap more carefully.'[1]

Why is managing the price gap so important, even for service-oriented mainstream retailers such as Ahold Delhaize? Because for the average consumer, price weighs heavily in their store choice. Price is also much easier to compare across retailers than added value. In Chapter 7, we talked about reducing prices on conventional retailers' assortments as a defensive strategy against hard discounters. Left undiscussed was how to do that without destroying the thin margins common in grocery retailing. Yet this is the million-dollar question retailers are struggling with, whether they are located in North America, Europe, or Australasia. The secret is to reduce procurement costs (cost of goods sold). This chapter will be devoted to strategies for achieving just that.

The dominant role of cost of goods sold in retailers' P&L statements

For grocery retailers, the costs of procuring the products sold in stores are the single most important cost factor. Take Colruyt, a price-oriented mainstream retailer with stores in Belgium, France and Luxembourg. Table 8.1

Table 8.1   Colruyt's P&L statement for 2016/2017

	€ million	%
Revenues from retail activities	9.493	100
Cost of goods sold	(7.079)	(74.6)
Gross profit	2.414	25.4
Selling, general, and administrative expenses	(1.782)	(18.8)
Depreciation and amortization	(250)	(2.6)
Operating income from retail sales	382	4.0
Other company income	111	1.2
Total operating income	493	5.2

SOURCE Based on Colruyt Annual Report, 2016/2017

shows its P&L statement for 2016/2017.[2] We see that Colruyt's cost of goods sold (COGS) are 74.6 per cent. Thus, on each euro earned by Colruyt Group, 75 cents are passed on to its suppliers. If Colruyt was able to cut its purchasing prices by 5 per cent, that would save the company €350 million. This is almost as much as their regular operating income from retail sales! Given the weight of COGS in the P&L statement of Colruyt, it is virtually impossible to save comparable amounts on other cost factors. For example, the second-largest cost factor by far for conventional retailers is labour costs, which for Colruyt Group are about 13.5 per cent of their total revenues. If Colruyt Group wants to achieve a saving of €350 million on labour costs, it would have to reduce its headcount by almost 27 per cent.

The lesson is clear. While other ways to reduce costs should not be neglected, the most direct and effective way to narrow the price gap with hard discounters without breaking the bank is to reduce procurement costs. To understand how to put this in practice, we need to recognize that the conventional retailer faces two different types of procurement costs: procurement costs of its own private-label products and procurement costs of national brand products.

P&L statements of branded versus private-label suppliers

Basically, grocery retailers do business with two types of suppliers: brand manufacturers and private-label suppliers. The group of private-label suppliers can be subdivided into suppliers of shelf-stable products (packaged foods and beverages as well as household and personal care products) and suppliers of fresh foods. In many categories, conventional retailers do business with both brand manufacturers and private-label suppliers. With soft drinks, for example, retailers buy their private-label cola from Refresco, for example, while they also have contracts with Coca-Cola and PepsiCo. For most conventional grocery retailers, brand suppliers account for anywhere between 35 and 50 per cent of total procurement costs, and private-label suppliers (including suppliers of fresh foods, which are largely unbranded) for about 50–65 per cent of total procurement costs.

To understand the potential for conventional retailers to save on procurement costs, we compare the P&L statements of brand manufacturers and private-label suppliers. Based on our consulting experience and a study of the performance of food suppliers, we developed an 'archetype' P&L statement for each type of supplier (see Table 8.2).[3]

COGS of a typical brand manufacturer account for 50 per cent of revenues. A brand manufacturer needs the high resulting gross margin to be able to pay for huge marketing expenses. But even after subtracting marketing and other expenses, the firm's operating margin is typically in the 15–25 per cent range. By contrast, COGS account for a much larger part of the total revenues of private-label suppliers (75 per cent), resulting in a much lower gross margin percentage – about 25 per cent. This is still adequate, as they spend much less on marketing. Yet the operating margin is usually somewhere between a third and a fifth of that of a brand supplier.

Table 8.2 Archetypal P&L statement for brand manufacturer and private-label supplier

	Brand manufacturer (%)	Private-label supplier (%)
Revenues	*100*	*100*
Cost of goods sold	(50)	(75)
Contribution margin	*50*	*25*
Marketing costs – brand-focused (eg advertising, product development, marketing research)	(12)	(4)
Marketing costs – sales-focused (eg price discounts, in-store marketing fees)	(8)	(4)
General and administrative costs, depreciation, and other costs	(10)	(12)
Operating margin	*20*	*5*

These very different P&L statements mean that the profits of brand manufacturers are much more sensitive to change in revenues than the profits of private-label suppliers. We will illustrate this with a simplified example. Suppose that, in order to increase category sales by $10 million, a large retailer considers either giving more support (display, shelf space, etc) to national brand A or to its own private label, produced by private-label player B. How does this impact their respective P&Ls? Referring to Table 8.2, this would mean that A's gross profit goes up by $5 million (50 per cent of $10 million) while B's gross profit increases by only $2.5 million (25 per cent of $10 million). And, as most of the operating costs have a more or less fixed character, the impact on the operating profit is also larger for A than for B. So if a conventional retailer is looking for ways to appropriate part of this incremental profit, brand supplier A has more potential to share the spoils than private-label supplier B. This is especially true when retailers can negotiate with more brand players (A1, A2, and A3) at the same time. In summary, the P&L structure of brand manufacturers with their relatively fat margins offers opportunities for conventional retailers to reduce procurement costs.

Capturing more value from brand suppliers

How can a conventional retailer capture more value from branded suppliers? To understand this, we have found it useful to consider two factors:

- the importance of the product category for the retailer's positioning; and
- the strength of the national brand in question in that category for consumer purchases.

When we combine these two dimensions, this results in a two-by-two matrix (Figure 8.1) with four cells. For each cell, the retailer can use a different approach in order to capture more value from its branded suppliers. Cells I and II are, at the end of the day, confrontational – you put pressure on brand manufacturers to fork over some of their profits to you in the form of lower procurement prices and/or higher slotting allowances. In Cells III and IV, the retailer seeks to extract more value through collaboration.

Cell I: reduce brand assortment

The first quadrant consists of brands that do not command high loyalty and operate in product categories that are not essential for the retailer's

Figure 8.1   Four strategies to capture more value from national brand manufacturers

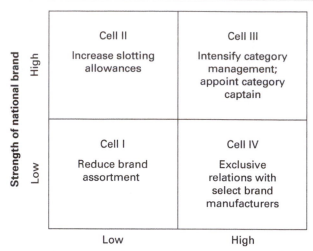

positioning. For many retailers, such categories include most brands in categories such as bathroom tissue, household cleaning products, canned soup, and other staple products. A retailer should focus on building a larger buying volume per branded item within the assortment. There are several ways to achieve this: first and foremost, by rationalizing the assortment by offering fewer of these (weak) brands, and second, by reducing the number of SKUs it offers of any given brand.

When a retailer seriously reduces the number of brands/SKUs in a category, three things typically happen:

1 The volume of the items that remain in the assortment will increase. This leads to some supply chain efficiencies in the procurement process (fewer contacts), as well as in transportation, warehousing, and store operations (eg easier restocking of shelves, fewer items out of stock).

2 Brand manufacturers that fear losing distribution for their SKUs, if not being outright delisted, are willing to negotiate deals that are more favourable for the retailer. After all, as we have seen, the P&L of branded suppliers is very sensitive to the total volume sold. This leads to a situation in which the retailer can apply the theory of the Prisoners' Dilemma to the brand suppliers: brand suppliers will lose some margin if they offer a better deal to the retailer, but they risk losing much more if they refuse to cooperate.

3 A third advantage for a retailer reducing its assortment is that, even in cases where manufacturers are not willing to offer better prices, the retailer can delist items with relatively low gross margins. This is especially true in situations where there are clear substitutes for items that might be delisted. Take Nettorama, a price-oriented grocery retailer in the Netherlands. Whereas market leader Albert Heijn offers many SKUs of the same brand, Nettorama usually offers a limited range of packaging formats and/or varieties. In Nettorama's selection process, the gross margin on each item weighs heavily. With this 'smart assortment' tactic, Nettorama offers low prices *and* is among the best financial performers, with an EBIT of around 7 per cent.

Overall, we expect that reducing the assortment of branded items in Cell I might lead to supply chain efficiencies and lower purchasing prices somewhere in the 4–6 per cent range. But this is only possible if the retailer dares to be ruthless. Reducing assortment holds some risks: it may backfire, as some consumers might miss certain items and switch stores for a while.[4] In our opinion, however, lower procurement costs for the remaining branded SKUs – and thus lower consumer prices – outweigh the risk for retailers serving a large base of price-conscious shoppers.

Superunie's 'Choose or Lose' programme

An interesting case of a retailer putting pressure on brand suppliers comes from Superunie, one of the largest buying organizations in the Netherlands. Its 13 members accounted for around 30 per cent of the Dutch grocery market in 2017. About a decade ago, it launched the 'Choose or Lose' programme in a number of categories, including bathroom tissue. Bathroom tissue is not important for Superunie's positioning, and brand preferences are low. Superunie offered three national brands: Edet (owned by SCA, now Essity), Page (Kimberly-Clark), and Lotus (Sofidel). Superunie informed the three brand suppliers that it was going to reduce the number of national brands in this category from three to two, and that the decision depended on which brand supplier offered the least attractive conditions. One of the suppliers did not cooperate, while the other two offered a significantly lower price – up to 20 per cent. That was a steep price cut but these two brand suppliers figured that they would capture a large part of the sales from the brand that was delisted. The next year, Superunie invited the same three brand manufacturers again, and now the supplier with the formerly delisted brand offered a much lower price and was relisted at the expense of one of the other suppliers. While

Superunie's actions did nothing to improve relations with these branded suppliers, the example shows that there is a considerable margin to be appropriated from weak brands in (for the retailer) unimportant categories.

Cell II: increase slotting allowances

The second cell in Figure 8.1 contains branded suppliers with strong brands in product groups that are not crucial for the retailer's positioning. Examples are product groups such as soft drinks, beer, confectioneries, detergents, and sauces. A retailer needs to offer these categories, but it is generally difficult to truly differentiate yourself with them. In these categories, multiple strong brands can be found, catering to different consumer segments. Thus, the retailer has little choice but to offer a wide brand assortment. It is virtually inconceivable for a conventional retailer (dependent on the country) not to offer Coca-Cola, Cadbury, Tide, Heineken, Heinz tomato ketchup, or Marmite. The sales margin for the retailer is often quite low on these brands, as the retailer cannot demand higher prices because the competitor next door also carries them. And, increasingly, hard discounters carry some of these brands too (to be discussed in Chapter 11), which makes it even more important to be price competitive.

Yet, retailers have considerable power. These strong brands have a lot to lose when they – or some of their SKUs – are de-emphasized in the store. For example, a retailer can decide to limit the number of in-store displays, reduce the number of shelf facings, or move the brand to a lower shelf. How much is it worth for a strong brand with ample marketing resources to remain at a favourable position on the shelf in a category that is not very important to the retailer? This is a lever with which the retailer can play.

Recall that the operating profit of these brands is very sensitive to volume changes (Table 8.2). We recommend that conventional retailers shift their focus from a front-margin system to a back-margin system. A front-margin system is one in which a retailer generates profits by selling a brand at a substantially higher price than the procurement price. So, the negotiations are all about gross margins for the retailer. In a back-margin system, the difference between selling and procurement price is modest. That is, the retailer sells the product for little more than the procurement price, and thus is price competitive with hard discounters. In that case, how does the conventional retailer earn money? By charging slotting allowances for all kinds of services it provides to the brand: a listing fee per SKU, per facing, per display, for space at eye level, for shopper data, etc. These slotting allowances are basically the retailer's fee for allowing the manufacturer to obtain valuable commercial space. It is somewhat comparable to the platform strategy adopted by online retailers such as Amazon and Alibaba.

If a brand manufacturer does not want to pay for these value-adding activities, they can still be business partners, but the position of its brand's SKUs within the store is minimized while the best space is given to its brand competitor or to the retailer's own store brand. In the meantime, the retailer's customers can still buy their favourite brands, but they are not found on prime shelf space. Brand sales will suffer as a consequence and, given high gross margins, so will profits. Manufacturers generally do not like the back-margin approach, but there is simply too much money on the table. In our experience, implementing a smart back-margin fee structure should lead to savings in the 2–3 per cent range.

Cell III: intensify category management

Conventional retailers should not only try to negotiate better deals with brand manufacturers, they could also choose to work more closely together in categories that might benefit from the expertise of these category experts. Conventional retailers typically sell thousands of products across hundreds of categories and realize that they can extract more value from the market by managing categories as opposed to individual SKUs. Category management involves the allocation of resources within sets of complementary and/or competing brands to maximize planned outcomes. This involves the analysis of category-level data, setting goals for category performance, and the formulation and execution of plans to maximize category-level results.

Category management can be applied to any product category, but empirical evidence shows that intensive category management is much more common in categories that are of strategic importance to the retailer.[5] For important categories, it makes more sense to spend time, effort, and resources on such category management activities as analysing prices, determining the impact of special displays, analysing profitability of individual SKUs, implementing and coordinating promotion and advertising plans, adjusting logistical arrangements, changing the assortment of SKUs, and developing detailed category performance objectives. Yet, many retailers realize they lack the market insights and financial resources to intensively manage even strategically important categories themselves. This offers opportunities for a brand manufacturer to take up the role as category captain. Indeed, by assigning the role of category captain to a brand manufacturer, the retailer can improve its financial performance in that category.

One study conducted in the United States compared the outcome for categories where the retailer assigned the role of a category captain to a leading brand supplier (eg Coca-Cola) versus categories where the retailer did not use a category captain.[6] The study found that, in categories where the retailer uses a category captain, channel conflict between suppliers – and with the retailer – was significantly lower. Better coordination through a category captain increased the efficiency of all suppliers' marketing efforts and therefore was often welcomed even by suppliers that were not selected to lead the category management efforts. More importantly, using a category captain led to higher retailer performance in that category. Categories with a category captain experienced growth in sales and profits that was double that of categories without a category captain.

By assigning category captains, a retailer profits from the resources of the manufacturers. The retailer gives up some independence, but the category captains can help the retailer keep its assortment up to date, as they have detailed knowledge of the product trends and the shopping behaviour in these product groups. The supply chain knowledge of a category captain can lead to significant savings; for example, they might combine the stock of slow-moving items of several manufacturers in a specialized warehouse or optimize the delivery schedule to minimize out-of-stocks. An interesting example of a category management project that focused on lowering supply chain costs was a project initiated by Coca-Cola. As Coca-Cola is one of the fastest-moving brands in the supermarket, considerable in-store handling is required. To save time, Coca-Cola and cooperating retailers invented a roller container that was able to restock the shelf much faster. This not only saved about one cent per bottle in the whole restocking process, but it also led to less out-of-stock and less consumer irritation caused by store employees restocking the shelves.

Overall, in our experience, intensive category management may lead to an increase of 2–3 per cent in margin due to supply chain savings and a more optimized commercial approach.

Cell IV: forge exclusive relationships with brand suppliers

In the fourth cell in Figure 8.1, we find weak brands in categories that are important for a retailer's positioning. For most conventional retailers, we should think about fresh foods, including produce, meat, seafood, cheese, bakery products, and ready-to-eat fresh meals. Gross margins in these categories are generally higher (30–40 per cent) than in dry grocery categories (10–25 per cent), so it is in the retailer's interest to increase category sales. They pay extra attention to these product groups in terms of services delivered, floor space, promotional coverage, and the location of these categories in the store.

Fresh foods are dominated by private-label suppliers, but national brands do exist (eg Driscoll's, SanLucar, Chiquita, Dole). To further differentiate themselves from their competitors, retailers are interested in obtaining exclusive distribution rights from national brands. For example, in a study among grocery brand manufacturers in the UK, 35 per cent said that they had been asked to enter into an exclusivity agreement with one of their retail customers. Two-thirds of those requests, which did not involve private-label production but dealt with the exclusive distribution of branded SKUs, came from one of the four largest supermarkets (Tesco, Sainsbury's, Asda and Morrisons). Overall, 19 per cent of all brand suppliers actually entered into at least one such exclusivity agreement.

For the brand manufacturer, an exclusivity arrangement guarantees shelf space and elicits more retailer support, but limits the total sales potential to one retailer. For the retailer, having a unique product in one's assortment can lead to increased store traffic by capturing market share from retailers not carrying the product, as well as generate a positive spill-over effect when consumers also buy other products while in the store. Moreover, given that the product is not available at other stores, intra-brand competition (between different retailers carrying the brand) that could drive the price down is avoided, allowing the retailer to extract monopoly rents from the market.

One study examined the gains and losses of exclusivity resulting from an exclusive distribution arrangement between Unilever and Albert Heijn in the Netherlands.[7] Unilever granted long-term exclusive distribution rights to Albert Heijn for five brands in the following categories: bread (three SKUs of Blue Band and two SKUs of Becel), soft cheese (three SKUs of Boursin), ice cream (two SKUs of Magnum), and tea (three SKUs of Lipton). What was the outcome?

Exclusive distribution turned out to be clearly beneficial for Albert Heijn. Total category sales and gross profits increased significantly. Unilever, in contrast, realized lower sales under this exclusive arrangement than it would have obtained with broad distribution. To render the situation profit neutral would necessitate a margin shift from Albert Heijn to Unilever in order to compensate Unilever for its sales losses from the exclusive deal. It was unclear whether that happened, but Unilever may very well have the market power to secure such a margin shift. Smaller brand manufacturers almost certainly do not have this power.

Because exclusivity arrangements are generally not very attractive for brand manufacturers and, at best, will cover only a limited part of the assortment, we believe that the incremental value captured by the retailer is small. Expressed in the metric of COGS, we expect this to be in the range of 0–0.5 per cent.

Saving money on private-label procurement

For most conventional retailers, the procurement costs of private-label products, including fresh foods, account for 50–65 per cent of their total buying costs. Private-label suppliers have less market power than brand suppliers, so the potential to negotiate better deals is greater. In our work, we have encountered two key routes conventional retailers can travel in their quest to capture more value from private-label suppliers: increase buying volume per SKU, and develop strategic relationships with preferred suppliers.

Increase buying volume per SKU

If a retailer manages to increase the volume of units purchased for any given SKU, that drives down production costs at the supplier and strengthens the retailer's negotiating position. Recall that high purchase volume per SKU is a key reason why hard discounters can offer high-quality private labels for a low price (Chapter 2). One way to achieve this is to rationalize your private-label assortment. The proliferation of private-label programmes in many conventional retailers has gone too far. For example, in 2017, Britain's Sainsbury's carried three broad lines of store brands – Basics (economy), Sainsbury's (standard), and Taste the Difference (premium) – as well as product lines sold under Be Good to Yourself, Deliciously FreeFrom, SO Organic, Tu, HOME, Home Collection, and On the Go. While these lines target different segments, they also cannibalize each other, which lowers the supply chain efficiency of the standard store brand workhorse. And do you really need 20 varieties of jam within your store brand range if the top six SKUs account for 80 per cent or more of the sales? Why not concentrate on the most preferred items with your regular store brand and relegate slower-moving SKUs to national brands? At least from an efficiency perspective, conventional retailers have made their store brand programme too complex. In order to create a better negotiating position, volume is still the name of the game.

We estimate that smart assortment rationalization can result in savings of 1–2 per cent on the procurement costs of private label, taking into account slightly lower sales due to less variety. The main reason for these savings is that larger buying volumes lead to better plant utilization, improved production processes, and higher purchasing efficiencies for suppliers. If conventional retailers or their buying groups are willing to negotiate longer-term contracts, suppliers will also be more willing to invest in new technology and additional production capacity.

Develop strategic relations with preferred suppliers

We have seen earlier that the potential gains from national brands in Cell IV of Figure 8.1 is small. Yet, the potential for conventional retailers to create and capture more value is significant, albeit that it involves developing strategic relations with carefully selected private-label suppliers. In these categories, which are dominated by fresh foods, it is very important for retailers to have skilled procurement managers that really understand the supply chains of perishable products, as well as knowing where to source them in order to get the necessary quality. Having the right set of suppliers is a key asset that can help the retailer differentiate itself from its competitors. In some cases, there might be even just one exclusive supplier per product group. Albert Heijn in the Netherlands, for example, works closely with exclusive suppliers such as Royal Vezet (chilled food and vegetable mixes), Hilton Food Holland (meat products), and Royal A-ware (cheese). Seen from the perspective of the retailer in question, the advantages of relying on exclusive suppliers are fourfold:

1 Other retailers cannot benefit from the knowledge and skills of this supplier.

2 The supplier can dedicate its full attention to you. This might lead to a more unique assortment that helps you to differentiate your chain from others.

3 Some exclusive relationships encompass an open-cost price calculation, in which the supplier discloses all its financial data to you and you guarantee the supplier a competitive EBIT. The supplier might receive bonuses if certain efficiencies are reached.

4 You may be in the position to guarantee a certain sales volume per year. This lowers the supplier's business risk. In this case it is also less risky for the supplier to invest in production capacity and IT solutions. Banks will

charge lower interest rates for loans if you guarantee a certain volume for multiple years, creating additional cost savings.

If executed well, this strategy might lead to a more differentiated assortment for the retailer, as well as lower buying and supply chain costs, since the manufacturer knows in advance what and when to produce. Overall, we estimate that this approach might lead to cost savings in the 1–2 per cent range if a retailer is able to bundle buying volumes to just a few strategic partners per category. In addition, extra margin of the same magnitude should be possible as the retailer increases the quality of its fresh operation.

Saving on total procurement bill by scaling up

There is another, complementary, way to decrease COGS applicable to the *total* procurement bill: namely to aggregate demand across retailers. Arguably, the most straightforward way to achieve this is through mergers and acquisitions. The Ahold Delhaize merger in 2016 is a good example. Royal Ahold and Delhaize estimated that cost synergies due to leveraging the scale of the combined company in branded and private-label sourcing would account for 50–60 per cent of total costs saved.[8]

Another way to aggregate demand is to join forces in a buying group. Conventional retailers can source brands and private labels together with (non-competing) conventional retailers. In Europe, most conventional grocery retailers are part of at least one international buying group such as EMD, Agecore, Coopernic, and AMS. These buying groups are not always used to their full advantage, as much of the procurement of even staple items is still done on a local scale.

We interviewed Philippe Gruyters, managing director of EMD, one of the largest European buying groups. He estimates that a cost price reduction of 5–10 per cent is possible if retailers bundle their buying effectively. Combining forces is easier for international brands – because there is no discussion about packaging or product specification – than for private labels, which are typically not standardized. Gruyters provides his perspective:

> Especially when manufacturers have the capacity to handle the extra volume, costs can go down significantly. This is often only possible if retailers cooperate and are willing to harmonize the product specifications of their store brands. In that case manufacturers can produce these items more efficiently as they don't have to switch lines all the time.

The rise of hard discounters is changing the perspective on how private labels can be sourced, especially with regard to non-perishable products such as detergents, chocolate, and canned soup. Aldi and Lidl have shown that many items can be sourced and sold successfully on an international scale. Aggregating demand across multiple conventional retailers drives down costs and can also result in higher product and packaging quality.

Corrected for higher logistical costs as a consequence of international sourcing, we conservatively estimate that savings in the 4–6 per cent range can be achieved if conventional retailers combine their private-label buying much more than is currently the case. For national brands, the savings are likely to be less, 2–4 per cent, because a significant number of brands are local brands and hence difficult to include in international buying arrangements.

Our experience suggests that the greatest barrier to achieving cost savings by international sourcing is that procurement managers of different retailers are reluctant to give up their autonomy, especially for their own beloved store brand products. Philippe Gruyters explains:

> [In some cases] this means the same kind of pizza for several countries. And probably that is the most important challenge. Are national operating retailers really willing to accept international product specifications for their pizza store brand if sales are currently satisfying and the category management department is proud of what they have developed?

How much can be saved on cost of goods sold?

Table 8.3 summarizes our estimates of potential savings and the main sources of these savings. Savings on the national brand bill of 4–8 per cent are realistic, while there is room for the private-label bill to be cut by 7–12 per cent. Total potential savings on COGS depend on the relative share of private-label products (including fresh foods) versus national brands in the total procurement bill, but we estimate that savings up to 5–10 per cent on the total procurement bill are possible if the conventional retailer really makes this a priority.

But these savings do not come easy. They can only be captured if the conventional retailer is willing to simplify its assortment and play hardball with suppliers to signal that it is serious. The retailer has to be willing to implement a brand boycott if necessary. Take European buying group Agecore (composed of German Edeka, Italian Conad, French Intermarché, Spanish Eroski, Swiss Coop, and Belgian Colruyt Group). In February

Table 8.3   Strategies for capturing more value from suppliers

Strategy	Potential savings on COGS (%)	Comments
National brand suppliers		
Scale up buying volumes by reducing number of brands/ brand SKUs (Figure 8.1: Cell I)	3–5	Brand manufacturers are willing to offer lower prices (or are willing to pay more slotting allowances) if they might lose or win a significant amount of sales. If a retailer reduces its assortment, supply chain efficiencies will go up. Some margin loss should also be taken into account as some consumers might buy the delisted item elsewhere.
Increase slotting allowances (Cell II)	2–3	Implementing a back-margin structure for valuable in-store marketing tools (eg shelf space, eye height, displays, coupons).
Intensify category management (Cell III)	1–2	Assigning category captains may lead to supply chain savings and a more optimal assortment.
Exclusivity arrangements with brands (Cell IV)	0–0.5	Substantial value can be generated through higher margins and more sales but the scope of application and willingness of brand manufacturers hinders widespread application.
Higher buying volumes per SKU through combining forces with other retailers (across all cells)	2–4	Due to bundling of buying volumes and increased market power, procurement prices will go down.
Total savings on national brands procurement bill	*4–8*	Total savings dependent on the share of each cell in total procurement bill paid to brands.

(Continued)

Table 8.3 (Continued)

Strategy	Potential savings on COGS (%)	Comments
Private-label suppliers		
Higher buying volumes per SKU through assortment rationalization	1–2	Rationalizing assortment for packaged private-label items by removing slow-moving items and simplifying store brand architecture reduces handling costs and creates shelf space to increase volume of faster-selling items. For the fresh foods product groups, a more efficient assortment may additionally reduce the costs from spoilage.
Develop strategic relations with preferred suppliers	2–4	Main savings are with regard to an improved supply chain (less product loss), higher volume per supplier (lower buying cost), and a more tailored assortment that is better appreciated by customers (margin gain).
Higher buying volumes per SKU through combining forces with other retailers	4–6	Due to bundling of buying volumes and/or reducing the number of different private-label items several things will happen. Procurement prices will go down as higher volumes are bought, but logistical costs will go up slightly if more products are sourced internationally.
Total savings on private-labels procurement bill	7–12	

2018, Agecore announced it would delist 160 SKUs from food giant Nestlé, if Nestlé was unwilling to offer significantly better buying conditions. This requires considerable courage. Nestlé is the largest food company in the world, and the delisting threat included strong brands like Nescafé, Vittel, San Pellegrino, and Maggi, among others.[9] Such a brand boycott hurts both parties; it is a matter who can bear the most pain.

Paradoxically, though, being squeezed is not all negative for branded players. In today's retailscape, the main engine behind the drive of conventional retailers to get better buying conditions from national brands is the price pressure they feel from hard discounters. It is certainly not in the best interests of brand manufacturers that hard discounters gain market share at the expense of conventional retailers. After all, conventional retailers sell a lot of your stuff, while hard discounters sell few brand SKUs.

Let us illustrate this with some numbers. In Western Europe, private labels account for around 35 per cent of the total sales of a conventional retailer and for around 85 per cent of the total revenues of a hard discounter. This means that each percentage point share loss of conventional retailers to hard discounters reduces the aggregate national brands' market share by half a percentage point. In the United States, the effect is even stronger, as private-label share among conventional retailers is lower (20 per cent) and among hard discounters is higher (90 per cent). As a consequence, one percentage point share loss by conventional retailers reduces national brands' share by 0.7 percentage points. In monetary terms, that is $7 billion for the United States alone.

In summary, unless you are one of the few lucky ones who also sell at the hard discounter (we will look at this in Chapter 11), every percentage point loss in market share by conventional retailers to hard discounters reduces your market share. Seen from this perspective, there is a strong mutual interest for national brand manufacturers and conventional retailers to limit the growth of hard discounters.

Finally, one might think that better deals for retailers automatically result in lower profits for manufacturers, but this is not always the case. Manufacturers have opportunities to become more efficient when they can produce larger volumes and can negotiate better deals with their own suppliers. This reduces COGS for branded players as well as for private-label suppliers.

Managerial takeaways

Procurement costs constitute the bulk of the total costs of conventional retailers. As such, reducing these costs is the primary way to reduce the price gap with hard discounters. Any effort to extract more value from suppliers – through direct reduction in procurement costs, increased slotting allowances, and higher margins through greater efficiency or exclusivity arrangements – should recognize that the procurement market consists of two distinct parties: national brand manufacturers and private-label suppliers. If you do this well, you can save up to 5–10 per cent on the total procurement bill. How to do this? Use the following checklists.

Checklist

To reduce the procurement bill for national brands,
do the following:

☐ Scale up buying volumes by reducing number of brands and brand
SKUs – especially applicable in categories 1) where brands are weak,
and 2) that are of low importance to the retailer's positioning.
Estimated savings on brand bill for the category: 3–5 per cent.

☐ Increase slotting allowances – especially applicable in categories 1)
where brands are strong, and 2) that are of low importance to the
retailer's positioning. Estimated savings on brand bill for the category:
2–3 per cent.

☐ Intensify category management and appoint a category captain –
especially applicable in categories 1) where brands are strong, and 2)
that are of high importance to the retailer's positioning. Estimated
savings on brand bill for the category: 1–2 per cent.

☐ Forge exclusive relationships with national brands – especially
applicable in categories 1) where brands are weak, and 2) that are of
high importance to the retailer's positioning. Estimated savings on
brand bill for the category: 0–0.5 per cent.

☐ Combine forces with other retailers, either through M&A or by
leveraging the power of (international) buying groups. Estimated
savings on brand bill for the category: 2–4 per cent.

Checklist

To reduce the procurement bill for national brands, do the following:

☐ Rationalize the private-label assortment by removing slow-moving items and simplifying your entire store brand architecture. Estimated savings on private-label bill for the category: 1–2 per cent.

☐ Develop strategic relations with preferred suppliers – especially attractive for fresh foods. Estimated savings on brand bill for the category: 2–4 per cent.

☐ Combine forces with other retailers, either through M&A or by leveraging the power of (international) buying groups. Estimated savings on private-label bill for the category: 4–6 per cent.

Notes

1 www.distrifood.nl/branche-bedrijf/nieuws/2017/12/dick-boer-hadden-lidl-scherper-moeten-volgen-101114093, last accessed 14 February 2018.

2 Colruyt Annual Report 2016/17.

3 Murk, M, van Aalst, M, Bod, M, and Ruigendijk, P (2011) The financial performance of food suppliers from 2002–2009, EFMI Business School.

4 Sloot, L M, Fok, D, and Verhoef, P C (2006) The short- and long-term impact of an assortment reduction on category sales, *Journal of Marketing Research*, **43** (November), pp. 536–48.

5 Gooner, R A, Morgan, N A and Perreault, W D (2011) Is retail category management worth the effort (and does a category captain help or hinder)? *Journal of Marketing*, **75** (September), pp. 18–33. These authors report a correlation of .68 between category strategic importance and category management intensity.

6 Ibid.

7 Gielens, K, Gijsbrechts, E, and Dekimpe, M G (2014) Gains and losses of exclusivity in grocery retailing, *International Journal of Research in Marketing*, **31** (2), pp. 239–52.

8 www.aholddelhaize.com/media/2156/board_report_ahold.pdf, last accessed 5 March 2018.

9 www.lebensmittelzeitung.net/european-view/Buying-Groups-Agecore-Putting-Nestl-Under-Pressure-134122, last accessed 6 March 2018.

PART THREE
Brand manufacturer strategies versus hard discounters

Competition – creating winning brand propositions versus private labels

Hard discounters will always be able to beat manufacturer brands on price. But that is OK. Most consumers do not aim for the lowest price but, rather, purchase the brand that most closely fits their needs. While price factors into that decision, brands need to focus on developing a compelling value proposition for consumers to buy brands instead of the hard discounter's private label. This is a battle the brand manufacturer has to fight on multiple fronts. At the most fundamental level, you have to critically assess whether your company can support the current number of brands and whether it has the right set of brands moving forward. Brand portfolio renovation might be the first step you want to consider.

Next, for those brands that you retain, you need to ensure they offer better quality than their hard discounter competitors, and that the brands are supported by regular meaningful innovations. Without a clear superiority grounded in the core offering, it will be an uphill battle. But quality superiority and innovation are not enough; brands have to be supported by advertising in order to communicate the differences and sales promotions (in moderation) to retain customers. These are all proven brand-building activities that are actually even more relevant today than in the past because the hard discounters have upped their own game dramatically in the last two decades. Finally, firms should pioneer new business models to create new sales opportunities and improve margins.

Figure 9.1   Five imperatives for creating winning brand propositions versus hard discounter private label

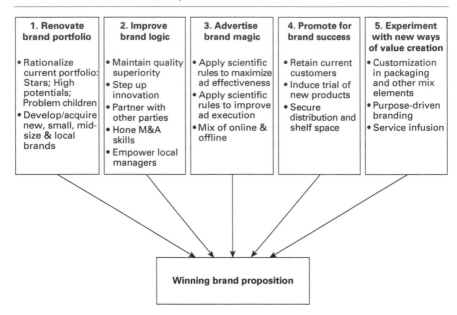

1. Renovate brand portfolio	2. Improve brand logic	3. Advertise brand magic	4. Promote for brand success	5. Experiment with new ways of value creation
• Rationalize current portfolio: Stars; High potentials; Problem children • Develop/acquire new, small, mid-size & local brands	• Maintain quality superiority • Step up innovation • Partner with other parties • Hone M&A skills • Empower local managers	• Apply scientific rules to maximize ad effectiveness • Apply scientific rules to improve ad execution • Mix of online & offline	• Retain current customers • Induce trial of new products • Secure distribution and shelf space	• Customization in packaging and other mix elements • Purpose-driven branding • Service infusion

Winning brand proposition

Building stronger brands against hard discounters' private labels therefore raises five imperatives (Figure 9.1):

1 Renovate the brand portfolio.

2 Improve quality and innovate to enhance the brand's rational logic.

3 Provide intensive advertising support to create brand magic.

4 Retain consumers with sales promotions.

5 Experiment with new ways of value creation.

We will take up each imperative in turn.

Brand portfolio renovation

Brand rationalization

The simple truth is that many CPG firms have too many brands. Roughly three-quarters of the Fortune 1000 consumer goods companies manage more than 100 brands each.[1] Yet, many of these firms generate 80–90 per cent of their profits from fewer than 20 per cent of their brands, while they lose money or barely break even on many of the other brands in their portfolio.

Perhaps that was workable when R&D and marketing costs were low and hard discounters were the ugly ducklings, but none of these conditions apply anymore. Firms find it increasingly difficult to manage such brand complexity, let alone to provide adequate marketing support for each brand in fierce competition with hard discounters.

Lack of marketing support is undermining brand differentiation in CPG markets. Research has shown that, on average, only 10 per cent of your current buyers think that your brand is different from other brands in the category.[2] Do the test yourself. Do you truly see meaningful differences between (regular) Chobani, Dannon, Fage, Siggi, Stonyfield, Yoplait, Maple Hill, Dreaming Cow, Liberté, Nancy's, and Mehadrin yogurt? Yet they were all offered by Kroger in 2017.

Given these facts, firms have started to rationalize their brand portfolio. Unilever was a trailblazer when it launched its 'Path to Growth' plan in 1999. Over a five-year period, Unilever reduced its portfolio of brands from 1,600 to some 450 so that the company could put more resources behind the remaining brands. Niall FitzGerald, Unilever's co-chairman at the time, explained the thinking: 'We weren't able to focus our innovation, our support – we were doing too many things.'[3] Unilever's operating margin increased from 11.1 per cent in 1999 to 15.7 per cent in 2003. In 2014, P&G initiated a programme to shed 116 of its 166 brands. In 2018, Nestlé's portfolio included over 2,000 brands, from global icons like Nescafé (instant coffee) to local favourites like Ninho (milk brand in Brazil). While that is still a large number, it is actually a quarter of the number of brands it marketed 20 years ago.

Yet, brand rationalization is a tricky undertaking. Traditional approaches like cutting the tail or discontinuing the lowest-share brands can introduce unintended consequences. By eliminating a low-volume brand, the manufacturer may inadvertently eliminate a brand that plays a unique strategic role in the portfolio. Or it might unknowingly drive up per-unit cost of other brands made on the same product line or with which they share raw materials.[4] Some local or smaller brands may have a loyal following. To help decide on which brands to prioritize and which to consider shedding, we recommend that management assign each brand to one of the following categories:

- *Stars*: carried by many retailers, cash-flow generator, high penetration, above average brand loyalty, clearly differentiated, high market share. Stars require continued investment in R&D and marketing to help them retain their position.

- *High Potentials*: caters to an unmet significant consumer need, captures growth in emerging trends (eg gluten-free, organic, local), reaches a new segment that is large and/or strongly growing, opens up new channels of distribution (eg online, hard discounters), has a clear identity. Ultimately, a High Potential needs to be turned into a Star. To assess this, ask the following questions: Can this be achieved in three years? How much investment in R&D and marketing is required? What do brand economics look like in that scenario? Develop a plan to achieve this. If three years is too short, how many years do you need? Is that acceptable? At the end of the day, you cannot build a company based on glittering future prospects that are always just beyond the horizon. Just ask your CFO.

- *Problem Children*: fall in neither of the above two categories. Use as benchmark that, for most firms, easily 50 per cent or more of their brands fall into this category. Examine brand economics. Can you develop a plan to turn brand performance around within three years? What are the brand's likely sales and profits under this scenario? How much money is saved by deleting the brand? Would deleting the brand have significant ramifications for procurement and production costs for Stars of High Potentials? Last but not least, do not be shy to shed Problem Children.

Adding new brands

Portfolio renovation should not end with brand rationalization. Cutting old and nonperforming brands frees up resources to support existing ones and to launch new brands (in moderation). In CPG, and especially in food, there is a movement away from large and established brands towards smaller and local brands that are seen as more authentic. For an increasing number of consumers in the West, Big Food has become synonymous with artificial colours and flavours, pesticides, preservatives, high-fructose corn syrup, growth hormones, antibiotics and genetically modified organisms. Campbell Soup Co CEO Denise Morrison spoke for many executives when she said to *Fortune* magazine, 'We understand that increasing numbers of consumers are seeking authentic, genuine food experiences. And we know that they are sceptical of the ability of large, long-established food companies to deliver them.'[5]

Yet there is hope. Most people do not necessarily know the company behind the brand (unless the two bear the same name, like Campbell or Hershey's). So when we are talking about large food companies, we actually mean large brands. New brands – even if introduced by large companies – do not necessarily suffer from this legacy. Thus, one way forward for Big Food is to rely less on its established brands and to introduce new brands. These brands can be either developed organically or acquired, something we will look at later in this chapter.

The potential for new brands is probably greater in foods and beverages than in other CPG categories. However, there is definitely room for new brands in these categories as well. Brands like Dollar Shave Club and Harry's have upended the razor blade market. The household products brand Honest was launched by Jessica Alba in 2011 and is known for 'safe' products (eg chemical-free baby wipes). Honest's sales in 2017 surpassed $300 million.[6] And in the 2017 proxy fight between P&G and Trian Partners, Trian released a white paper 'Revitalize P&G Together' that emphasized the growth potential of 'new small, mid-size, and local brands'. It cited research by Kantar Worldpanel that local brands are growing twice as fast as their multinational counterparts.[7]

Improve brand logic

Maintain quality superiority

Historically, consumers preferred brands over hard discounters because of their assumed quality superiority. Unfortunately for many brands, over time, this quality superiority has all but disappeared. Figure 9.2 demonstrates this for colour laundry detergent brands in the Netherlands. We can see that only Ariel (called Tide in the United States) holds a (small) quality

Figure 9.2   Price and quality of colour laundry detergent brands in the Netherlands in 2015

NOTE Ariel and Dash are owned by Procter & Gamble, Omo and Robijn by Unilever, and Persil and Witte Reus by Henkel.
SOURCE Based on 2016 data from *Consumentengids*

edge over Aldi and Lidl, albeit one that consumers have to pay a steep price for. Per 10 washes, Ariel costs €4.13 versus €1.45 (Aldi) and €1.23 (Lidl). The other national brands, all owned by the global Big Three in laundry care (P&G, Unilever, Henkel), deliver lower quality. It seems that the only thing on which they excel is charging a higher price. Hardly a recipe for success.

This is not an isolated case. Table 9.1 presents the results for a number of other tests conducted by consumer organizations in Australia, Europe, and the

Table 9.1 Quality of hard discounter private labels versus leading national brands in 2014–2018

Category	Country	Hard discounter quality score (0–100)	National brand quality score (0–100)
Ice-cream cones	Netherlands	Lidl: 69 Aldi: 67	Cornetto (Unilever): 66
Milk chocolate	Australia	Aldi: 66	Lindt (Lindt & Sprüngli): 75 Green & Black's (Mondelez): 47
Hazelnut spread	Germany	Lidl: 60 Norma: 56 Aldi: 48	Nutella (Ferrero): 72 Gepa (Fair Trade): 64
Margarine	Germany	Aldi: 74 Lidl: 68 Plus: 44	Deli Reform (WR): 72 Rama (Unilever): 56 Flora (Unilever): 52 Sana (WR): 28
Bacon	US	Trader Joe's: 71	Oscar Mayer (Kraft Heinz): 74
Veggie frozen pizza	US	Trader Joe's: 62	California Pizza Kitchen: 64 Dr. Oetker (Oetker Group): 61 Newman's Own: 58 DiGiorno (Nestlé): 54 Freschetta (Schwan's Consumer Brands): 49
Plain Greek yogurt	US	Trader Joe's: 71	Fage (Fage): 85 Stonyfield (Danone): 76 Oikos (Danone): 72 Chobani (Chobani): 59
Diapers	Australia	Aldi: 88	Pampers (P&G): 91 Huggies (K-C): 84
Baby wipes	Germany	Lidl: 66 Aldi: 44	Pampers (P&G): 72

(continued)

Table 9.1   *(Continued)*

Category	Country	Hard discounter quality score (0–100)	National brand quality score (0–100)
Shampoo	Germany	Lidl: 72	Dove (Unilever):72 Garnier Fructis (L'Oréal): 70 Schwarzkopf (Henkel): 70 Pantene (P&G): 66 Nivea (Beiersdorf): 66
Facial cream (men)	Germany	Aldi: 64 Lidl: 64	L'Oréal: 66 Nivea (Beiersdorf): 66 Clarins: 64 Vichy (L'Oréal): 52
Sunscreen: spray	US	Trader Joe's: 100	Banana Boat (Edgewell): 96 Neutrogena (J&J): 82 Coppertone (Bayer): 64
Sunscreen: lotion – SP20	Germany	Aldi: 78 Lidl: 74	Nivea (Beiersdorf): 66 Clarins: 62 Garnier Ambre Solaire (L'Oréal): 58
Bathroom tissue	Netherlands	Aldi: 76 Lidl: 74	Edet (Essity): 79 Page (K-C): 74 Popla (K-C): 56
AA batteries	UK	Aldi: 74 Lidl: 63	Duracell (Berkshire Hathaway): 78 Energizer (Edgewell): 70 Panasonic: 58 Kodak: 42
Dish soap	Germany	Norma: 80 Aldi: 74 Lidl: 74 Penny: 60	Pril (Henkel): 84 Fairy (P&G): 82 Palmolive (C-P): 14
Laundry capsules & pods	UK	Lidl: 59	Ariel (P&G): 61 Persil (Unilever): 54 Surf (Unilever): 48
Laundry detergent HE	Australia	Aldi: 80	Omo (Unilever): 82 Cold Powder (C-P): 81 BioZet (Kao): 77 Drive (Unilever): 74

(continued)

Table 9.1 *(Continued)*

Category	Country	Hard discounter quality score (0–100)	National brand quality score (0–100)
Laundry detergent HE	US	Trader Joe's: 29	Tide (P&G): 82 Persil (Henkel): 82 Gain (P&G): 62 Arm & Hammer (Church & Dwight): 53 Woolite (R&B): 41
Dishwasher tablets	UK	Lidl: 77 Aldi: 72	Fairy (P&G): 79 Finish (RB): 56 Ecover (Ecover): 54
Dishwasher tablets	Australia	Aldi: 72	Ecover (Ecover): 74 Finish (RB): 68 Fairy (P&G): 60
Dishwasher detergent	US	Trader Joe's: 42	Cascade (P&G): 84 Finish (RB): 82 Sunlight (Sun): 76
Fabric conditioner	UK	Lidl: 64 Aldi: 53	Lenor (P&G): 74 Comfort (Unilever): 71 Fairy (P&G): 60
All-purpose household cleaner	Netherlands	Lidl: 82 Aldi: 62	Dettol (RB): 87 Ajax (C-P): 70

NOTE If there are multiple variants of the same (hard discounter or national) brand, we listed the highest-scoring variety. Not all national brands shown. The company is given in parentheses; C-P = Colgate-Palmolive, J&J = Johnson & Johnson, K-C = Kimberly-Clark, P&G = Procter & Gamble, RB = Reckitt Benckiser, WR = Walter Rau. German quality scores transformed from original scale. So 0–100 scale.
SOURCE Based on 2014–2018 data from *Consumer Reports* (US), *Choice* (Australia), *Which?* (UK), *Stiftung Warentest* (Germany), and *Consumentengids* (Netherlands)

United States comparing the objective quality of leading national brands with those of hard discounters. While national brands invariably charge a much higher price, it is remarkable that, in many categories, they do not enjoy an appreciable quality superiority. In many cases, there is at least one national brand that outperforms its hard discounter competitors, but other leading national brands frequently suffer a quality deficit. For example, Aldi's diapers are rated higher on quality than Kimberly-Clark's Huggies in Australia. Aldi and Lidl's bathroom tissue rates higher than Kimberly-Clark's Popla in the Netherlands, their dishwasher tablets rate higher than Reckitt Benckiser's

Finish in the UK, and their margarine rates higher than Unilever's Rama in Germany. Trader Joe's plain Greek yogurt scores higher than Chobani, the brand that virtually invented the category.

Taken together, this evidence suggests that, in Australia and Europe, the quality gap between leading national brands and hard discounters, especially Aldi and Lidl, has become worryingly small. The situation is more favourable in the United States. While Trader Joe's scores well in many food categories, its performance in household care suggests it is less reliable than brands. Take the laundry detergent category, where Trader Joe's private label scored only 29 versus 82 for P&G's Tide Plus Ultra and Henkel's Persil Pro Clean. However, neither Aldi nor Lidl were included in those tests, and Trader Joe's is focused on foods and beverages.

The appeal of national brands

In such an environment, where the quality gap has narrowed dramatically while national brands continue to be much more expensive, the question becomes, why don't even more people switch to buying the hard discounter private label? The answer is because brands continue to appeal to consumers for whom at least one of the following conditions apply:

1 *Store accessibility*: consumers who live far away from a hard discounter store. While over 90 per cent of German households are within a 10-minute drive of a hard discounter, distribution coverage is less intensive in other countries.

2 *Consumer ignorance*: consumers who are unaware of the true quality of the hard discounter brands, and instead perceive national brands to be of superior quality and value this difference enough to pay the price premium.

3 *Risk avoidance*: consumers who know that no individual hard discounter offers quality parity in all categories, and have neither the time nor interest to figure out in which categories it offers excellent quality. These consumers rely on buying a well-known national brand under the assumption that these brands are unlikely to provide bad quality, something that is generally true (see Table 9.1).

4 *Emotional benefit seekers*: consumers who derive emotional benefits from national brands (eg L'Oréal's 'Because I'm Worth It') beyond those available from hard discounter brands and see the resultant higher value worth the price premium. A relatively recent development is imbuing brands with a higher purpose – something we will discuss later in this chapter.

No room for complacency

At least one of these conditions will apply to many consumers, which puts national brands in a favourable position. Yet there is no room for complacency. As discussed in Chapters 4 and 5, hard discounters are opening new stores at a rapid pace in countries ranging from Australia, the UK and the United States, to Poland and Brazil, substantially increasing store accessibility.

Consumer ignorance declines steadily with the advent of social media and press stories highlighting the quality of hard discounter brands. An example is a 2011 article in Britain's *Daily Mail* with the headline, 'For hands that do dishes... choose ALDI washing up liquid: budget brand knocks Fairy [called Dawn in the United States] off top spot after 20 years.'[8] These and other articles convey the message that hard discounter brands are just as good as named brands. One thing that Aldi and Lidl need to do is to be included in product tests conducted by the United States' Consumers Union.

Moreover, although modern branding was pioneered by CPG companies like P&G and Unilever, national brands have steadily lost relevance to consumers in the West. Figure 9.3 shows the importance brands play in consumer purchase decisions (measured on a seven-point scale) in the United States and Europe, as well as the market share of hard discounters in 2016. A score

Figure 9.3   Importance of brands vs hard discounter share in the United States and Europe in 2016

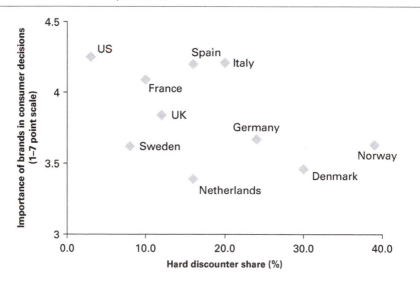

SOURCE Based on 2017 data from Planet Retail and Europanel, plus authors' own research

above four is evidence for continued brand importance, with a score above five providing strong evidence. The figure generates the following insights:

- In countries where brand importance is lower, hard discounters are more successful. (Sweden and the Netherlands are a bit of an exception, which is due to the overwhelming market power of one mainstream retailer: ICA and Albert Heijn, respectively.)

- Brand importance is highest in the United States and the Southern European countries, but even there, brand importance is barely above a four. Moreover, in Italy – where CPG brand importance is comparable with the United States – hard discounter share doubled in the decade 2007–2016. True, it took a brutal recession to accelerate the growth of market share of the hard discounters from 12 per cent in 2012 to over 20 per cent in 2017, but sooner or later, a recession will hit the United States again.

The solution is to invest more resources in quality improvement. To illustrate, we took a closer look at the detailed test results for ice-cream cones and colour laundry detergents as published in the Netherlands' *Consumentengids* in 2016 and 2015 respectively. This yielded remarkable insights. How is it possible that hard discounter ice-cream cones score higher on vanilla taste and contain more nuts than Unilever's Cornetto? Or, take the test results for colour laundry detergents. Two key quality attributes in this test were stain removal and (absence of) colour bleeding. How is it possible that Aldi and Lidl score higher on stain removal (both score 80) than Henkel's flagship brand Persil (70) or Unilever's Omo (66)? How can Aldi score more favourably on colour bleeding (64) than market leader Ariel (46)? When we discuss such test results with brand managers, they are often not aware of them or tend to disparage them as being inconsistent with their own lab studies. Perhaps. But consumer testing agencies around the world have built a solid reputation and are generally seen as more impartial than manufacturers' own lab tests.

Innovation

Continuous quality improvement is usually the result of gradual product improvements. While gradual product improvements are necessary, they are unlikely to lead to large increases in brand sales. For this, the firm needs to develop and introduce major new products, whose quality can be further improved over time until the next innovation is introduced. Major innovations use new technology, deliver new benefits or existing benefits in a significant new way, and, ideally, create entire new product categories. Tide created the synthetic detergent category, Coca-Cola the carbonated soft drinks category, Pampers stood at the base of the disposable diapers category, and Gillette pioneered the disposable razor blade category. Global sales in these categories run into countless billions of dollars every year.

Major innovations continue to be a key element in CPG brands' activities. Recent examples include Tide Pods (Ariel Pods in Europe), which created a new subcategory whose main benefit is the delivery system. It crossed the billion-dollar per year mark within five years of its introduction. Another example is in-wash scent booster Downy Unstopables (Lenor Unstoppables in Europe), which delivered a new benefit and sold $300 million in the first year alone. Food company Hormel (2017 revenues: $9.2 billion) saw an opportunity in solving a conundrum: US consumers love bacon, but food-service operators hate it because of the laborious clean-up after a breakfast shift and the danger of overcooking. Hormel spent five years on R&D creating a machine that produces fully cooked bacon that can be reheated on-site *and* has proper taste and texture. Branded 'Hormel Bacon 1', the new product eliminates the hassles of cooking raw bacon; frees up people, equipment and space; saves time from order to plate; and delivers the flavour, texture, and appearance of freshly-cooked premium bacon. It has been a success for institutional customers.[9]

These examples illustrate that major innovations really do move the needle, can rejuvenate the brand, and provide meaningful new benefits that consumers value – and are willing to pay for – to put the hard discounter at a distance.

New product activity by small companies

Innovations are not the prerogative of large CPG manufacturers with deep pockets. Turkish-American entrepreneur Hamdi Ulukaya launched Chobani Greek yogurt in 2007. This Greek-style yogurt is widely credited with starting a Greek yogurt craze in the United States. It surpassed $1 billion in annual sales within five years and, in 2016, became the United States' top-selling yogurt brand with sales close to $2 billion, surpassing General Mills' Yoplait. Indeed, small companies and startups are driving category growth in food and beverages, more often than not through their new products. According to Nielsen, 20,000 small companies (below the top 100) drove 49 per cent of all sales growth in food and beverages, with an annual growth rate of 6.3 per cent over the period 2011–2016, versus an annual growth rate of 0.1 per cent for the 25 largest manufacturers.

Take Halo Top, a privately held low-sugar, high-protein ice cream, which moved from a kitchen experiment in 2010 to become the best-selling ice cream at grocery stores in the United States in July 2017, surpassing Unilever's Ben & Jerry's and Nestlé's Häagen-Dazs, which had previously held that distinction for years.[10] Halo Top's innovation is two fold: it uses erythritol, a no-calorie sugar alcohol as a sweetening agent which adds texture and reduces the sugar count, and it has higher levels of protein compared to regular ice cream. These are undoubtedly important benefits to consumers. But why could Nestlé or Unilever, with their vastly larger R&D budgets and decades of consumer insights, not come up with this idea? It is not like inventing the iPhone. Why are small companies increasingly leading the innovation race?[11]

For one, they operate much faster, unencumbered by bureaucracy and vested interests. While it took P&G seven years from idea generation to the launch of Tide Pods, Chobani conceived, developed, and shipped a successful new offering in six weeks. Small firms are frequently 'owner-operated' and sweat the details, immersing themselves in consumers rather than relying on reports and subordinates to filter and organize the outside world's messiness. Big companies are taking note. In 2016, P&G's CEO David Taylor launched a drive to shed layers of bureaucracy and empower managers who are closer to their market than to Cincinnati.

Moreover, today's fragmented media have reduced the traditional scale-buying advantages of large firms. Smaller firms actively embrace the cost-effectiveness of digital media, unhindered by a legacy of traditional media that served existing firms so well in the past. (Recall that P&G invented the 'soap opera'.) Halo Top's 38-year-old CEO Justin Woolverton said to the *Wall Street Journal*, 'We are very, very differentiated from old-school brands. We understand social media out there because we are a younger company.'[12]

Being small has become something of a badge of honour in an era in which many consumers are increasingly distrustful of big brands, seeing them as remote and not speaking to their needs for natural, organic, and local. These small companies are also more concerned with being authentic and relevant. They actively embrace new business models, which disrupt the scale economics of large firms' integrated operations. They do not have the investments in production or distribution, so they are able to operate without the pressure to utilize or finance fixed assets.

Stepping up innovation activities by large CPG firms

Increase R&D

The development of the Gillette Fusion cost $700 million. While this may be an exceptional case, there is no denying that R&D is getting more expensive by the year. Table 9.2 details R&D expenditures by leading global CPG firms. We can see that, on average, R&D expenditures increased by

Table 9.2 R&D and advertising intensity of major consumer packaged goods firms in 2016

| Company (currency) | Primary category | R&D expenditures | | | | Advertising expenditures |
		2010 (millions)	2016 (millions)	Change 2010–2016 (%)	% of revenues 2016	% of revenues 2016
Colgate-Palmolive ($)	Household and personal care	256	289	13	1.9	10.6
Procter & Gamble ($)	Household and personal care	1950	1879	–4	2.9	11.1
Henkel (€)	Household and personal care	391	463	18	2.5	6.9
L'Oréal (€)	Personal care	665	850	28	3.3	30.1
Danone (€)	Food	209	333	59	1.5	3.4
Campbell Soup ($)	Food	123	124	1	1.6	4.8
General Mills ($)	Food	218	222	2	1.3	4.6
PepsiCo ($)	Food and beverages	488	760	56	1.2	4.0
Nestlé (CHF)	Food and beverages	1403	1736	24	1.9	5.2
Reckitt Benckiser (£)	Consumer products	125	149	19	1.5	17.3
Unilever (€)	Consumer products	928	978	5	1.9	15.5
Average across these firms		*6879*	*7934*	*15*	*2.0*	*10.3*

NOTE Numbers calculated across all firms based on constant exchange rates to eliminate distorting effect of currency fluctuations; Reckitt Benckiser advertising expenditures as % of revenues refer to 2014.
SOURCE Authors' calculations based on annual reports from Ad Age, S&P Capital IQ and Statista

15 per cent in the period 2010–2016. But if we take inflation in the same period into account (around 10 per cent in the western world), the real increase is only 5 per cent. And these firms are generally seen as being at the top of their game. An industry study conducted by Deloitte revealed that only 4 out of 10 CPG companies are investing more in product research than they were 10 years ago!

While we are strong proponents of increasing R&D intensity, it does not seem to lead to an increased outpouring of really innovative new products. What is wrong? The reason might be psychological, rooted in group thinking. If you join a team of R&D engineers, studying the same issues day after day, it unconsciously frames your mind to seek a solution within these boundaries. It nudges the mind towards incremental steps. But starting with a *tabula rasa* is required for truly innovative thinking. Involving outsiders may help.

Partner with other market parties

Spending more on R&D is one route. Another is to form networks and alliances with other parties. P&G launched its Connect + Develop programme, which helps P&G engage with innovators and patent holders to drive discontinuous, sustainable innovation and productivity. P&G has a global team dedicated to empowering Connect + Develop, searching for innovations, working with prospective partners and shepherding breakthrough innovations through the company and into market. Its website features current needs and what P&G looks for in its innovation partnerships.

France's Danone places big bets on the microbiome, the 100 trillion microorganisms that live in us – most of them in our gut. They do vital work for us: manufacturing vitamins and essential acids, building and stimulating the immune system, and regulating digestion. Danone is well placed to come up with pertinent functional foods for the microbiome. Yogurt, one of the best-known gut-friendly foods, is Danone's bestselling product globally (sold under the Dannon brand in the United States). Yet it neither can nor wants to do microbiota research all by itself. Therefore, it funds and collaborates with more than 40 academic or commercial partners in the field. Gérard Denariaz, director of strategic R&D partnerships at Danone, describing the company's scatter-the-seeds philosophy, said in *Fortune*, 'Who knows who will come up with the next breakthrough?' The rewards of a breakthrough innovation are huge – global sales of fortified/functional foods exceeded $300 billion in 2016.[13]

Become an acquisition machine

Increasingly, the brightest graduates want to work for a small company rather than for a large company with its bureaucratic procedures and lack of speed. Large CPG firms can follow the example of Big Pharma and specialize in honing their competencies in identifying and acquiring the 'right' companies. In 2014, General Mills bought Annie's Inc. for $820 million. Annie's is a maker of 'natural' and organic pastas, meals, and snacks. General Mills extended the brand to new products such as yogurt and soup. In 2016, France's Danone bought WhiteWave Foods Co. for over $10 billion. WhiteWave makes Silk nondairy (soybean, almond, etc) milk and Horizon Organic dairy. In 2017, Campbell Soup Co. bought Oregon-based Pacific Foods, an organic and healthy meal company for $700 million. This is just the tip of the iceberg.

Unilever has made a habit of acquiring hit consumer brands and scaling up their successes. One such example is Ben & Jerry's, which it acquired in 2000. Since its acquisition, the brand has managed to maintain its quirky and socially conscious edge while going on a growth binge. Its sales have roughly tripled over the past 15 years to $1.3 billion in 2016, making it the Anglo-Dutch conglomerate's fastest-growing ice-cream brand, and the fourth-largest ice-cream brand in the world. More recently, Unilever acquired several buzzy companies, including the Jennifer Aniston-approved Living Proof hair-care line; natural skin-care brand Ren; Seventh Generation, a maker of plant-based detergents and household cleaners; Dollar Shave Club; condiment maker Sir Kensington, known for its artisanal, non-GMO ketchups, mustards, and mayonnaises; Pukka Herbs, a British-based organic herbal tea maker; and Carver Korea, a large maker of toners and moisturizers, to buy into the growing global popularity of Korean skin-care routines and products.

Following this path to innovation poses two challenges. First, you need to find the balance between the efficiency that comes with large-scale production and distribution, and retaining and nurturing the entrepreneurial talent that prefers small companies. That is why Unilever went to great lengths to ensure that Ben & Jerry's remains a separate entity. When Hormel bought Applegate Farms in 2015, Applegate employees had serious concerns about what the new owners – referred to as 'Hormellians' – would demand. Applegate's social media team still spends a lot of time assuring customers that nothing has changed and that Applegate (largely) operates independently. Of course, too much independence means that the benefits of scaling the brand nationally, if not globally – which is the rationale for the acquisition price – may not be realized.

This leads to the second challenge. The worth of the acquired company is critically dependent on its potential for growth. The danger, of course, is that the established CPG firm overpays. Unilever paid $326 million for Ben & Jerry's, which turned out to be a bargain. Yet its acquisition of nutritional supplement Slim-Fast on the same day for $2.6 billion was a failure. The business was hit by the subsequent success of the Atkins diet, causing double-digit growth to disappear. Slim-Fast was sold in 2014. Financial terms were not disclosed, but since Unilever wrote off nearly half the acquisition value in 2005, the loss had to be substantial. What about Hormel, paying $774 million for Applegate, more than twice its $340 million in sales? Or the acquisition of Seventh Generation for a ratio of 3.5 to 1, let alone Dollar Shave Club's whopping 5 to 1? Only time will tell whether these investments are worth the money.

Minority investments

Realizing the challenges with full ownership, several major CPG companies, including Kellogg Co., General Mills, Campbell Soup Co., and Tyson Foods, are trying out a middle path. They have started venture capital funds to invest in startups, betting that younger companies can generate a healthy return on investment and teach the big companies to be more entrepreneurial and innovative. For example, in January 2017, General Mills' venture capital fund, 301 Inc., invested $6 million in Rhythm Superfoods, maker of 'zesty nacho' kale chips. According to Rhythm Superfoods Chief Executive Scott Jensen, many emerging brands are more open to a minority investment than a full acquisition. Some have heard cautionary tales of startups that slipped after teaming with big food companies, such as what happened when all-natural cereal maker Kashi was bought by Kellogg's in 2000. A few years into its ownership, corporate headquarters started to exert more control over planning and product approval. Kellogg's merged Kashi with its broader operations, and the once-ahead-of-the-curve brand began falling behind on innovation, according to former Kashi employees interviewed by the *Wall Street Journal*.[14] Kashi was also hit by a scandal. The USDA found that its products contained genetically modified soy, and that certain grains contained pesticides that are known carcinogens and hormone disruptors. Kellogg's response was seen by many as less than forthcoming. It even blamed the USDA for not regulating the term 'natural'.[15] Not surprisingly, Kashi's market share in the breakfast cereals market declined from 3.4 per cent in 2013 to 2.3 per cent in 2016.

So, what is in it for the entrepreneurs? Involvement with an established firm gives the startup validation with grocery store buyers. Moreover, deep production knowledge possessed by the large companies is a plus. Rhythm Superfoods CEO Scott Jensen said that his kale chip company benefited from the food giant's array of specialists, such as an engineer who works only on bagging machines. However, General Mills kept itself at a distance – it was not telling Rhythm Superfoods how to run their business. This model seems to work. According to Jensen, 'Now that other people can see that, I have a lot of people who come to me and say, "Can you introduce me to them?"'[16]

Advertising

Advertising remains indispensable for communicating the brand's functional benefits and for creating brand imagery. While hard discounters do advertise, their business model does not allow them to provide the level of advertising support CPG brands can muster. The advertising support for national brands is indeed enormous. Table 9.2 shows that leading CPG firms spend five times as much on advertising than on R&D. The 2016 top 100 largest advertisers in the world includes 26 CPG firms, with them spending, in total, $76.4 billion that year on advertising.

But given the increase in market share of private labels in general, and the rise of discounters in particular, one might wonder whether this is money well spent. A century ago, John Wanamaker – one of the founding fathers of marketing – famously said, 'Half the money I spend on advertising is wasted; the trouble is I don't know which half.' Fifty per cent wastage might actually be too optimistic. A study of TV ads run in Australia found that the average ad recognition among people that had watched the programme during which the ad was played was barely 40 per cent. And of that 40 per cent, a mere 40 per cent were able to correctly identify the brand that was advertised. Eighty-four per cent was wasted![17]

What can be done to increase advertising effectiveness? Here are some guidelines for CPG managers.[18]

Advertising effectiveness

- Set your priorities right. In general, do not expect a strong impact on sales. For CPG brands, a 1 per cent increase in brand advertising expenditure increases brand sales by 0.05–0.10 per cent. Why is that? Because everybody advertises and competitive effects largely cancel each other out. Advertising's main effect is to prevent what (without advertising) would otherwise be a gradual decline in sales. So, advertising causes sales even if sales are flat.

- Advertising is highly synergistic with innovation. Advertising for new products is five times more effective than advertising for existing products.

- Advertising has important indirect effects. Heavy advertising increases the perceived quality gap with private labels, decreases consumers' price sensitivity, and increases their willingness to pay a price premium. It creates brand imagery that is difficult for hard discounters to copy.

- Advertising clutter diminishes the effect of one's own advertising by 50 per cent. Smaller brands, especially, should avoid going head-to-head with competitors when scheduling their advertising. Focus on media and markets where there is less advertising from competing (larger) brands.

Advertising execution

- Much advertising money is wasted because viewers cannot recall the brand that was advertised or they think it was for a competitor. Prominently mentioning/showing the brand and its packaging is crucial. Show the product in use. Although this seems obvious, many ads fall short on this.

- Novelty in message, media, and creative content is more likely to lead to an increase in sales than spending more money on existing ads. But beware! Do not confuse novelty in execution with inconsistency in message. Stick to the same brand values, but vary execution format.

- Message effectiveness increases if you combine an emotional appeal with a reason to believe. Use of an emotional appeal grabs consumers' attention, breaks through the clutter, and makes the ad more memorable. Linking it to a functional attribute increases credibility and taps into the primary reasons why most consumers purchase the product, viz, performance, taste, purity, and other functional attributes.

- Comparative ads generate 22 per cent more purchases than non-comparative ads. The effect is strongest for new brands and leader-comparison brands.

Online versus offline

- Online advertising is more successful at increasing loyalty and purchase volume among existing buyers, while offline advertising is more effective in attracting new buyers.

- Strong offline TV and print advertising increases traffic to brand websites by up to 20 per cent.

- A strategy that uses both online and offline media yields, on average, 50 per cent more 'bang for the advertising buck' than an online-only strategy. Conversely, the combination of TV and digital advertising can increase brand recall by 33 per cent and message recall by 45 per cent compared to TV ads alone.

Connecting with millennials: Knorr's 'Love at First Taste' campaign

Many millennials are passionate about food.[19] Some 63 per cent consider themselves foodies versus 34 per cent for all ages. Yet this generation tends to be more distrustful of established food brands. This posed a problem for Knorr (known as Continental in Australia), Unilever's biggest brand, with 2016 sales exceeding US $3 billion. It is a leading seller of bouillon cubes, soups, and sauces. The biggest creative challenge Knorr faced in connecting with millennials was in finding a highly engaging topic on which Knorr had credibility. Knorr had long been obsessed with flavour and interviews with millennials around the world taught Knorr that, to them, flavour was not just taste but also had emotional connotations. Flavour preferences had become some of the most common descriptors used online by millennials to characterize themselves and others. Knorr further noticed that this behaviour was especially prevalent on the dating platforms frequented by millennials. Combining these insights led to the creative idea of 'Love at First Taste'. The ensuing campaign had three objectives:

- Get people talking about Knorr: achieve 1 billion free media impressions globally.

- Make an emotional connection with millennials: help people recognize the emotion of flavour in order to make Knorr's functional product strengths matter to a new generation.

- Jump-start growth in Knorr's brand equity measures, including differentiation, recommendation, and purchase intent.

To achieve these objectives, Knorr developed the Flavour Profiler and a three-minute content film, 'Love at First Taste', based on a real, unscripted social experiment. Based on their flavour profiles, Knorr paired up single strangers over a table of their favourite flavours and served them foods based on their shared tastes. Knorr asked them to feed each other and captured the spontaneity and awkwardness of what happened while the cameras were rolling.

To generate impressions beyond the paid-media budget, Knorr used a multipronged approach. It created initial buzz via influencers; launched the content via social media (eg using YouTube); drove click-throughs, shares and comments via Facebook, Twitter, and Snapchat; and ran content partnerships with Playbuzz and Tastemade to create promoted recipe videos in social media.

The campaign was launched in 2016 and resulted in 2.2 billion impressions, of which 1.6 billion were free (ie earned through voluntary engagement, reporting, and sharing). Furthermore, Knorr was able to establish a stronger emotional connection with millennials, measured by brand appeal, favourability, and agreement with 'my sort of brand', all of which increased by 7–10 per cent. Third, Knorr's scores on the brand equity measures improved by 5–7 per cent. This also showed up in the value of the Knorr brand name, which increased from $1.5 billion in 2016 to $2.0 billion in 2018, according to *Brand Finance*.[20] Finally, Knorr's global market share increased 1.4 per cent.

Use sales promotions – in moderation

Results-oriented managers often justify their use of sales promotions by pointing out their immediate, tangible and, usually, substantial effect on sales. The average price promotion elasticity is -3.6, meaning that a 10 per cent price discount leads to a 36 per cent increase in unit sales. Brand switching (including from private labels) accounts, on average, for around 30 per cent of the sales bump, forward buying (stockpiling) accounts for 40 per cent, store switching (buying your favourite brand at another store where it is on promotion) accounts for 25 per cent, and increase in consumption by brand buyers for 5 per cent. So, only 35 per cent of the sales promotion bump is actually an increase in brand sales. Moreover, even that bump is ephemeral.[21] After a promotion has run its course, customers quickly return to their old buying patterns and sales drop back to normal levels. The (temporary) category expansion effect of 40 per cent represents existing brand customers stockpiling – but these are now bought for a lower price than these people would otherwise have paid.

Over time, frequent promotions 'teach' brand loyals to lie in wait for the next promotion and stock up. Who these days still purchases a 12-pack of

Coca-Cola for $6.99? Further, you direct the consumer to attend to price information – a battle no brand can win – rather than to brand quality or brand values. Over time, this generates a price promotion cascade from loyal brand buyer to promotion buyer to hard discounter buyer. For example, in Germany, in the heavily promoted laundry detergent category, over a three-year period, 23 per cent of loyal brand buyers switched to a lie-in-wait buying mode, while 15 per cent of the lie-in-wait brand buyers switched to hard discounters. To add to the woes, despite the large immediate sales spike, promotions seldom pay for themselves because they directly eat into the contribution margin.

So, why promote at all? Price promotions have a role to play in attracting new or occasional customers to your brand, albeit that they do not increase the likelihood of repeat purchase (since the long-term effect of price promotions is essentially zero). However, they bind existing customers to your brand. The reality is that your competitors promote, so if you do nothing, you will lose customers. Moreover, price promotions are effective to clear out unwanted inventory quickly to make room for an improved version. Finally, if you need to meet your sales volume target and have run out of other ideas to stimulate brand sales, running a price promotion will solve your problem – at least for this quarter. These are all essentially defensive reasons. Promotions play two more offensive, brand-building roles.

First, price promotions have longer-lasting effects when done in combination with a new product introduction. Our research has shown that the likelihood that a retailer will adopt your new product is strongly affected by the extent of promotional support you offer. Furthermore, in the crucial first year after adoption by the retailer, price promotion intensity, as well as feature and display promotions, are key factors in determining sales volume. This is because consumer awareness for your new CPG product is lower and many potential customers are uncertain about its benefits. Offering price promotion provides an effective inducement to give it a try. If consumers like what they get, repeat sales follow.[22]

A second brand-building role played by sales promotions concerns the distribution channel. Retailers like price promotions because they help them project a favourable price image (recall that promotions are one of the components of the store choice model discussed in Chapter 7), and attract customers to the store who may buy many other items at the same time. Seen from this perspective, price promotions can be regarded as a legitimate part of distribution costs, necessary to maintain good relationships with your retail customers. We have frequently heard this argument, and it is often a valid one. However, we have rarely seen formal, quantified evidence that relationships are better, and more importantly, that the monetary benefits of better relationships exceed lost profit.

Experiment with new ways of value creation

Customization

Packaging is a key element of winning at the first moment of truth: the point of sale. It communicates the product's benefits and drives purchase. In recent years, some brands have started to experiment with personalized packaging. Coca-Cola showed the potential of personalized packaging with its highly successful 'Share a Coke' campaign, which began in 2011 in Australia. It involved digital printers putting people's first names on millions of bottles and cans. The campaign tapped into self-expression and individual storytelling, and deepened the connection between the famous brand and millennials. It was launched in the United States in the summer of 2014. Coke took the 250 most popular first names for teens and millennials and slapped them on the front of 20-ounce bottles. In addition, the company printed out more than 1 million personalized 7.5-ounce cans across the United States at roving kiosks where more than 100,000 names were available. The campaign's website also let visitors type names to make 'virtual' Coke bottles that they could share on social media; more than 6 million bottles have been created. This new initiative was credited with increasing the price paid for Coca-Cola by 2.1 per cent. It also led to a (temporary) increase in sales volume of 0.4 per cent for the 12 weeks ending August 2014 amidst a general decline in consumption fuelled by ever-increasing health concerns.[23]

Other CPG companies have also started experimenting with personalized packaging using digital printing technology. A 400g bag of Oreo cookies retails for $1.99 in the United States, but consumers are willing to pay $10 for the same bag of cookies in fancy wrapping and a customized message. Valerie Moens of Mondelez said to the *Financial Times*, 'Once people arrived at the Oreo website, purchase conversion was three times higher than the industry's average.'[24] Customized jars of Nutella became a top-selling item for Christmas in Australia, despite their hefty price of AU $12.95.

While it is likely that the price premiums paid for personalized packaging will decrease in the future as they become more common, it will be a way to differentiate your products from the standardized offering of hard discounters. Moreover, it increases your brand's relevance for the new generation of consumers.

Customization can be extended beyond packaging to other elements of the marketing mix. For example, Coca-Cola Freestyle is a touch-screen soda fountain featuring over 150 different Coca-Cola drink products, as well as custom flavours. The machine allows users to select from mixtures of flavours of Coca-Cola branded products which are then individually dispensed.[25]

Purpose-driven branding

Purpose-driven branding is the process of trying to be relevant and different based on participation in a meaningful purpose that can better our world or our community. In its simplest form, purpose-driven branding provides people with a chance to help change the world for the better. Today's consumers, and especially millennials, are attracted to brands that serve a higher purpose, over and above delivering good quality. Take Tony's Chocolonely, a Dutch confectionery company focused on fair-trade chocolate, which strongly opposes child labour by partnering with trading companies in Ghana and Côte d'Ivoire to buy cocoa beans directly from the farmers, providing them with a fair price for their product and combating exploitation. The message is printed on the inner side of the wrapper. In the period 2009–2016, its revenues grew from €1.1 million to €46 million. It is now the market leader in chocolate bars in the Netherlands, leaving local darling Verkade and global giant Milka behind. In 2017, it was also sold at Whole Foods in the United States.[26]

According to Jan Zijderveld, President of Unilever Europe, cut-throat promotions have devalued CPG brands across Europe, but brands that have purpose can inject value into a business. In 2016, 'purpose-driven brands' accounted for 60 per cent of sales growth, expanding at twice the rate of other brands across Unilever's portfolio. Dove is one such example. Unilever's global research found that only 2 per cent of women considered themselves beautiful. In response, its personal care brand Dove chose to fight distorted views of female beauty. Unilever promotes Dove's 'Real Beauty' with print advertisements, billboards, and TV ads. Its positioning and use of real women who do not look like Gigi Hadid has set itself apart in its industry. It also yielded strong dividends. Dove's brand value stood at $6.0 billion in 2018, up 4 per cent from the previous year, making it the eighth-most-valuable personal care brand in the world, according to brand consultancy Kantar Millward Brown.[27]

Service infusion

Many leading manufacturers are adding services to their existing products. Why? Because tangible goods are more easily copied than intangible services. Experience from companies ranging from GE to Caterpillar has shown that service infusion makes the brand's value proposition more unique and valuable to customers.[28] CPG firms are starting to experiment with service infusion, too. Germany's Henkel aims to derive a greater share of its earnings from providing services to customers rather than selling products. Henkel's CEO Hans Van Bylen explained, 'If you look at automobiles, the product is moving from the automobile to mobility. We also see this in our business, and we want to expand our product with a more complete service offering.'[29] Henkel has started Persil Service in Germany, which collects laundry from customers before cleaning and returning it. P&G is doing something similar, Tide Spin, in the United States. Customers can use a smartphone app to order laundry pickup and delivery from Tide-branded couriers. The service targets younger people in dense cities where apartments often come without washers or dryers. In 2018, it charged $1.59 per pound for wash-and-fold laundry service. Its couriers also pick up items to be dry cleaned at Tide-branded locations.[30]

Large packaged food companies are under pressure from the increasing popularity of meal kit companies, which ship parcels of ingredients and recipes to consumers who do not have the time or inspiration to create their own dinners. Meal kit revenues stood at $2.2 billion in 2017, with one out of four US people having purchased a meal kit in the past year. The predicted annual growth rate in revenues will be 25–30 per cent over the next half-decade, according to food consultancy Pentallect.[31] Meal kits are eating into sales of brands. For example, sales of ConAgra Foods at the grocery retailers that generate about 85 per cent of its sales declined for three consecutive years. In response, in 2016 it started to sell meal kits in partnership with Ahold Delhaize's online retailer Peapod. It sells kits to make dishes such as buffalo chicken quinoa and zucchini noodle primavera, and, of course, the kits contain ConAgra branded products such as Hunt's canned tomatoes. ConAgra is not the only one. Hershey partnered with online meal kit retailer Chef'd to offer co-branded dessert meal kits, and Tyson Foods launched its kits through AmazonFresh, working its chicken and beef into tacos, stews, and roasts.

In 2017, Campbell Soup Co. invested $10 million in Chef'd in an effort to learn from its e-commerce capabilities. Under the terms of the partnership,

Chef'd will help with infrastructure and distribution of meal solutions through the Campbell's Kitchen site. Denise Morrison, Campbell's CEO, said in a statement, 'The [e-commerce] movement is irrevocable and irreversible. In the future, shopping for and preparing meals will be flexible, fully automated and even anticipatory. Chef'd will help Campbell connect with our consumers where they are today, and, more importantly, where they're headed.'[32]

That same year, Nestlé bought a stake in the startup Freshly, a US subscription meal company that offers rotating menus, including options that are gluten-free, high protein, low carbohydrate, and vegetarian. In addition to broadening Nestlé's menu of products, the stake in Freshly provides direct access to customer data – a sought-after asset for CPG companies because it may allow them to sell in a more targeted fashion. Nestlé US Chief Executive Paul Grimwood explained, 'Nestlé will gain visibility into Freshly's advanced analytics and its highly effective distribution network, and Freshly will benefit from our R&D, nutrition and sourcing expertise.'[33]

It remains to be seen which meal kit initiatives will succeed. The Hershey partnership was panned in 2016 by Whitney Filloon, senior reporter with Eater.com. She wrote:

> The amount of energy and resources consumed by someone measuring out ingredients that the vast majority of Americans already have in their kitchens… is, frankly, grotesque… I don't need this, you don't need this, nobody needs this… Just don't let a desire for fresh, warm baked goods with a minimum of effort lure you into the overpriced insanity that is these 'dessert meal kits'.[34]

Yet Hershey and other branded food companies may not have a choice. Meal kits will continue to cut into brand sales. One of the authors of this book is an example; in the past, he and his wife bought all their foodstuffs at the local supermarket, but nowadays, almost all their in-home dinners come from meal kits.

When national brands win: hair care

Hair care is a category where hard discounters find it very difficult to gain a foothold despite the large price difference.[35] What makes it so difficult to break into this category? A lot has to do with effective brand strategies:

- *High innovation rate*. New products launched within one year make up more than 4 per cent of same-year total category sales. Launches are big (generally millions of dollars in sales) and require significant investment, which makes it more difficult for hard discounters to compete.

- *High product differentiation.* Manufacturers have developed products to serve a wide array of needs, including anti-dandruff, colour protection, and damage repair, among others. The degree of real and perceived differentiation is high.

- *Strong advertising support.* Brand manufacturers spend over $7 billion on advertising personal care products annually, creating the illusion that only their brand gives the elusive shine and volume that makes the user irresistible. Brand manufacturers' investments in innovation and advertising have created strong brand preferences and loyalty among consumers.

- *Heavy promotional activity.* Hair-care products are often heavily promoted, lowering the price differential between national brands and hard discounter products, which appeals to smart shoppers.

- *High brand relevance.* Since hair is very important to the vast majority of consumers, the higher price tag for brands is less of a barrier and actually often acts as quality indicator. Consumers associate considerable performance risk (who wants to have dandruff or go bald?) and emotional benefits (eg Pantene's slogan, 'Hair so healthy you shine') with the category, favouring brands.

The result? Half of the 10 most valuable personal care brands in 2018 have a strong presence in hair care (L'Oréal Paris, Nivea, Garnier, Dove, and Pantene).[36] Even in Germany, national brands reign supreme. The combined market share of hard discounters' private labels was less than 5 per cent in 2018. At the same time, leading brands like Pantene (P&G), Schwarzkopf (Henkel), Dove (Unilever), Nivea (Beiersdorf), and Garnier Fructis (L'Oréal) retail at a price premium of 200–350 per cent over Lidl's private-label shampoo, although Lidl actually trumps all these brands except Dove on quality (Table 9.1)!

Managerial takeaways

In a world where CPG brands are increasingly challenged by hard discounters, they need to vigorously pursue a set of activities to strengthen their value proposition. Building stronger brands raises five imperatives.

#1 Renovate your brand portfolio:

☐ Get ready to cut the number of current brands in your portfolio and direct all resources to the remaining set to win against hard discounters.

☐ Assign each brand to one of the following categories: Stars, High Potentials, and Problem Children.

☐ Problem Children are prime candidates for deletion unless you are able to address their problems within three years. As a benchmark, for most firms, at least 50 per cent of their brands are Problem Children.

☐ Add (with moderation) new, small, mid-size, and local brands to your portfolio to accommodate shifting preferences in the marketplace. Consider both organic development and M&A.

☐ After an incubation period of several years, classify the new brands as Stars, High Potentials, and Problem Children, and act accordingly. Not every new, hot, or local brand will succeed!

#2 Improve your brand's rational logic:

☐ Maintain quality superiority over hard discounters. This is slipping in category after category, and in various countries.

☐ Step up innovation activity. In the last decade, this has been falling rather than increasing in many companies.

☐ If you struggle to develop truly new products yourself, partner with others or hone your acquisition skills.

☐ Push responsibilities from headquarters to line managers who are closer to the market in order to achieve some of the entrepreneurial flexibility characteristic of small companies.

#3 Advertise brand magic:

☐ Understand how advertising really works. Its main effect on sales is to prevent what (without advertising) would otherwise be a gradual decline in sales. Indirect effects come through quality perceptions and willingness to pay a price premium. Collect evidence and present this to your CFO to make your case.

☐ Leverage the synergetic effect of advertising and innovation. Advertising for new products is five times more effective than advertising for existing products.

☐ Increase the novelty of your advertising – message, media, creative content – while remaining consistent with your brand values.

☐ Combine functional benefits with emotional payoff in your messages.

☐ Evaluate whether the comparative advertising format works for you, especially when you are a new brand.

☐ Resist the siren call of online only. Instead, leverage the synergistic effect of online and offline advertising – it yields 50 per cent more bang for the buck than using online advertising alone.

#4 Promote for brand success:

☐ Use sales promotion in moderation.

☐ Have the right expectations; the long-term effect of promotions on sales for existing products is negligible.

☐ Over-index promotional support for new products in your allocation of the sales promotion budget.

☐ Quantify the profitability implications of sales promotions. Which ones pay for themselves? Which do not?

☐ Quantify the effect of sales promotions on distribution. Do we spend the right amount on each retailer?

#5 Experiment with new ways of value creation:

☐ Are you actively exploring possibilities for customization of packaging, product, or other marketing elements?

☐ Do you use purpose branding to create a distinction from hard discounters?

☐ Are you experimenting with service infusion models?

Notes

1 condomcollective.com/2015/03/20/manage-your-portfolio-through-brand-rationalization-aka-how-to-kill-a-brand/, last accessed 1 June 2017.

2 Sharp, B (2010) *How Brands Grow*, Oxford University Press, Melbourne (Australia).

3 Jones, A (2004) Stumbling blocks on Unilever's Path to Grow, *Financial Times*, 22 August, p. 13.

4 Adams, C *et al* (2016) Simpler is (sometimes) better: managing complexity in consumer goods, McKinsey & Company, December.

5 Kowitt, B (2015) The war on Big Food, *Fortune*, 21 May; fortune.com/2015/05/21/the-war-on-big-food/, last accessed 5 January 2018.

6 Ng, S (2018) No longer a unicorn, *Wall Street Journal,* 5 January, p. B1.

7 www.revitalizepg.com/wp-content/uploads/2017/09/Trian-PG-White-Paper-9.6.17.pdf, last accessed 5 January 2018.

8 www.dailymail.co.uk/news/article-2027361/ALDI-budget-brand-Magnum-knocks-Fairy-spot-20-years.html, last accessed 5 January 2018.

9 Otterbourg, K (2016) Hormel's new recipe for success, *Fortune*, 15 June, pp. 198–209; www.hormelfoodservice.com/products/hormel-bacon-1-all-natural-1822-style-288-slice/, last accessed 5 January 2018.

10 Chaudhuri, S (2018) Outfoxed by small-batch upstarts, Unilever decides to imitate them, *Wall Street Journal*, 3 January, p. A1.

11 Based on Hall, T, Wengel, R and Yoon, E (2016) Nielsen breakthrough innovation report, The Nielsen Company; Gasparro, A (2017) Top food brands are losing the battle for shelf space, *Wall Street Journal*, 1 May, p. A1.

12 Chaudhuri, S (2018) Outfoxed by small-batch upstarts, Unilever decides to imitate them, *Wall Street Journal*, 3 January, p. A1.

13 Fry, E (2015) Danone's big bet on tiny bacteria, *Fortune*, 1 June.

14 Kashi case based on Kesmodel, D and Gasparro, A (2015) Inside Kellogg's effort to cash in on the health-food craze, *Wall Street Journal*, 31 August, p. A1.

15 ecosalon.com/behind-the-label-the-kashi-controversy/, last accessed 22 March 2018.

16 Gasparro, A (2017) Big food looks to startups for ideas, innovation, *Wall Street Journal*, 18 February, p. B1.

17 Sharp, B (2010) *How Brands Grow*, Oxford University Press, Melbourne, Australia.

18 Based on Hanssens, D M (2015) *Empirical Generalizations About Marketing Impact*, Marketing Science Institute, Cambridge, MA, 2nd edn; Knäble, S (2016) The importance of digital communication: what we have learnt from GfK crossmedia link, Presentation at the 35th Kronberg Meeting, GfK; Sethuraman, R, Tellis, G J and Briesch, R A (2011) How well does advertising work? Generalizations from meta-analysis of brand advertising elasticities, *Journal of Marketing Research*, 48 (June), pp. 457–71; Sharp, B (2010) *How Brands Grow*, Oxford University Press, Melbourne, Australia; Steenkamp, J B E M, van Heerde, H J and Geyskens, I (2010) What makes consumers willing to pay a price premium for national brands over private labels? *Journal of Marketing Research*, 47 (December), pp. 1011–24; Tellis, G J (2004) *Effective Advertising: Understanding when, how, and why advertising works*, Sage Publications, Thousand Oaks, CA.

19 Knorr case based on Morgan, R (2017) Case study: How Knorr's 'love at first taste' bonded the brand with millennials, *Campaign US*, 14 April. The content film (ad) can be found at www.youtube.com/watch?v=xwx7NnPQ44U; the food profiler at myflavour.knorr.com/en-US/profiler/#I3SQmlFkgSujYxQv.97, both last accessed 27 June 2017.

20 brandfinance.com/, last accessed 18 June 2018.

21 van Heerde, H J, Leeflang, P S H and Wittink, D R (2004) Decomposing the sales promotion bump with store data, *Marketing Science*, 23 (Summer), pp. 317–34.

22 Steenkamp, J B E M and Gielens, K (2003) Consumer and market drivers of the trial rate of new consumer products, *Journal of Consumer Research*, 30 (December), pp. 368–84; Lamey, L, Deleersnyder, B, Steenkamp, J B E M, and Dekimpe, M G (2018), New product success in the consumer packaged goods industry: A shopper marketing approach, *International Journal of Research in Marketing*, 35 (3).

23 Esterl, M (2014) 'Share a Coke' credited with a pop in sales, *Wall Street Journal*, 25 September, p. B1.

24 McGee, P (2016) Consumers courted amid push into personalised product packaging, *Financial Times*, 15 June, p. 13.

25 www.coca-colafreestyle.com/, last accessed 3 January 2018.

26 For more on Tony's Chocolonely: us.tonyschocolonely.com/, last accessed 5 February 2018.

27 Kantar Millward Brown (2018) Brand Z Top 100 Most Valuable Global Brands 2018.

28 Fang, E, Palmatier, R W and Steenkamp, J B E M (2008) Effect of service transition strategies on firm value, *Journal of Marketing*, 72 (September), pp. 1–14.

29 Shotter, J (2016) Henkel chief renews focus on growth, *Financial Times*, 31 October, p. 16.

30 Terlep, S (2016) P&G seeks to turn Tide by direct selling, *Wall Street Journal*, 20 July, p. B5.

31 Meyer, Z (2017) Meal kit dinners soar in popularity, *USA Today*, 3 July, p.1B.

32 Gee, K (2016) Big Food tests meal-kit startups, *Wall Street Journal*, 6 December, p. B1; Springer, J (2017) Campbell Soup, FreshDirect invest in online meal kit retailer, *Supermarket News*, May 24.

33 Chaudhuri, S (2017) Nestlé buys into delivered meals, *Wall Street Journal*, 21 June, p. B2.

34 www.eater.com/2016/9/7/12817942/dessert-meal-kits-nope, last accessed 22 March 2018.

35 This example is taken from The Nielsen Company (2014) The state of private label around the world.

36 Kantar MillwardBrown (2018) BrandZ Top 100 Most Valuable Global Brands 2018.

Cooperation – producing private labels for hard discounters

10

Private-label sales are growing in most Western countries, and hard discounters account for a large portion of that growth. As hard discounters manufacture only a small portion of their private-label products themselves, this offers opportunities for manufacturers to directly profit from hard discounter success. There are two alternative strategies for manufacturers to pursue with respect to supplying hard discounters:

- First, as a dedicated private-label producer. Here, the manufacturer only produces private labels, supplying to hard discounters as well as conventional retailers (few only supply hard discounters).

- Second, the manufacturer can pursue a dual strategy where it makes both its own brands and private labels for the hard discounter.

Dedicated private-label manufacturers

There are literally thousands of companies employing hundreds of thousands of people that focus exclusively on the production of private labels. They can be found in Europe, North America, Australasia, and elsewhere. Many of them belong to the Private Label Manufacturers Association (PLMA).[1] Founded in 1979, PLMA is the international trade organization dedicated to the promotion of private-label brands. With offices in Amsterdam and New York, it represents more than 3,500 suppliers worldwide, ranging from companies that specialize in private labels to those that produce private-label products in addition to their own brands. PLMA held its first trade show in the United States in 1980, in Europe in 1986, and in

Asia in 1994. Today, it provides services to member manufacturers in more than 70 countries. At the 2017 show in Chicago, more than 1,400 companies from over 50 countries exhibited their products, ranging from food and beverages to household and kitchen products, from health and beauty aids to general merchandise. In addition to three annual trade shows in Amsterdam, Chicago and Shanghai, PLMA also offers conferences, executive education programmes, market research, and trade reports.

The large majority of private-label manufacturers are small (less than $50 million in annual sales) and operate within one country only. More recently, a new breed of manufacturers has emerged. They are large (sales exceeding $500 million), technologically sophisticated, and operating internationally, if not intercontinentally. They represent the best and the brightest in private-label manufacturing. They include companies like McBride (household and personal care), Dalli Group (household and personal care), Homann (foods), Cascades Tissue Group (tissue), Global Tissue Group (tissue), Groupe Leclerc (cookies, snack bars, crackers), Perrigo (over-the-counter healthcare products and infant formula), and Refresco (soft drinks and fruit juices). But leading the pack in 2017 was TreeHouse Foods.

TreeHouse Foods – 'the biggest company you've never heard of'

US-based TreeHouse Foods Inc. was founded in 2005 as a spinoff from Dean Foods. It has grown through successive acquisitions, ranging from the private-label soup and infant-feeding business of Del Monte in 2006, to the Flagstone Foods snack business in 2014, and its biggest acquisition to date: ConAgra Foods' private brands business (known as Ralcorp) in 2015 for $2.7 billion. By 2010, the trade magazine *Food Processing* was already calling TreeHouse 'the biggest company you've never heard of'.[2] Yet, with more than 13,000 employees in over 50 plants across the United States and Canada, and sales of $6.3 billion in 2017, there are few households in the United States where its products cannot be found. It manufactures shelf-stable, refrigerated, frozen, and fresh products in five product groups: baked goods, beverages, condiments, meals, and snacks. In a sign of the times, it also offers natural, organic, and preservative-free ingredients in many categories. TreeHouse's goal is to be the leading supplier of private-label food and beverage products by providing the best balance of quality and cost to its retail customers. TreeHouse sells its products to more than 200 retail food customers in North America, including over 50 of the

75 largest non-convenience food retailers. However, in 2017, the top 10 customers accounted for approximately 61 per cent of TreeHouse's sales. The company is especially dependent on Walmart (accounting for 22.0 per cent of TreeHouse's sales in 2017) and Costco (10.3 per cent).[3]

TreeHouse is undertaking efforts to build a B2B brand, 'TreeHouse Brand', which is 'a promise to our customers that we will meet their needs and levels of service'. It has designed TreeHouse Brand as a pyramid, with cost, service levels, quality, and customer responsiveness as the base; customer insights, category management and new product development as the middle layer; culminating in a broad portfolio of products at the top of the pyramid. TreeHouse Brand is an innovative initiative. Too often, private-label manufacturers just bid on and fulfil orders. However, there is ample evidence that branding not only creates value for B2C companies, but also for B2B companies – companies where the customer is another firm – where the brand reduces purchase risk. Retailers, and especially hard discounters with greater emphasis on long-term relationships with a select set of suppliers, want a reliable partner, not only one that is cost-efficient. TreeHouse Brand is an attempt to guarantee this.

A recurring theme in TreeHouse Foods' strategy is the acquisition of private-label dual tracker businesses that have failed to generate adequate profitability. Yet that also carries significant risks. The acquisition of ConAgra's private brands business proved to be a real drag on TreeHouse's operational performance, even though TreeHouse bought it just for 54 per cent of the price ConAgra had paid for it a few years earlier. Integration of a business that was about as large in terms of revenues as the original TreeHouse company proved challenging, and the costs of servicing the additional debt (total debt exceeded $2.5 billion at the end of 2017) dragged down earnings. Its profitability was further hurt by stiff competition, intense promotional headwinds, a shift in demand from packaged foods to unprocessed products, additional investments in sales force, and escalated commodity and freight expenses.[4]

As a result, TreeHouse's financial performance deteriorated sharply. In hindsight, it appears that TreeHouse paid too much for ConAgra's private brands business. In 2015, TreeHouse had a healthy operating margin of 7.5 per cent on a gross margin of 20.1 per cent. This was achieved by keeping its operating expenses at 12.6 per cent, which was considerably below that of leading branded food manufacturers like Smucker, General Mills, Kellogg, or Hershey (Table 10.1). In 2016–2017, TreeHouse's financial performance deteriorated considerably. COGS increased from 79.9 per cent of revenues

Table 10.1 Financial performance of TreeHouse Foods vs leading branded food companies

Company	Year	Gross margin (%)	SG&A (%)	Other operating expenses (%)	Operating margin (%)
Smucker	2015	34.6	18.1	2.9	13.6
General Mills	2015	33.7	18.9	(2.2)	17.2
Kellogg	2015	38.8	24.6	0	14.2
Hershey	2015	45.8	26.7	5.0	14.1
TreeHouse	2015	20.1	10.6	2.0	7.5
TreeHouse	2016	18.2	12.1	7.7	(1.6)
TreeHouse	2017	17.2	11.2	12.5	(6.5)

NOTE The year 2015 was chosen for the comparison because it was the year before TreeHouse Foods acquired ConAgra's private brands business.
SOURCE Based on company annual reports

in 2015 to 82.8 per cent in 2017, reflecting among other things an increase in commodity costs. While this also hit brand manufacturers, as a private label manufacturer, TreeHouse is less able to increase prices. However, the real culprit was a sharp increase in 'other' (ie non-SG&A) operating expenses, from 2 per cent (2015) to 12.5 per cent (2017). ConAgra's private brands business did not achieve forecasted results and expectations for the future were lowered, leading to a goodwill and other intangible assets impairment of $352 million in 2016 (5.7 per cent of revenues) and $550 in 2017 (8.7 per cent of revenues). As a result, TreeHouse's operating margin declined from +7.5 per cent in 2015 to -6.5 per cent in 2017.

TreeHouse's experience shows that private-label manufacturing is a tough business even for strong companies. Given that gross margins for dedicated private-label suppliers are much lower than those for brand manufacturers, they cannot afford a major misstep as there is little 'fat' to cut.

McBride – the limitations of dedicated private-label manufacturing

McBride is one of Europe's leading dedicated suppliers of household and personal care products, manufacturing for 49 out of Europe's 50 largest hard discounters and conventional retailers in 2017. One element of McBride's strategy is to be extremely fast in copying new products launched by brand manufacturers. Retailers expect McBride to be able to supply innovations at about the same time as (or shortly after) they are introduced by brand manufacturers. This means that McBride's substantial R&D department is focused on spotting and forecasting the R&D activities of brand manufacturers. To achieve this, they visit trade shows, conduct desk research, and investigate patterns and trends in the marketplace.

A second component of McBride's strategy is unrivalled flexibility in production. Its production lines are set up around delivery of flexible products that can be requested at very short notice by the retailers. In effect, the machines are programmed to recognize a basic set of product attributes, eg height of product or size of base, and they are able to add flexibility to the process by changing the mould. Basically, the same machine can make many different-looking products, in rapid succession, at a cost-efficient price.

Third, McBride has strong operating excellence, including detailed knowledge of its production costs and production capabilities. This gives it an edge in internet bidding auctions, which are becoming more common. Internet bidding allows a group of selected manufacturers to bid for large contracts. These bids can be for individual retailers or for international consortia of retailers. Internet bidding takes place under heavy time pressures; the 'bidders' may have only one or two hours to submit a bid. Profitable internet bidding is only possible if the company has detailed knowledge of its cost structure and production capabilities on a day-to-day basis. If McBride wins the bid, it adapts the product (marginally) to the requirements of local markets and formats.

Fourth, McBride tries to build long-term relationships with retailers based on trust. To achieve this, account managers stay on the same account much longer than is usual for brand manufacturers. Moreover, compared to salespersons for a brand manufacturer, McBride salespersons have broader knowledge, including current technology, production, legislation, and the cost structure of their products.

Yet despite these formidable strengths, McBride suffers from a basic weakness which it shares with other private-label manufacturers – that consumer appreciation for hard discounter fancy brands (or store brands of conventional retailers, for that matter) is still not equal to those of national brands. If the price difference is small, consumers overwhelmingly prefer national brands. In the period 2010–2014, McBride faced tough economic challenges, most notably from increased promotional activities by national brands – which were concerned about the loss of market share in the financial and economic crisis that hit Europe at the time – and pressure from retailers to reduce prices in response to the competitive environment. Its revenues fell from £812 million in 2010 to £744 million in 2014, and operating profits more than halved, from £50 million to £22 million. The stock market reaction was even stronger. McBride's share price collapsed, from a high of 238 pence in 2010 to 80 pence by the end of 2014.

To right the capsizing ship, McBride launched a three-phase programme in 2015, named 'Repair, Prepare, Grow'. The core element of the Repair phase was substantial simplification of the firm's activities. The goal was to reduce operational complexity by exiting three-quarters of its customers and reducing the number of SKUs produced by at least 20 per cent. Costs were reduced by cutting overhead, closing plants, and closing the defined benefits pension plan in the UK. To increase revenues in the longer term (Prepare and Growth phases), more emphasis was given to Asia. By 2017, McBride's financials had improved substantially. While revenues in 2017 (£705 million) were lower (due to shedding many small customers), the operating margin doubled from 3.0 per cent in 2014 to 5.9 per cent in 2017.

McBride was nearly undone by the triple whammy of national brand pushback, retailers' pressure to cut prices in response to national brand actions, and McBride chasing volume (many small orders) over profits (focusing on a smaller set of larger accounts), which added complexity and hence costs. It illustrates that hard discounters might be more attractive customers than conventional retailers. While they are tough negotiators, with their limited set of SKUs and large market presence, they generate high volume with low complexity.

Crossing the Atlantic

Historically, private-label manufacturers have been more limited in their geographical reach than their national brand counterparts. Few had a truly continental reach, and hardly any players operated on both sides of the Atlantic. But this is changing. Germany's Krüger Group (2017 revenues: €1.8 billion) has become one of the world's largest private-label manufacturers of chocolate spreads and chocolate candy. It does business in over 100 countries, including the United States, where it uses its country of origin to gain credibility among hard-nosed purchase managers.[5] Ads in US trade journals proclaim that Krüger delivers 'German-engineered products made with exceptional European quality', and also proclaims, 'Our German quality, efficiency and innovation combine to make delicious private brand solutions!' Italian private-label manufacturers are often too small to cross the Atlantic on their own. They combined forces under the Italian Trade Agency to offer their services in the United States.[6]

Founded in 1887 in Michigan, Perrigo is the world's largest dedicated manufacturer of over-the-counter healthcare products and infant formula. Its revenues in 2017 were $5 billion, and its adjusted operating margin was a healthy 22 per cent. Perrigo had over 30 operating locations in the United States, Mexico, the UK, France, Germany, Austria, and Australia, and its products were sold in over 80 countries in North America, Europe, Australasia, China, India, Japan, and Brazil. Perrigo was somewhat unusual among dedicated private-label manufacturers in that it invests around 4 per cent of net sales in research and development and, as such, it launched over 100 new products in 2017.[7]

Among the most aggressive trans-Atlanticists is Netherlands-based Refresco (2017 sales: €2.3 billion, adjusted EBITDA: 9.4 per cent). Refresco is a leading supplier of juices and soft drinks for retailers and a contract manufacturer (co-packer) for national brands. Private-label manufacturing accounted for 63.7 per cent of production volume in 2017, while contract manufacturing accounted for the remaining 36.3 per cent. It has 32 facilities located in Europe and 27 facilities in North America. Refresco provides full service, from idea, to planning and sourcing, product development, production, warehousing, and transportation. Founded in 1999 with a management buyout of Menken Drinks and Refrescos de Sur Europa S.A., Refresco steadily increased revenues through a series of acquisitions in Europe and organic growth: 'buy & build strategy'.

In 2016, Refresco took its first step into North America by acquiring Whitlock Packaging – one of the largest independent contract manufacturers of liquid refreshment beverages in North America – for $129 million. In 2017, Refresco took another, much larger step by buying the bottling activities of Canada's Cott Corp. for $1.25 billion. Cott's bottling activities comprised a full portfolio of non-alcoholic beverages, focused on retailer brands and contract manufacturing. The deal added 29 production sites, 19 of them in the United States, making Refresco the largest bottler there. Refresco CEO Hans Roelofs explained:

> This transaction marks a step change in the industry that reinforces Refresco's position as a leading independent bottler for retailers and A-brands… This is a truly transformational deal, right at the heart of our buy & build strategy… The bottling activities of Cott are a perfect strategic fit to our current activities. With the acquisition we create nationwide coverage in the US.[8]

Compared to Europe, the US private-label manufacturing industry is more fragmented and is seen as technologically less sophisticated, making it more difficult for hard discounters to place large-scale orders of consistent quality.[9] Indeed, consumer test results reviewed in Chapter 9 indicate that the quality gap between national brands and hard discounter brands is generally larger in the United States than in Europe (or Australia), especially in personal care and household care. Aldi and Lidl attempt to address this problem by sourcing some private-label products from Europe. For example, in 2017, Lidl's dishwasher tablets were sourced from the Netherlands. However, this is not a viable long-term solution, if only due to transportation costs.

We believe that the demand for high-quality, innovative private-label products from hard discounters and from conventional retailers, who will need to emphasize their own private-label assortment to remain price competitive, will push the private-label manufacturing base to consolidate. This offers unique opportunities for other sophisticated manufacturers like McBride, Dalli, Homann, or COPACK (foods) to cross the Atlantic through acquisitions. This consolidation will allow private-label manufacturers to fill large orders and to invest in more sophisticated/flexible manufacturing technology.

However, as the TreeHouse example shows, private-label manufacturers should be conservative in their estimates of synergy effects and future sales. Build in a buffer for disappointing results, as your gross margin leaves little room for error. If the saying 'better safe than sorry' applies to any business situation, we believe it is in M&A involving dedicated private-label suppliers. Paying too much is much worse than foregoing the opportunity to acquire another company.

Key success factors and challenges for dedicated private-label manufacturers

Our research and these company examples reveal that successful dedicated private-label manufacturers possess multiple skills. Some of them are more important when supplying to hard discounters, others more important when supplying to conventional retailers. However, as few dedicated private-label manufacturers supply only to hard discounters, the successful ones need to have the entire set.

First and foremost is cost leadership. Cost leadership is absolutely crucial when dealing with hard discounters. Cost leadership not only requires superior production efficiencies and economies of scale, but also commensurate accounting procedures – more specifically activity-based costing.

Activity-based costing is a costing methodology that identifies activities in an organization and assigns the cost of each activity to all products and services according to the actual consumption by each. Companies rely on activity-based costing to better understand the true costs of manufacturing. It is an alternative to traditional accounting in which a business's indirect costs are allocated in proportion to an activity's direct costs. Activity-based costing requires that the firm breaks down all business activities into their discrete components, whose purpose and cost must be determined, and then assigned proportionally to every individual unit produced based on its consumption of those activities.

Let us illustrate the key principle with a simplified example. Suppose a company spends $10 million per year on equipment setup, and produces 20 million units, with volumes of 10 million, 5 million, 4 million, and 1 million private-label units for four retailers A, B, C, and D respectively. Under traditional accounting rules, it would allocate $0.50 setup costs to each private-label unit. Using activity-based costing, if equipment setup time is the same for all four orders, it allocates $2.5 million to each order, which results in a cost allocation of $0.25, $0.50, $0.625, and $2.50 per unit for retailers A, B, C, and D, respectively. This reveals dramatic differences in profitability, unless prices reflect these cost differences (which is unlikely). Now, suppose retailer B's order entails quite different packaging and product specifications which require equipment setup time that is twice as long as for the other orders. Then the cost picture changes further. Activity-based costing dictates that the firm should allocate twice as much equipment cost to this order ($4 million versus $2 million for the other orders). This leads to cost allocation of $0.20, $0.80, $0.50, and $2.00 per unit for retailers A, B, C, and D respectively. As one can see, retailer C is now more profitable per unit than retailer B (assuming equal prices).

A second key success factor is being a fast follower. Retailers want to be able to quickly put a private-label copycat innovation on their shelves. In the past, that was more important for conventional retailers, with their desire to match national brands in quality and innovation, but, increasingly, hard discounters are no longer satisfied with being late to the party. Being a fast follower requires market intelligence focused on identifying and copying innovations by the time they appear in the marketplace.

Third, the firm has to be able to produce large production runs of uniform quality. This is especially important for hard discounters because their small number of SKUs in any given category means the required volume for each SKU is vastly higher than that of almost any conventional retailer.

Fourth, the successful private-label manufacturer needs to be able to handle a high degree of production complexity and unsurpassed flexibility in its production lines. This is especially important for being successful with conventional retailers. Production runs for these customers are typically relatively small, and thus require the private-label supplier to quickly make frequent changes in machine settings in order to accommodate different product formulations, packaging shapes, and labels.

Fifth, internet auction skills are required. Many private-label contracts are awarded every year in internet auctions where you have to bid and counter-bid in a matter of hours. Yet, regularly, a contract won in an internet auction is loss-giving. Experience has shown that this happens if an auction participant is desperate for business, bases its bids on poor cost calculations (activity-based costing is required), or is caught up in the heat of the moment. Internet auction skills are less important when dealing with hard discounters because they work more often with long-term contracts, as we discussed in Chapter 2.

Dual trackers

In the United States alone, it has been estimated that over half the brand manufacturers are 'dual trackers', ie, they also engage in private-label production. More often than not, they are weaker brand players, of which there are many in the Western world. These manufacturers are typically secretive about it, lest it reduce the equity of their own brands. Whether or not to engage in private-label production for hard discounters is not a simple black-or-white decision, but requires a careful trade-off of the pros and cons. The potential pros are threefold: to generate additional profits, to gain strategic advantages, and to build relationships with hard discounters. For *opportunistic dual trackers,* generating additional profits is most pertinent, while all three pros come into play for *full dual trackers*.

Opportunistic dual trackers

The most common situation involves what we call opportunistic dual trackers. The brand manufacturer has some spare capacity, due to a temporary imbalance between supply and demand. A hard discount order can be used to fill the spare capacity. In this case, any contribution over and above the variable costs of production is incremental profit. Opportunistic dual trackers favour their own brand over private labels. These manufacturers are not willing to invest in a dedicated private-label commercial organization, as the supply of private labels is a matter of opportunity rather than a long-term business strategy. Under these conditions, opportunistic dual tracking makes excellent business sense. Indeed, there is a strong correlation between capacity utilization and operating margins. Filling your capacity with private-label production might be an important step to maximize the utilization of your production capacity.

However, the long run is nothing but the accumulation of many successive short runs and, when seen from that perspective, the enhanced profitability is often illusionary. Only when the company fills capacity on a purely *ad hoc*, strictly *occasional*, and *temporary* basis is it sound business practice to consider any income above variable costs as a contribution to profits. However, what starts as an ad-hoc opportunity often leads to repeat business. Then, full costs should be calculated, and the profitability picture usually changes dramatically. Just ask your CFO. If the firm has structural overcapacity, it should reduce capacity to bring it in line with demand for its brands.

Full dual trackers

For full dual trackers, private-label manufacturing is an integral component of their strategy. They proactively invest in production capacity to be able to meet the future requirements of private-label demand. Full dual trackers often have separate commercial organizations for their own brands and for private labels, with separate account and trade marketing teams – and sometimes even separate R&D teams – who have their own key performance indicators. The national brand and private label are of equal importance when it comes to allocating production capacity. An example of a full dual tracker in 2018 was Hormel Foods. Its commercial retail division offered private-label products in canned meat, dry mix desserts, sports nutrition and supplements, and other shelf-stable foods. Hormel positioned itself as a full-service supplier, with the promise, 'We are your trusted partner for the development, production, and distribution of private-label products that help retailers thrive.'[10]

Firms adopt a full dual tracking strategy to achieve all three pros mentioned earlier: additional profits, strategic advantages, and relationships with hard discounters.

Additional profits

Full dual trackers benefit from economies of scale, as the average cost per unit declines with production volume. If demand for the firm's own brand is not sufficient enough to generate maximum economies of scale, it can reduce its costs by engaging in private-label production. To illustrate, say the average cost of production per unit is $1 if the firm produces 1 million units, but falls to $0.75 if the firm produces 2 million units. If demand for the branded product is only 1 million, and the firm can produce an additional 1 million units for the hard discounter, it generates $250,000 in extra profits on its own branded sales. As long as the firm covers all costs involved in private-label production, firm profits are higher.

Strategic advantages

The brand manufacturer learns more about the needs and behaviours of hard discounter buyers, which, after all, constitute a rapidly growing segment in many categories and countries. Production for hard discounters may also be used as a competitive tool. You are better able to influence the positioning, product formulation, and packaging of the hard discounter's products, lowering the risk of cannibalization of your own brands. The firm can attempt to weaken a competitor by producing a product whose quality characteristics imitate those of a leading competitive brand.

A third strategic advantage is that supplying to hard discounters can buffer sales over time. Hard discounter sales tend to grow especially strong in hard times, exactly when brand sales are under pressure.[11] Producing both one's own brand and supplying hard discounters will dampen the effect of the business cycle on your firm's sales and improve overall capacity utilization.

Strengthen relationship with hard discounter

A third argument favouring full dual tracking is that it may strengthen the relationship with the hard discounter. But why should a dual tracker care about this, given the hard discounter's focus on private label? Because hard discounters are increasingly interested in adding a strictly limited set of national brands to their assortment, something we will discuss in detail in the next chapter. By making a pledge of private-label production for the hard discounter, a dual tracker effectively signals good faith and cooperative behaviour. The hope is that this may lead to discounter goodwill. But is this hope realistic? Research has shown that it actually is.

One study covered 37 food categories where Aldi chose to add one or more national brands to its assortment in Germany. The study found that in 44 per cent of the cases where the brand manufacturer engaged in private-label production for Aldi, Aldi had included the manufacturer's brand in its assortment. Examples include FrieslandCampina (with its brand Tuffi in the yogurt category), and the namesake brands of Rugen Fish (canned fish), Hochland (processed cheese), and Lambertz (cookies). If a brand manufacturer did not engage in private-label production for Aldi, the likelihood that Aldi would nevertheless include its brand in its assortment was only 14 per cent. In other words, the chances that your brand will be listed by Aldi increases threefold if you produce for Aldi as well.

The beneficial effects of private-label production for listing are not restricted to Aldi. The same study also investigated assortment decisions across 53 food, beverage, household, and personal care categories at the Spanish (soft) discounter Mercadona (with over 50 per cent private label). The likelihood that your brand is carried by Mercadona is twice as high if you also cooperate with them on private-label manufacturing.[12]

Essity – how to be a successful full dual tracker

Sweden's Essity is a global leader in what can be broadly described as 'paper' products. Its three business areas are personal care (37 per cent of revenues in 2017, including incontinence products, diapers, and feminine care), consumer tissue (39 per cent, eg toilet paper, kitchen towels), and professional hygiene (24 per cent, hygiene solutions for the B2B market). Its focus on paper products is no coincidence. Essity used to be part of SCA, a global paper giant. Historically, SCA's basis was the exploitation of Swedish forests the size of Switzerland to produce timber as well as wood pulp. In fact, SCA was Europe's biggest private owner of forests. Essity was spun off because the forestry business and the three business areas covered by Essity are very different. The return on capital of the forest division was only one third that of the other business.[13] By separating them, shareholder value was unlocked.

Essity's revenues in 2017 were $13.3 billion and its adjusted EBITDA was 12.3 per cent. Essity's products are sold under its own and retailers' brands, supplying Aldi, Lidl, and other retailers. Private-label manufacturing accounted for 17 per cent of Essity's revenues in 2017, including 34 per cent of revenues in consumer tissue and 10 per cent in personal care. Table 10.2 provides more information.[14]

For Essity to follow a dual-tracking approach made sound business sense given its production economics and the relatively modest strengths of its

Table 10.2   Essity's operations in 2017

Company/ business unit	Share of total revenues (%)	Share of private label in revenues (%)	Adjusted EBITDA (%)	Adjusted return on capital (%)
Essity	100	17	12.3	14.9
Consumer tissue	39	34	9.7	9.8
Personal care	37	10	14.6	20.5
Professional hygiene	24	0	15.0	19.7

SOURCE   Based on Essity's 2017 Annual and Sustainability Report

brands. Why? First, making pulp-based products – such as toilet paper, tissues, and diapers – requires huge investments in production lines with significant economies of scale. Large volumes are necessary to drive down costs. Second, the tissue category (the largest source of pulp demand, and Essity's largest division) is a category where brands are not particularly relevant to consumers. Third, Essity's own brands, such as Libero (diapers), Libresse (feminine care), Edet (kitchen towels), and Tempo (tissue), command less consumer equity than competing brands like Pampers, Always, Bounty, and Kleenex, respectively. The result is that, while Essity needs to sell a large production volume to achieve economies of scale in supply chain and manufacturing, it cannot do so under its own brands. In such a case, private-label manufacturing makes eminent sense. And its core competencies in large-scale production made it an attractive partner for hard discounters and other retailers.

Essity's challenge in aligning supply and demand is not unique. For example, Netherlands-based dairy cooperative Royal FrieslandCampina (2017 revenues: €12.1 billion) processes 1.2 million kilograms of (perishable) milk per hour supplied by its members (dairy farmers), 24 hours per day, 7 days per week. Relatively few consumers strongly prefer branded milk and, as a cooperative, FrieslandCampina does not have the financial resources to build strong brands in yogurt to rival those of Danone (called Dannon in the United States) or Nestlé. Not surprisingly, FrieslandCampina derives more than half of its revenues from private labels. Its vertically integrated structure can be challenging at times. In 2016, it experienced increased milk supply, which could only be sold under private label, resulting in reduced margins.

How had Essity been able to do both brand marketing and private-label production in the same company profitably and on an enduring basis? By keeping them apart. According to Hans Kisjes, Essity's Regional Director North/West Europe, the best organizational structure for a dual tracker is separate organizations. Essity had separate sales divisions for its own brands and for private labels, with separate account managers defending the interests of their main accounts. Essity served its retail brands with dedicated commercial teams with a high level of speed, flexibility and responsiveness. However, in this industry, efficiency and capacity utilization are make-or-break factors. Therefore, in the supply chain and other support functions, it combined branded and private-label activities.

Essity was more willing than most dual trackers to incorporate innovations in private labels. Kisjes explained:

> With regards to passing innovations to the retailers' brand, I think it's important that one should make clear agreements in advance about which and when innovations will become available for the retailers' brands. But the moment that an innovation is copied by competitors, I think you should not limit that innovation to your own labels. An advantage of being a dual tracker is you have a large R&D department and there are many ways to improve a product or packaging.

A failed dual tracker: how ConAgra lost over $2 billion in 30 months

Becoming a dual tracker might seem an easy thing on paper, but it is hard to make it work in practice. The ConAgra–Ralcorp case is an example of what might go wrong. In January 2013, ConAgra Foods, a major US food company with brands like Hunt's, Bertolli, Pam, and Swiss Miss, acquired Ralcorp Holdings for almost $5 billion. Ralcorp was a well-known private-label specialist whose big customers included Trader Joe's. It had strong positions in breakfast cereal, crackers, snack foods, chocolate, and peanut butter. Combined sales of ConAgra and Ralcorp were $18 billion. Private label accounted for a quarter of revenues. ConAgra Foods expected to use the ability to buy ingredients in greater bulk, along with its manufacturing and distribution capacity, to run the combined business more efficiently and boost margins.

However, it did not work out as planned. Within two years, its CEO, Gary Rodkin, resigned after ConAgra was the only food products maker in the S&P 500 whose share price had declined in the preceding 18 months, making it one of the industry's cheapest stocks. In November 2015, ConAgra announced it would sell Ralcorp to TreeHouse Foods for $2.7 billion, incurring a loss of almost $2.3 billion within 30 months. What went wrong?[15]

First, ConAgra overpaid. It offered a hefty 28 per cent premium after Ralcorp's stock already had a nice run-up. Second, it had to take on nearly $6 billion in new debt to finance the deal, which left it vulnerable to any deterioration in the underlying business. Third, the private-label business turned out to be more competitive than ConAgra had anticipated. Demand for private label in the categories supplied by ConAgra had grown in previous years, but this growth had drawn more competition, while at the same time, grocery chains were demanding higher quality without higher prices. Margins for private-label contracts declined and could no longer bear the relatively high overhead costs of the ConAgra conglomerate.

Last but not least, the much-touted synergies never materialized. Ralcorp proved difficult to integrate because the businesses are so different. There was little overlap in product lines. This was a virtue in that the store brands did not compete directly with ConAgra's brands, but limited synergies and the acquisition spread management's focus. ConAgra found out that building and maintaining brands with sophisticated marketing is a different ball game compared to collaborating as a private-label supplier with retailers continually insisting on increased quality at lower prices. Bidding for private-label contracts also requires different expertise than planning product promotions and vying for shelf space in grocery stores.

Key success factors and challenges for dual trackers

ConAgra's experience shows that becoming a successful dual tracker is anything but easy. Why is this the case? This can best be understood by examining the key success factors for brand manufacturers and dedicated private-label manufacturers. To be a successful brand manufacturer, you need to excel in brand management, continuously introduce innovations to keep the quality edge versus other brands and private labels, and develop deep insight into consumer trends. In short, the firm has to excel in R&D

and marketing, and the manager's mind must be focused on creating brand imagery.

On the other hand, as we have seen, dedicated private-label manufacturers have to excel on cost leadership, being able to account for every expense. They have to be a fast follower, flexible in production, able to handle high production complexity, and skilled in internet auctions. In short, these firms have to excel on production and have a mindset focused on cutting costs wherever possible without compromising quality.

A successful full dual tracker needs to be on a par with low-cost producers on price and quality, and on a par with brand manufacturers on supporting its brands with innovation and marketing. Otherwise, you get stuck in the middle, being competitive neither on cost nor on brand equity. The Essity example shows the challenges. Recall that its brands command lower equity than major competing brands in those same categories. Only in incontinence products does it have the leading consumer brand (Tena). Essity was the first to spot this important market opportunity (interestingly, private labels only accounted for 1 per cent of Essity's revenues in incontinence products in 2017). Essity's aim is to grow the branded share of total sales in total revenues.[16] This makes sense. Table 10.2 shows that EBITDA is lower, the higher the private-label share in a business unit's revenues. To grow the branded share, Essity focuses on innovation. In 2017 alone, it launched seven innovations in consumer tissue, including a moist toilet paper under the Lotus and Tempo brands, among others. A new Tempo handkerchief was also launched.[17]

Full dual trackers combine the core competencies and the mindsets of two very different types of company. This can – and often does – create tension between image-oriented brand managers in their nice offices and down-to-earth private-label sellers in their austere offices. Who is the swan? Who the ugly duckling?

Managerial takeaways

Private-label sales are getting a major boost from the growth of hard discounters. This is bad news for brands, but offers opportunities for manufacturers to supply hard discounters and conventional retailers with private labels. Yet the road to success in private-label manufacturing is narrow and winding. Here are the key requirements for success for three types of companies:

Dedicated private-label manufacturers need to:

☐ have an organizational culture that is single-mindedly focused on efficiency, austerity, and driving down costs, without compromising on functional quality;

☐ implement activity-based costing;

☐ be fast followers who employ market intelligence focused on identifying and copying manufacturer brand innovations by the time they appear in the marketplace;

☐ be able to produce large production runs of constant quality;

☐ have unsurpassed flexibility in their production lines;

☐ excel in internet auctions;

☐ be very cautious about what you pay to acquire other companies. Do not follow rosy scenarios of growth in an industry where profit margins are thin and volatile.

Opportunistic dual trackers need to:

☐ have only temporary overcapacity;

☐ only engage in private-label manufacturing if price exceeds variable costs of production;

☐ reduce capacity if brand demand is structurally below production capacity.

Full dual trackers need to:

☐ have separate organizations for their own brands and private labels;

☐ be able to compete with competing brands on brand-building skills and with dedicated private-label suppliers on cost leadership;

☐ develop strict guidelines to protect brand innovations from the demands of hard discounters to also offer them in their private-label products;

☐ think hard about whether they can manage the organizational schizophrenia associated with combining two very different organizational cultures (brand building versus austerity and cutting costs to the bone) in one company.

Notes

1 plma.com/, last accessed 5 March 2018.

2 www.foodprocessing.com/articles/2010/processor-of-the-year/, last accessed 5 March 2018.

3 TreeHouse Foods Inc. annual report for the fiscal year ended 31 December 2017.

4 www.just-food.com/analysis/treehouse-foods-wrestles-with-former-conagra-foods-assets-6-things-to-learn_id134879.aspx; www.omaha.com/money/after-disappointing-quarter-treehouse-foods-sees-share-value-plunge-by/article_e997a354-c014-11e7-b63e-0720631a7f2e.html, last accessed 25 March 2018.

5 www.krueger-unternehmen.de/en/group, last accessed 4 March 2018.

6 www.italianprivatelabel.com/, last accessed 4 March 2018.

7 Information obtained from Perrigo's annual report and presentation at the annual general meeting.

8 https://www.prnewswire.com/news-releases/refresco-acquires-cotts-bottling-activities-300493516.html, last accessed 25 March 2018.

9 Powers, S *et al* (2017) Global consumer: will private label swallow up $48 billion of branded US consumables value? UBS report, 11 July.

10 www.hormelcommercialretail.com/, last accessed 4 March 2018.

11 Lamey, L (2014) Hard economic times: a dream for discounters? *European Journal of Marketing*, 48 (3/4), pp. 641–56.

12 ter Braak, A, Deleersnyder, B, Geyskens, I, and Dekimpe, M G (2013) Does private-label production by national-brand manufacturers create discounter goodwill? *International Journal of Research in Marketing*, 30 (4), pp. 343–57.

13 Authors' calculations based on SCA's 2016 annual report.

14 Information about Essity based on Essity's Annual and Sustainability Report 2017.

15 Based on Gasparro, A (2015) ConAgra plans to exit private brands, *Wall Street Journal*, 30 June, p. B1.

16 Essity's Annual and Sustainability Report 2017.

17 Essity's Annual and Sustainability Report 2017.

Co-opetition – generating successful sales in hard discounter stores

11

'If you can't beat them, join them', is a time-honoured strategy. While hard discounters are characterized by a strong focus on private labels, that does not mean they carry no national brands at all. For example, in 2017, Aldi's assortment in the United States included one or more SKUs of M&Ms, Snickers, Hershey's, KitKat, Reese's, Haribo, Cheerios, Coca-Cola, Sprite, Gatorade, Duracell, and Kraft. Procter & Gamble was particularly well represented with Always, Tide, Pantene, Febreze, Crest, Secret, Old Spice, and Tampax. Overall, in 2017, about 5–15 per cent of the SKUs carried by Trader Joe's and Aldi were brands, about 30 per cent for BIM and for Lidl in Germany (lower elsewhere), and over 40 per cent of DIA's assortment were national brands. Increasingly, brands try to prosper in a retailscape increasingly dominated by hard discounters by developing trade relations with them.[1]

Yet, this poses two major challenges to brand managers. First, listing your brand at a hard discounter is not for the faint-hearted. Brand managers are concerned about margin pressure, possible reputational damage, and, most of all, cannibalization of existing brand sales at full-service retailers. Second, if you decide the hard discounter is a good option, getting a listing is difficult. Hard discounters are very picky about which brands they will include in their assortment. Their primary concern is not brand cannibalization but private-label cannibalization, with shoppers simply switching from their private label to the national brand.

Pros and cons of listing your brand at a hard discounter

Getting their brands included in the hard discounters' assortment has several benefits for CPG firms:

- Most obviously, you increase distribution coverage. The relationship between distribution coverage and market share is convex (J-shaped). That means that increasing distribution from, say, 10 per cent to 20 per cent has a smaller effect on the brand's market share than increasing distribution from 80 per cent to 90 per cent.[2] The lesson is clear – you cannot have high market share and grow your brand without being present in most, if not all, distribution channels. In 2018 and beyond, this means being present at hard discounters.

- It allows CPG firms to counter sales and margin pressure in conventional retail channels. Conventional retailers increasingly rely on their own brands and demand better conditions from national brands. This creates a double jeopardy for the brand manufacturer: not only do they lose shelf space to retailer brands, but their (reduced) sales suffer from lower margins. Getting discounters to carry their brands compensates for some of these losses.

- Selling through hard discounters is an opportunity to slow private-label growth. After all, hard discounters are the main engine behind the growth in private-label share that we can see in Western countries.

Nonetheless, we have noted in our work that many brand managers are reluctant to go the discounter route. Why?

- *Lower prices.* Hard discounters are tough price negotiators and lower prices hurt margins. This effect is exacerbated if other retailers strive to match hard discounter prices for the national brands. This does indeed happen. One study found that in Germany, a brand name product's price plummets by 17 per cent on average nationwide once discounters start stocking it on their shelves.[3] Another study reported that, after a brand was introduced in Aldi's assortment, within one month its price at conventional retailers was cut by 9 per cent.[4] We can be confident these retailers did not fully finance this drop in prices themselves.

- *Damage to brand equity.* Brand equity may be damaged if the brand is sold at hard discounters. The store atmosphere is austere and shelf facings are not always very tidy. For example, when we visited an Aldi store in Durham, NC, we were struck by the messy presentation of leading brands such as Tide, Tampax, and Always. Products were presented scattered over the shelf rather than being neatly aligned and some outer cases had shifted. The in-store brand experience was clearly inconsistent with their premium positioning.

- *Fear of retaliation.* There is also the concern of retaliation by conventional retailers. We have frequently heard managers of other retailers utter threats that they would diminish support for – or even delist – brands that sleep with their worst nightmare. In the past, Carrefour even imposed fines on manufacturers whose brands were included in Lidl's assortment – until that was deemed illegal by anti-trust authorities.[5]

Yet these burdens are worth bearing if listing your brand at a hard discounter increases total sales. In our work, we have noted that brand managers are worried that this may not be the case. They think that most of the sales revenues obtained in the discounter channel are from consumers who previously bought the brand at conventional retailers. However, the dangers of cannibalization are less than many managers fear. A large-scale study examined the cannibalization rate for 146 brand listings across multiple discounters in France, Germany, the UK, the Netherlands, and Spain. The results were encouraging. Although the cannibalization rate differed somewhat between countries depending on local market conditions, in all countries, the average brand cannibalization was below 25 per cent (Table 11.1). In our work, we use brand cannibalization of 20–25 per cent as the benchmark against which to judge actual cannibalization rates.

When is listing at hard discounters more beneficial to brands?

While, on average, cannibalization is quite low for brands, results for individual brands can vary strongly. For example, 72 per cent of the sales of Procter & Gamble's Always panty liners brand at Lidl in Germany came from existing buyers of Always who merely switched retailers. On the other hand, when Müller Vitality yogurt drinks were listed at Netto in the UK, the brand cannibalization rate was 0 per cent! What explains this difference? Under which conditions is cannibalization lower? Here are guidelines:[6]

- Innovative brands suffer less from cannibalization than less innovative brands. Innovative brands regularly introduce new and improved

Table 11.1 Brand and discounter cannibalization after brand listing at a hard discounter

Country	Brand cannibalization (%)	Discounter cannibalization (%)
France	15.4 [a]	55.4 [b]
Germany	22.0	67.0
Netherlands	19.8	80.5
Spain	22.0	80.2
UK	11.1	63.9
Average	**18.1**	**69.4**

NOTES Average is the unweighted average across countries.

a) To be read as: on average, one year after a national brand is listed at a French hard discounter, 15.4 per cent of that brand's sales at the discounter come from buyers who previously bought that national brand at another retailer.

b) To be read as: on average, one year after a national brand is listed at a French hard discounter, 55.4 per cent of that brand's sales at the discounter comes from buyers who previously bought another brand at that discounter (typically the retailer's private label).

SOURCE Based on Koll *et al* (2007) and 2014 data from GfK

products, which grow the category, attract new buyers, and induce people to increase their consumption intensity.

- Brands with a low market share experience lower cannibalization than brands with a high market share. A brand with a small market share can only gain when listed at a discounter. Its exposure to potential buyers multiplies, the danger of cannibalization is very low, and current retail partners are less concerned about its availability in the discount channel because the brand is unimportant to their revenue objectives. High-share brands, in contrast, face the opposite situation: they have to grow from what is already a large customer base. Their distribution coverage before the listing was high already, increasing the odds that existing buyers switch channels and that existing partners will be unhappy. To give you an idea about the magnitude of the difference, the cannibalization experienced by brands that are in the top quartile (top 25 per cent) in market share is, on average, six times larger than the cannibalization of brands that are in the bottom half – 37 per cent versus 6 per cent. Always' high market share (47.7 per cent) was the main reason why cannibalization at Lidl in Germany was so high.

- Brands for which the price gap between hard discounters and conventional retailers is small incur less cannibalization. There is little reason to switch stores to buy your favourite brand. But why would price-focused hard discount shoppers buy your brand if the price advantage is small? Because you reach new customers – people who like your brand but are unwilling to make the effort to go to another store to purchase it. Do the test yourself. Are you willing to go to another store to purchase Tresemmé shampoo, let alone Del Monte canned tomatoes? You can still offer superior value by delivering a larger volume for broadly the same price. Such SKUs appeal to heavy users and grow the category. Nestlé, for example, sold two-litre containers of Vittel mineral water at Lidl in Europe.

- Brands in perishable categories (eg dairy) have a cannibalization level that is one-third below the cannibalization rate of non-perishable brands. In perishable categories, consumers are less likely to purchase the products in bulk as they do not store for a long period of time. Thus, there is not as much saving to be had for the consumer, meaning the incentive for switching stores is less. For example, when Müller listed its Yogz Corner brand at Netto in the UK, only 6 per cent of its sales at Netto came from consumers who had previously bought Yogz Corner at conventional retailers.

- Brands in impulse categories (eg confectioneries, gum) have a 30 per cent lower cannibalization rate than brands in categories where purchases tend to be planned (eg rice, baked beans). In impulse categories, consumers are generally less willing to delay gratification to get a better deal by switching stores. Kraft's chocolate brand Toblerone is a case in point. Cannibalization after it was included in Lidl's assortment in Germany was only 20 per cent and, one year after listing at Lidl, its share of the German confectionery market had increased by 75 per cent.

- Brand cannibalization also depends on the specific hard discounter where your brand is listed. Evidence from Germany and Spain suggests that brand cannibalization following listing at Aldi and Lidl is higher than at other hard discounters, with cannibalization at Lidl generally being highest. To illustrate, cannibalization at Lidl in Germany was, on average, about one-third higher than at Aldi and twice the cannibalization rate at Penny, while Lidl's cannibalization rate in Spain was twice that of DIA.

The Brand Cannibalization Scorecard

What is the cannibalization risk of your brand? To help you assess the rate of cannibalization, Table 11.2 presents a diagnostic tool. The scoring guidelines

Table 11.2   Scorecard for assessing brand cannibalization by listing your brand at a hard discounter

Score your brand on a number of cannibalization factors, tally the scores, and then use the key at the bottom to gauge the cannibalization risk

Cannibalization factor	Scoring guidelines	Score
Brand innovativeness	0 = Multiple major innovations	
	2 = One major innovation	
	4 = New packaging design or sizing strategy	
	4 = Multiple minor innovations	
	6 = One minor innovation	
	8 = No innovations in the past three years	
Brand size	0 = market share under 2%	
	4 = market share of 7.5%	
	6 = market share of 15%	
	8 = market share above 15%	
Price difference with conventional retailers	0 = price gap below 10%	
	3 = price gap 10–20%	
	6 = price gap above 20%	
Perishability	0 = Perishable product	
	2 = Non-perishable product	
Impulse product	0 = Impulse product	
	2 = Non-impulse (planned) product	
Hard discounter	0 = Other hard discounters	
	3 = Aldi	
	4 = Lidl	

Total Score

Total score	Expected brand cannibalization is
0–10	Low
11–20	Average
21–30	High

NOTE The benchmark for the average cannibalization rate is 20–25 per cent and the range in scores per factor are based on field studies conducted by ourselves and our colleagues.[7] We illustrate its use for the listing of Mars candy bars at Kwik Save in the UK. The confectionery manufacturer is innovative with developments and extensions of the Mars Bar line, keeping consumers interested and loyal to the brand. In the three years before the listing at Kwik Save, it introduced Mars Delight – an indulgent chocolate bar described as 'Milk chocolate with a rippled wafer centre surrounded by a caramel cream and chocolate-flavour cream' (brand innovativeness score: 2). With a market share of 3.7 per cent, Mars was a moderately large player in the British candy bar market (brand share score: 2). The price differential with mainstream retailers was between 10 and 20 per cent (price gap score: 3). Candy bars are non-perishable (score: 2) and are generally seen as an impulse category (score: 0). Finally, since neither Aldi nor Lidl was involved, the score for hard discounter is zero.

This yields a total score of 9, indicating that the expected cannibalization is expected to be below average. (Recall that the benchmark cannibalization rate, based on hundreds of brand listings, is 20–25 per cent.) In Mars' case, the cannibalization rate was 10.5 per cent. That is, around 90 per cent of the sales of Mars at Kwik Save came from people who had not bought Mars candy bars before. One year after listing at Kwik Save, Mars' market share had increased from 3.7 per cent to 3.9 per cent – an increase of 5.4 per cent, a good result in a mature category.

As another example, let us take a closer look at the aforementioned listing of Müller Vitality yogurt drinks at Netto in the UK, where the cannibalization rate was 0 per cent. How does it score on our scorecard? Vitality yogurt drinks were positioned as a breakfast product aimed to provide consumers with essential nutrients to start their day. The company was very innovative in this category, introducing multiple major innovations in the functional foods market with products targeting consumers concerned about issues such as heart and digestive health (brand innovativeness score: 0). Products launched in the preceding years included Müller Vitality Probiotic Low-Fat Yogurt Drink, Müller Vitality (contains omega-3), and Müller Vitality Fat-Free Probiotic Yogurt Drink (contains probiotics and omega-3). However, its market share was below 1 per cent (brand share score: 0). The price gap for Müller Vitality between mainstream retailers and Netto was less than 10 per cent (price gap score: 0), the product is perishable and buying is typically on impulse (product type score: 0). Thus, the cannibalization score is the lowest possible score: zero. The brand listing was a great success and one year after listing at Netto, market share had increased to 4.7 per cent.

Why are hard discounters increasingly interested in brands?

Hard discounters have grown to prominence in market after market with their no-frills store formats and strong reliance on private labels, which allows them to offer a price–quality combination that is second to none. So, why would they even be interested in considering adding national brands to their assortment? There are three reasons. First, their very success means that, increasingly, hard discounters are competing with each other rather than against conventional retailers. Growing within-format competition increases the need for differentiation. A carefully constructed portfolio of their own brands and national brands is part of this differentiation. Second, national brand buyers are generally less price sensitive – and hence more profitable – than private-label buyers. By putting national brands on the shelves, such high-contribution shoppers might be lured into the hard discounter.

Third, in many categories, there are large segments of consumers who are attached to their favourite national brand. Take carbonated soft drinks: the segment of people just not willing to purchase a private-label cola is large, probably closer to 80–90 per cent than to 50 per cent in most countries. As hard discounters grow in market share, they start to approach the upper limit of their success, especially in categories where brand relevance is still high. The only way to continue on their growth trajectory may be to add one or more national brands to their assortment. For example, in the period 2005–2008 in Germany, Aldi retained its exclusive focus on its own brands in the detergent and coffee categories, while Lidl added national brand SKUs to its assortment. The result? In both categories, Aldi's market share declined while Lidl was able to significantly grow its category share (Table 11.3).[8] These are not isolated cases. The growing success of Lidl vis-à-vis Aldi in the period 2005–2017 is generally attributed to its greater willingness to include national brands in its product offering.

The hard discounter has to weigh these benefits against the adverse effects that carrying national brands have on their profitability and price image. While hard discounters hope that brands allow them to grow their market share in the category in question, brand sales may instead come from the discounter's own private label. This danger is very real (Table 11.1). Our research has shown that, on average, 70 per cent of brand sales come from in-store brand switching – current shoppers who previously bought another brand at that store, usually the hard discounter's private label. This hurts

Table 11.3   Brands help Lidl grow category share

	Category share (%)			
	2005	**2006**	**2007**	**2008**
Detergents				
Aldi	14.3	14.1	12.0	11.7
Lidl	7.8	11.3	13.9	14.9
... of which national brands	*3.3*	*6.3*	*9.6*	*10.6*
Ground coffee				
Aldi	17.2	17.0	15.9	16.6
Lidl	10.0	11.3	13.1	15.3
... of which national brands	*4.4*	*6.2*	*8.8*	*10.5*

SOURCE Based on 2009 data from GfK

profitability as brands typically generate lower margins than the hard discounter's own brands.

A second danger will reveal itself in the longer term. As hard discounters keep adding national brands, their costs increase and their no-frills proposition may become blurred, opening the back door for a new format. Recall that department stores started as low-cost outfits. So did supermarkets. Over time, they expanded their offering to cater to other shopper segments until they had become bloated with high assortment complexity and high overhead, holding, and sourcing costs. So, it is crucial that hard discounters keep their assortment fairly small and strictly limit the number of national brand SKUs. We believe a good rule of thumb is that they limit the number of brand SKUs to a maximum of 25 per cent of the assortment, excluding fresh (where brands play a small role). Hard discounters need to be primarily outlets to buy high-quality private labels at rock-bottom prices. If they lose that proposition, they will go the way of department stores and supermarkets.

Making your case to the hard discounter

How does the national brand manager get their brand listed at a hard discounter? Obviously, you have to offer attractive margins and marketing support. This is no different from other retailers. Second, you can consider manufacturing the hard discounter's private-label production.

In Chapter 10, we presented evidence that the likelihood that your brand will be listed by Aldi increases threefold if you produce for Aldi as well. You can further strengthen your case if you are able to present evidence that discounter cannibalization will be relatively low for your brand listing. While you may not be unduly upset by discounter cannibalization, the hard discounter is. Here are the criteria that you can use to craft the argument:

- *Innovative brands*. Innovative brands not only have lower brand cannibalization but also reduce discounter cannibalization because they expand the category.

- *Price premium versus the hard discounter's private label*. If the price premium is below 50–75 per cent, cannibalization of private-label sales at the hard discounter becomes substantially higher.

- *Hard discounter share in the category*. Retail cannibalization is lower the smaller the hard discounter's market share in the category. If relatively few buyers purchase that category at the hard discounter, there is more room for attracting new shoppers.

- *Number of national brands carried in the category*. If the hard discounter already carries multiple national brands, it already caters to the needs of most of its customers who prefer to buy a national brand in that category. An additional national brand will have limited ability to draw new category buyers to the discounter.

- *Product type*. While brand cannibalization is higher for non-perishable and planned products, the reverse is true for retail cannibalization. Retail cannibalization is higher for perishable and impulse products because consumers are less willing to switch stores for such products.

This is summarized in Table 11.4.[9] We will now discuss two examples of brand listings: one that experienced low retail cannibalization and another for which retail cannibalization was very high.

Carling beer at Netto (UK)

Listing Carling beer worked out well for hard discounter Netto in the UK. Cannibalization at the retailer was only 33.6 per cent, less than half the norm for retail cannibalization of 70 per cent. What accounted for this low cannibalization rate? First, Carling was an innovative brand. In the year before the listing at Netto, it had launched the low-alcohol beer Carling C2, which was the result of eight years of research, and 'was brewed to taste great'. Low-alcohol beer was a popular trend in the category, appealing to health-conscious consumers.

Table 11.4   Checklist to assess extent of discounter cannibalization

These five questions will help you determine if listing your brand at the discounter will lead to significant in-store cannibalization of the discounter's current offering. Check the response box if the answer to the question is 'yes'.

If you answered 'yes' to:

0–2 questions: expected cannibalization at the discounter is high

3–4 questions: expected cannibalization at the discounter is average (norm is 70 per cent)

5 questions: expected cannibalization at the discounter is low

Question	Yes?
Does your brand regularly introduce meaningfully new products in the market?	
Does the price premium of your brand at the discounter versus the hard discounter's private label exceed 50–75%?	
Does the hard discounter have a small market share in your category?	
Does the hard discounter carry no or very few (1–2) national brands in the category?	
Is it a non-perishable product *and* is the purchase typically planned (non-impulsive)?	
Total	

Carling was 150 per cent more expensive than the average price of all private labels sold in the category in Netto, which clearly separated the brand from Netto's private labels. In addition, this beer was presented as a premium lager, as indicated by the packaging. Netto had a low share in the beer category (0.8 per cent) and did not stock other national brands. Finally, beer is neither perishable nor predominantly an impulse purchase. Using the checklist (Table 11.4) results in five affirmative responses, which is the maximum score, indicating low discounter cannibalization.

Cuetara cookies at Plus (Spain)

In contrast, hard discounter Plus in Spain did not benefit from listing Cuetara cookies. The retail cannibalization was a whopping 97 per cent. Why? On the positive side, the price premium over Plus's private label was 130 per cent. However, innovation in the cookie category was rather low, and this also applied to Cuetara. Cookies are non-perishable (which is good for retail cannibalization), but they tend to be impulse purchases (which is bad for retail cannibalization). But most problematic was that Plus already stocked four cookie brands and its share in the category before the listing of Cuetara already stood at 22 per cent. Thus, Plus already catered to brand shoppers in this category and, with such a dominant presence in the category, its ability to attract new category buyers was low. Using the checklist (Table 11.4) results in one affirmative response (for price), indicating high discounter cannibalization.

Win–win at hard discounters

The ideal case is a brand listing that leads to low cannibalization of existing brand sales and low cannibalization at the discounter. Such a win–win outcome is what economists call a stable equilibrium. Both parties benefit. When is such an outcome more likely to transpire? Two factors stand out. First, listings of *innovative brands* are more likely to result in win–win outcomes. This, again, underlines the key importance of innovation in brand success, something we have also seen in previous chapters. Second, win–wins are more common in categories where *the discounter has a low market share*. While this factor plays a large role in creating a win for the hard discounter, it has a negligible effect on brand cannibalization.

Gillette at Lidl in Germany

An example of a win–win is the listing of Gillette shaving foam at Lidl in Germany. Lidl had a 2.4 per cent category share in shaving foams before listing Gillette. One year after the listing, this increased to 3.3 per cent (+38 per cent). Procter & Gamble also benefited from listing the Gillette brand at Lidl in Germany. Gillette's market share in the shaving foam category increased from 18.0 per cent one year before the listing, to 19.4 per cent one year after listing at Lidl (+8 per cent). A key factor in this win–win outcome was that both brand cannibalization rate and discounter cannibalization were at or below the benchmark.

Brand cannibalization was 23.1 per cent, which is about average. Gillette had introduced multiple major innovations in the shaving cream market, most prominently products that moisturize and put less stress on the user's skin, such as Gillette Fusion HydraSoothe Balm, HydraCool Skin Gel, Gillette Fusion HydraGel, and Gillette Mach 3 Parfümfrei Turbo Gel (brand innovativeness score in Table 11.2: 0). This complemented trends in cosmeceuticals, as more food and drinks make claims about their ability to help moisturize the skin. As a result, Gillette was able to attract a large number of new buyers and grow the category. Moreover, the price difference with conventional retailers was small (score: 0). On the negative side (at least with respect to brand cannibalization), with 18 per cent market share, Gillette was a large player (brand share score: 8). Moreover, the product is non-perishable (score: 2) and non-impulse (score: 2), and brand cannibalization is higher at Lidl (score: 4). The total cannibalization score of 16 puts it at the average level of cannibalization.

The success of Gillette for Lidl was due to several favourable characteristics (Table 11.4). The brand was innovative, and the price gap of 310 per cent with the Lidl private label dampened in-store switching from Lidl's private-label products. Shaving foam is non-perishable and non-impulse, and Lidl did not stock any other national brand in the category. Last but not least, Lidl was clearly underperforming in the category. Listing a large brand in an underperforming category meant that Lidl could increase store traffic and reach new consumers. Only 38 per cent of buyers in the category were existing category buyers.

Managerial takeaways

Brands have always followed consumers, wherever they went. They did this when department stores were reshaping the retail industry, and when, subsequently, supermarkets, hypermarkets, and warehouse clubs rose to prominence. Now, brands need to do the same with hard discounters. However, with any channel addition, the manager faces a real danger that current brand customers are merely switching to the new channel with no net sales gain. Moreover, with hard discounters being tough price negotiators, you may be worse off than before. Here are the key issues to consider:

- Expect that listing at a hard discounter will exert downward pressure on your prices – both at the discounter and in conventional retailers.

- Brand reputation may suffer because of austere selling context and messy shelf presentation. Design nice outer-case boxes and find other ways to minimize the fallout.

- Some brand cannibalization is unavoidable. The benchmark is 20–25 per cent. Assess cannibalization for your brand using the Brand Cannibalization Scorecard (Table 11.2).

If you have decided that listing at a hard discounter is suitable for your brand, you still need to convince the retailer to accept your brand. Given their heavy focus on private labels, getting on a hard discounter's shelf is challenging. Apart from the price and other delivery conditions, here are two ways to improve your odds:

- Engage in private-label production for the hard discounter. If you do that, the likelihood of having your brand listed increases by up to a factor of two to three. But only do this if the brand economics are favourable. Chapter 10 provides details.

- Make your case that listing your brand leads to below-average cannibalization for the hard discounter. The benchmark is 70 per cent. Discounter cannibalization below 50 per cent can be regarded as an outright success. Use the checklist (Table 11.4) to assess your situation.

The best-case scenario is a win–win where listing of the brand leads to below-average brand cannibalization and below-average retail cannibalization. Win–win is most likely for innovative brands that are introduced in categories where the hard discounter has a low market share.

Notes

1   In developing this chapter, we benefited greatly from discussions with – and comments by – Barbara Deleersnyder of Tilburg University. Much of the empirical evidence and case studies reported in this chapter are based on the following publications: Deleersnyder, B, Dekimpe, M G, Steenkamp, J B E M and Koll, O (2007) Win–win strategies at discount stores, *Journal of Retailing and Consumer Services*, **14** (5), pp. 309–18; Deleersnyder, B and Koll, O (2012) Destination discount: a sensible road for national brands? *European Journal of Marketing*, **46** (9), pp. 1150–70; Koll, O, Deleersnyder, B and Sadler, J (2007) Brands in discounters, Business Insights & Europanel.

2   Kruger, M W and Harper, B (2006) Market share and product distribution: re-tested and extended, INFORMS Marketing Science Conference, Pittsburgh, 9 June; Wilbur, K C and Farris, P W (2014) Distribution and market share, *Journal of Retailing*, **90** (2), pp. 154–67.

3   Kimball, S, Roth, T and Underhill, W (2017) The unstoppable rise of Aldi and Lidl, *Handelsblatt Global*, Fall.

4   Consumers and Retail 2015/2016, presentation at the 35th Kronberg Meeting, GfK, 28 January 2016.

5   Berkhout, C (2017) A-merken bij Aldi, Lidl, AH en Jumbo, *FoodPersonality*, October, pp. 21–23.

6   Koll, O, Deleersnyder, B and Sadler, J (2007) Brands in discounters, Business

Insights & Europanel; Consumers and Retail 2012/2013, presentation at the 32nd Kronberg Meeting, GfK 2013.

7 See note 1 for key sources.

8 Einfluss von Preiserhöhungen und Wirtschaftskrise auf das Konsumverhalten 2008, presentation at the 28th Kronberg Meeting, GfK, 22 January 2009.

9 We combine non-perishability and planned purchase in a single criterion. A 'yes' response is only obtained if both criteria are fulfilled. We do this on purpose. The scoring key weighs each criterion equally but in our experience, the first four criteria have a greater impact on reducing in-store cannibalization than product type. By combining the two aspects of product type, we impose a higher hurdle for a yes response.

A look into the future of disruptive retailing

12

In our discussions with retailers and brand managers, we have often heard the complaint that hard discounters allegedly impoverish the shopping experience, direct people to focus on a single choice criterion (price), and stifle innovation. While it is certainly true that the average Aldi store, let alone a Biedronka or BIM store, does not stimulate the senses like an Albert Heijn, Woolworths, Waitrose, or Kroger store does, they obviously do something right, given their phenomenal success in so many countries. And when it comes to innovation, hard discounting is actually the biggest innovation in brick-and-mortar retailing in the past quarter of a century.

The success of hard discounters contributes significantly to consumer welfare in the sense that their dollar or euro goes further than before. The effect is twofold. Buying at hard discounters can save you anywhere between 30 and 50 per cent on your grocery bill. Moreover, hard discounters 'democratize' innovations. For example, in the Netherlands, organic products sold by conventional retailers like Plus and Albert Heijn were so expensive that they were out of reach for most people. After Aldi and Lidl moved aggressively into organics, prices at these retailers dropped by 40 per cent. Thus, beyond the direct effect, there is an indirect effect. Once hard discounters become a meaningful market presence, conventional retailers respond by dropping their prices. Conventional retailers put pressure on national brands to reduce their prices, cut the prices of their own private labels, and expand their private label assortment with lower-priced economy lines. So, even consumers who do not shop at a hard discounter benefit from their market success.

A cautious estimate of the total welfare effect of hard discounter success is that, in Europe and Australia, consumers save 10 per cent on their grocery bill. This translates into savings of €20 billion *annually* for German shoppers, £16 billion for British shoppers, and AU $13 billion for Australians.

Now that is real money! These savings can be used to pay off student loans, purchase better healthcare, add to a retirement fund, or something else.

As of the time of writing, the welfare effects in the United States are smaller, since hard discounters are earlier in the process of expansion. However, wherever Lidl entered an area in 2017, grocery prices on average dropped by about 10 per cent, and Aldi's expansion has generated a strong response by Kroger, Walmart, and others. For example, Aldi's entry into Southern California in 2016 triggered an epic price war, turning this area from one of the highest-priced markets in the country to the most competitively priced within 18 months.[1] In response to increasing competition from Aldi, Walmart demanded that branded goods manufacturers like P&G, Unilever, and ConAgra reduce the cost they charge the retailer by 15 per cent.[2] We estimate that burgeoning hard discounter success allows the average consumer to save 2–3 per cent on their grocery bill, or around $20–$30 billion per year.

And let us not forget emerging markets. The success of hard discounters in countries like Poland, Turkey, Brazil and Argentina highlights the global appeal of the hard discount concept and brings much-needed price relief to millions of shoppers every day.

Who will be worse off? National brand manufacturers will lose market share due to the rise of hard discounters and the increased focus on private label by conventional retailers. However, they can limit their losses and grow at the expense of other brands by ramping up true, meaningful innovation activity. This requires CPG companies, especially large firms, to up their game significantly. A fair number of large firms appear more concerned with cost-cutting – embracing zero-based budgeting – than in introducing really innovative products that create new categories, accelerate organic growth, and improve the lives of consumers. Cost reduction is necessary to remain price competitive, but, ultimately, pricing is a game brands cannot win. No brand has ever cut itself to greatness. It is an ominous sign that many innovations come from small companies and startups, ranging from Dollar Shave Club and Seventh Generation to Halo Top and Annie's. If large CPG companies struggle to develop innovations themselves, they can become sophisticated acquisition machines instead. You let startups develop and commercialize new product concepts, and, after acquiring them, they can be scaled to a national or even global scale using the acquirer's marketing expertise and access to distribution channels.

Conventional retailers are hurt more by hard discounter success than national brand manufacturers. While the latter lose one unit, the former lose an entire shopping cart. Yet conventional retailers are far from powerless. They can create their own 'blue ocean' by adding more value to their offering, something that retailers like Wegmans (US) and Waitrose (UK) are doing. They can also set up their own hard discounter chain or move aggressively into the online channel. They can slug it out by dropping their prices, or increase their market power with mergers and acquisitions. For example, Dutch retailer Royal Ahold and Belgium's Delhaize merged in 2016, making it the fifth-largest retailer in the United States alone. There are consistent rumours that Ahold Delhaize might join forces with Kroger. The experience in France has shown that a judicious combination of these strategies can be effective in fighting off hard discounters, albeit at such high costs that some might argue that the cure is worse than the disease. Finally, conventional retailers and brand manufacturers may realize that they face a common threat, which can be countered more effectively by cooperation. Currently, their relationships are often adversarial rather than collaborative. It is time to change that.

So where does this all end? Experience thus far suggests that hard discounters will rarely capture more than 20–25 per cent of the market, the upper limit being reserved for countries where conventional retailers are relatively weak. Of course, that is little consolation for retailers and manufacturers in countries ranging from the United States to the UK and Australia, where each percentage point lost to hard discounters is worth billions.

While hard discounters are set to grow further, we are not oblivious to the clouds on their horizon. Two stand out. First, the growth of online grocery retailing puts hard discounters at a disadvantage, for now. Although predictions for the market share of online groceries vary widely – from anywhere between 5 and 20 per cent in the United States alone by 2025 – this channel is bound to grow, with Amazon being the big engine behind it. Hard discounters are experimenting with online delivery models but their low-cost operations and limited assortment put them at a disadvantage to conventional retailers. We note, though, that their higher operating margins makes it easier to absorb extra costs associated with online retailing than mainstream retailers. Moreover, their limited assortment makes order fulfilment much easier – and hence cheaper – and their website easier to navigate. Thus, they may be at a disadvantage but the growth of the online channel also offers opportunities for hard discounters.

Second, there is the wheel of retailing, one of the most widely accepted theories regarding institutional changes in retailing. This theory states that changes in a retail concept take place in a cyclical manner. The new retail format enters the market as a low-status, low-cost, low-price store. Over time, it moves to up-market locations and starts to stock premium products to cater to new shopper segments. Stores become bigger to keep the growth momentum and to differentiate themselves from imitators. Eventually, it matures as a high-cost, high-price retail format, leaving its former niche to be filled by a new low-cost concept. This new concept will, in turn, go through the same cycle of retail development. We can see the process of hard discounter upgrading occurring at Aldi and, especially, Lidl. Stores and assortments are increasing in size, national brands are becoming a more prominent fixture, and services like bakeries are being added. The first wave of US stores opened by Lidl in 2017 are illustrative of this trend. We wonder if Lidl's initial approach of opening stores in the United States of more than double the average size of their European counterparts has been a wise entry strategy given the limited assortment they still have. This might also be the reason the roll-out of Lidl in the United States is somewhat slowed, giving them time to work on their store concept. Another danger of hard discounters moving up is that they give space to other low cost operators, such as the Dollar stores in the United States and Action in Europe.

It remains to be seen whether hard discounters can find and hold onto the sweet spot between bare-bone austerity and costly services and large assortments, or if they will follow the siren song of upgrading to expand sales, while leaving the back door open for a new concept. Given the amount of self-restraint they have shown over the last 30 years, we advise you not to hold your breath.

The conclusion is clear. Hard discounters are – and will remain – a permanent fixture in the grocery retailscape. The ultimate winner is the consumer. And that is the right outcome in a competitive society.

Notes

1   www.ocregister.com/2017/10/23/prices-drop-in-southern-california-as-aldis-march-west-is-causing-upheaval/, last accessed 6 March 2018.
2   https://www.reuters.com/article/us-walmart-pricing-exclusive-idUSKBN1660I4, last accessed 6 March 2018.

INDEX

Note: Page numbers in *italics* indicate Figures or Tables.